GREEN DAY
★ REBELS WITH A CAUSE ★

BY GILLIAN G. GAAR

OMNIBUS PRESS
London/New York/Paris/Sydney/Copenhagen/Berlin/Madrid/Tokyo

Exclusive Distributors
Music Sales Limited,
14-15 Berners Street,
London W1T 3LJ, UK.

Music Sales Corporation,
257 Park Avenue South,
New York, NY 10010, USA.

Macmillan Distribution Services,
53 Park West Drive,
Derrimut, Vic 3030,
Australia.

To the Music Trade only:
Music Sales Limited,
14-15 Berners Street,
London W1T 3LJ, UK.

Every effort has been made to trace the copyright holders of the photographs in this book but one or
two were unreachable. We would be grateful if the photographers concerned would contact us.

Typeset by Phoenix Photosetting, Chatham, Kent
Printed in the United States of America by Quebecor World

A catalogue record for this book is available from the British Library.

Visit Omnibus Press on the web at www.omnibuspress.com

Contents

To my mother, Marcella Gaar,
for always being there

INTRODUCTION

Kings Of The World

"They'd been superstars all along. The only difference was that now the whole world knew it."
— *Lawrence Livermore*, Metal Hammer Presents Green Day, *2005*

Date: September 24, 2005. Place: SBC Park, a 41,000-seat outdoor stadium in San Francisco, California, where Green Day will perform yet another date on the seemingly never-ending tour promoting their wildly successful album, *American Idiot*. So far, the record's racked up sales of nine million worldwide, and the previous February won a Grammy award for Best Rock Album. It's been hailed as a stunning return to form for the band: "the album of their career," in the words of the *London Times*. It's also — surprisingly from a group previously regarded as bratty punk rockers — something of a political statement, marking the first time the band members have spoken out extensively about several issues on the minds of many Americans today: the machinations of the Bush administration; the "war on terror"; the US invasion of Iraq; and how all this has been distilled, dumbed down, and relayed to the nation via "reality" TV. As Billie Joe Armstrong, Green Day's lead singer and guitarist, told a reporter at the time of the album's release, "The country's divided, and there's a lot of confusion... and it's not only confusing for my kids, it's confusing for adults, too. Everybody just sort of feels like they don't know where their future is heading right now, you know?"

But today isn't just any date on the tour. The San Francisco gig, held the same day as yet more anti-war protests are being held across the country (including one in San Francisco), is the closest the band will come to doing a homecoming show. (Billie Joe Armstrong and Mike Dirnt having made their live debut at a now-closed rib joint in Vallejo, some 30 miles to the north.) And at a time when other stadium acts are charging as much as $300 a ticket, Green Day has kept their ticket prices relatively inexpensive (around $50). Opening acts Flogging Molly and Jimmy Eat World have each received a warm welcome, but it's obvious who the crowd has come to see. Giant screens on either side of the stage, bearing the Verizon logo in a nod to tour sponsor Verizon Wireless, display text messages from the attendees: "Green Day Rocks" and "Scream if you love Green Day!" along with jokes ("Go Dodgers!" which elicits boos from fans of the San Francisco Giants) and personal pleas ("I'm sorry Jan. Everyone makes mistakes. Call me."). It's also predominantly a young crowd, including plenty of kids and pre-teens who have come in the company of their parents, like the seven-year-old girl who walks by in a pink Green Day shirt and matching boots, holding her mother's hand. Fans who haven't been following the tour through online websites debate what the opening song will be: 'American Idiot' or 'Welcome To Paradise'?

In the run up to Green Day's set, the music playing over the PA system is mostly punky pop/poppy punk like Devo's 'Whip It' and The Go-Go's 'We Got The Beat'. Five years ago, Billie Joe sang on stage with The Go-Go's in San Francisco and went on to co-write the song 'Unforgiven' for the group's 2001 reunion album. Not too many in the crowd seem familiar with Bikini Kill's 'Rebel Girl' (whose lead singer, Kathleen Hanna, makes a cameo appearance on the *American Idiot* album), but The Beastie Boys' '(You Gotta) Fight For Your Right (To Party)' gets a lot of cheers. Then a familiar trumpet fanfare brings the crowd to its feet. It's the Village People's 'YMCA', of all things, and as the song reaches the chorus, the audience stands and obligingly spells out "Y-M-C-A" with their arms *en masse*, as someone clad in a pink bunny suit bounces out on stage, goofing around, chugging beers, winding up the already expectant crowd even more.

Then comes a song by one of Green Day's chief influences, The Ramones' 'Blitzkrieg Bop'. It's a song Green Day themselves have played in concert, most notably in a short tribute set at the 2002 Rock and Roll Hall of Fame induction ceremony when The Ramones joined the other illustrious names already in the "Rock Hall". When the song comes to its abrupt end, the lights go out and the crowd snaps. Those in the stands rush to the front of the seated sections, and those on the field push even tighter together in the standing-room area in front of the stage. Everyone unleashes their emotions in a fusillade of screams "probably audible on the Berkeley shoreline," *The Contra Costa Times* later observes. (Contra Costa county being where Billie Joe and Mike originally hail from.)

Now the music is Richard Strauss' majestic 'Also Sprach Zarathustra', better known to modern audiences as the theme from Stanley Kubrick's sci-fi classic, *2001: A Space Odyssey*, as well as the music that welcomed Elvis to the stage for most of his Seventies-era shows. (As it happens, Billie Joe's first album purchase was an Elvis record.) The screams reach a fever pitch when the members of Green Day finally appear — the core trio of guitarist Billie Joe Armstrong, bassist Mike Dirnt, and drummer Tré Cool augmented by Jason White and Mike Pelino on guitars, and Jason Freese and Ron Blake on horns, keyboards, and assorted percussion. The ensemble blasts into 'American Idiot'.

When Tré first hits his drums, the red curtains at the back of the stage drop to reveal three huge vertical red banners, two of which have the "zapped man" logo used in the cover artwork for *Warning*. The middle banner is emblazoned with the now-iconic cover image from *American Idiot*: a hand gripping a heart-shaped grenade (but which Billie Joe said "looks more like a strawberry" in the program for the spring and summer 2005 tour). Two additional large banners with the zapped man logo flank the stage. The band members are all dressed in black, with little individual touches adding a bit of colour: Billie Joe and Tré wearing striped ties, Billie Joe wearing a white armband with the words "Rage" on his right arm and a black wristband with the red heart grenade/strawberry logo on his left wrist, and Mike's trousers having a thin white stripe down each leg.

After the song's first chorus, Billie Joe shouts out, "*San Francisco!*" to massive cheers; he'll go on to yell the city's name at some point during just about every song in the set to the same enthusiastic response. He also begins the audience interaction that will continue throughout the show. During the instrumental breaks he dashes from one side of the stage to the other, singing, "*Hey — oh!*" and then pointing at the crowd who dutifully sing, "*Hey — oh!*" right back at him. He also endeavors get the audience to do "the wave", pointing to his right to get the crowds there to start the ritualistic raising of arms, continuing all around the ballpark. Before charging back into the final verse of the song, Billie Joe says, "I want you to sing so *fucking* loud that every redneck in America hears you tonight, all right?" to more delighted screams. At the song's conclusion, he races back to center stage and on the final note strikes a crucifixion pose, standing straight, both arms thrust out to the sides. He holds the pose for a full 30 seconds.

"Welcome to the Green Day world tour 2005!" he finally shouts above the crowd noise. "And this is our *homecoming show*, bay-bee!" He dedicates the next song to "everybody that came here from the East Bay" — as the area across San Francisco Bay is referred to — and launches into 'Jesus Of Suburbia'. This is the first of *American Idiot*'s song-suites, which runs just over nine minutes, one of the longest songs Green Day's ever recorded. ('Homecoming', also on *American Idiot*, runs 10 seconds longer.) During the 'City Of The Damned' segment, Billie Joe gets the crowd to wave their arms from side to side, shouting, "Get those fists in the air! Get those hands up!" As the number segues into the 'Dearly Beloved' segment of the suite, Billie Joe cries, "Stand up! Stand up and be heard!" It's a demand that goes right to the heart of *American Idiot*'s appeal and its multiple layers of meaning. Is it a call to arms or merely a request to enjoy yourself? It's ultimately your decision; as Billie Joe told *Guitar World* in discussing the album, "I'd rather have people work out for themselves what it means to them." At the end of the 'Tales Of Another Broken Home' segment, where on the album there's a brief pause before the song thunders to its conclusion, in concert the moment seems to stretch into eternity. Billie Joe, standing still for a change, takes in the spectacle of a stadium packed with fans screaming at the top of their lungs, then backs up, slowly raising his arms to heighten the crowd's screams, and dives back into the song as flash pots explode.

Afterwards, Billie Joe bows deeply, holds his right fist in the air, blows kisses, then gives a few "I'm not worthy" bows before saying, "You guys fucking rule!" as the crowd excitedly chants, "Green Day! Green Day!" "And this next song is a big *fuck you* to George W. Bush!" says Billie Joe, and the band launches into 'Holiday', with its bitter critique of "President Gasman" and threats of "bombs away" to those who have the audacity to be critical of the government. However, "This song isn't anti-American!" Billie Joe shouts as he plays the song's intro, "It's anti-war!" At one point, he calls for "Lights out!" then, shining a flashlight into the audience, starts reciting the American Pledge of Allegiance, in the eerie glow of a red spotlight. The last line of the pledge, "With liberty and justice for all," provides a defiant reminder of what real American values are.

"Hi! How you guys doing out there tonight? Welcome to the biggest hometown show that we've ever had — thank you! Thank you! Thank you! Thank you!" Billie Joe says at the song's end. "We've been a band now — I should say, we've been a Bay Area band now — for the last 17 years," he continues, going on to talk about the their first-ever show at Rod's Hickory Pit in Vallejo. Among the packed audience down front is 17-year-old Robin Paterson, also from Vallejo. She's a senior at John Swett High School in Crockett, where Billie Joe was once himself a student, until the number of his unexcused absences piled up too high. She's been a Green Day fan ever since a friend told her about *Dookie*, the band's major-label debut, released 11 years earlier in 1994. She is especially fond of *International Superhits*, Green Day's greatest-hits collection. She wasn't immediately won over by *American Idiot* on its release: "At first I didn't like it that much because they sounded so different," she says. "But after I heard it more and more, I liked how it sounded. And I really liked how they made it all one story, but each separate song had a different meaning behind it."

Paterson and her friends got in line for the show around 4 pm, and managed to get close to the catwalk that juts out from the front of the stage. They've all brought T-shirts with "John Swett" on them, in the hopes Billie Joe will see them. Paterson throws hers on stage, but not knowing what it is, Billie Joe ignores it. Finally, he notices the group wearing the red and white T-shirts (the high school's colours) and points to them. Other people in the crowd try to grab the shirts for themselves, but the Swett group is determined to get one to Billie Joe. Joe Pallotta and Rick Williams each throw shirts up, but Billie Joe can't catch them. At last, during an instrumental break in 'Hitchin' A Ride', Charles Wetmore makes a perfect toss and the shirt lands right on top of Billie Joe's microphone stand. Billie Joe picks it up and displays it for the crowd. "This is the high school I went to in Crockett, California," he says, amending that to, "One of the high schools I went to. Didn't graduate though." He pauses, then can't resist adding, "And look at me, mom!" grinning broadly, his arms open wide in a gesture of triumph. From somewhere in the audience, Ollie Armstrong, Billie Joe's mother, is surely smiling back. In her story about the concert for the *John Swett Signal*, Paterson quotes fellow student Tarah Rhine saying jokingly of the moment, "For once it made me proud to go to John Swett."

There are more *American Idiot* songs during the show, including 'Are We The Waiting', which has the crowd waving their arms in the air again, then segues into the rollicking 'St. Jimmy', during which Billie Joe races from one side of the stage to the other, breathlessly spitting out the lyrics, as the crowd claps along in time. Then come the classics; the loping drum beat that kicks off 'Longview', from *Dookie*, which introduced the band to the rock mainstream. It's an ironic slacker anthem from a band that's rarely sunk into a "no motivation" slump like the protagonist in 'Longview'. Perhaps one of the primary reasons Green Day has such a loyal and devoted fan base is that they spent much of their formative years touring as extensively and as frequently as possible, a regimen they've basically maintained ever since. To start one number, Billie Joe quickly plays a single chord, then stops. He does it again. And again. And again, provoking the crowd into screaming louder each time he does it. Finally, on the tenth time, he continues past the first chord, and the song turns out to be 'Brain Stew', a favourite track from *Insomniac*. It's embellished by the copious use of flame pots; as the flames rhythmically shoot upward, the whole band begins jumping up and down in time with the song. Toward the end, Billie Joe picks up a large hose and sprays the crowd. Then, spotting a little boy in the audience, he brings him onstage and hands him the hose so he can spray the packed, sweaty masses in the mosh pit before him. And then there's 'Minority', the first hit single from *Warning*, whose anti-authoritarian message would've fit quite nicely on *American Idiot*. Underscoring this message, Billie Joe will later shout during the show, "No matter who are the powers that be, do not give up your civil liberties! And speak out against the bullshit that the bastards throw in your face!" The call to maintain an active interest in current events is the same reason you'll find booths for organisations like Amnesty International, Punkvoter, USA Harvest, and Greenpeace at Green Day shows.

There are a few surprises in the set list as well. Tré comes down front from behind his drum stool after 'Longview' to sing 'All By Myself', a hidden track on *Dookie*, which — as befits the gregarious drummer — is both goofy and a bit endearing. And after asking, "How many old-school Green Day fans are out there tonight?" Billie Joe presents a real blast from the past with '2000 Light Years Away', the lead-off track from *Kerplunk!*, their second album for Lookout Records, released over a decade ago, all the way back in 1992. Billie Joe then takes the time to introduce the band, saying of Mike, "a man that I've been standing next to since I was 10 years old. And the *greatest bass player in the history of punk rock music!*" Tré, says Billie Joe, is "a man I like to shower naked with" — Tré winks and nods at that — as well as "a man that is close childhood friends with Mr. Michael Jackson… and… *the greatest drummer in the history of rock'n'roll!*" "And my name," Billie Joe concludes, "is George W. Bush." The crowd boos and jeers in response, but Billie Joe gets the last laugh when, after a pause, he continues, "But you can call me *asshole!*"

There's typically a lot of interaction with the audience on 'Hitchin' A Ride', and this night is no different. First Billie Joe gets the crowd chanting, "Hey! Hey! Hey!" At one point, the music drops out completely, and Billie Joe points to various sections of the audience, encouraging each side to out-yell the other. Pleased with the results, he says, "Now that's how you do it San Francisco, *bay-bee!*" Before the song starts up again, he teases the crowd further by fondling himself with his left hand, while moaning provocatively into the mic he's holding in his right. Inevitably, as the moaning builds, he reaches into his trousers and finally shrieks,

"*Somebody fuck me!*" as the crowd roars in delight. Having "recovered", he grins and says, "I smell some of that Northern California marijuana out there! It's going down good with that hot dog about now!" — a scent that he'd certainly recognise, given that the band's name was inspired by pot smoking. "This is what I need," he continues. "This is what I need. This is what it's going to take. I need every single person in this park, in SBC Park in San Francisco, California, to scream, 'One, two, one, two, three, four.' Are you ready?" The crowd is. 'Hitchin' A Ride' finally resumes, and as flames shoot up, the crowd howls even more.

Audience participation reaches its height when it's time to play 'Knowledge', a song originally by East Bay legends Operation Ivy. It's the opening track from OpIvy's sole album, *Energy*, released in 1989 on Lookout. The album went on to sell over half a million copies, a remarkable achievement for an independent label, then or now, and especially so considering that it's been promoted almost exclusively by word of mouth. *Energy*'s record release party was held May 28, 1989 at the equally legendary Berkeley venue 924 Gilman. You could easily fit a few clubs the size of Gilman on the stage Green Day now occupies at SBC Park. Green Day opened for OpIvy that night in 1989; in fact it was their first show at Gilman playing as "Green Day", having only recently changed their name from Sweet Children. The Lookouts, Tré's band before he joined Green Day, played the same show.

Green Day covered 'Knowledge' on their second EP, *Slappy*, released in 1990. Nowadays, in a spirit of all-inclusiveness, they pull up kids from the audience to play the song. First, the band plays through the song, then Billie Joe announces, "Now, this is what we're gonna do. We're going to do something that's never been done here in San Francisco at SBC Park, ever! We want to start a band on stage, right now! So we need three volunteers." Naturally, everyone clamours to have the opportunity, but Billie Joe grills the prospective players intensely. "Do you know how to play drums?" he asks a young man in the crowd tonight. "Swear to God? How long have you been playing for? Seven years? Right, get your ass up here, let's go!" The new drummer scrambles up and gets behind the kit, with Tré watching over him, smacking him in the head each time he tries to do a fancy fill; "We got a show boater here tonight!" exclaims Billie Joe. Then a young woman is chosen to play bass; "This one's for the ladies — get your ass up here!" says Billie Joe. The drummer and bass player get their parts down, to an approving, "All right! We're making history!" from Billie Joe. Rounding out the new band is a young man with a mohawk, who, on taking the stage, hugs Billie Joe, then pulls a guitar pick off Billie Joe's mic stand; Billie Joe pulls him back and gives him a big kiss on the mouth in return, and the young man literally leaps for joy. Billie Joe then urges the bassist and guitarist to the front, where they let rip and strike all the classic rock-star poses while Billie Joe runs around the stage singing the lead vocal. "That was the greatest band we've ever had up here, ever!" he says afterwards. Then he calls the guitarist back; "Hey you! Come here! What are you doing? What's your name? Javier? Where are from, Javier? You're from Peru? That's awesome. Javier, you get to keep the guitar." Javier holds the guitar up in delight. "Now get your ass off my fucking stage!" Billie Joe thunders in mock anger. He then directs the drummer to do a stage dive. As Tré plays a drum roll and Mike thumps his bass, Billie Joe leads the crowd in shouting, "Jump! Jump! Jump!" The drummer gears himself up, then executes a perfect dive into the crowd.

The celebratory mood continues with Billie Joe donning a crown for 'King For A Day', a giddy celebration of cross-dressing. The rest of the players also don funny hats, and a wizard puppet pops up on stage and dances on top of some gear. It wouldn't be a Green Day show if Billie Joe didn't bare his bottom at least once, and it happens during this song, as he turns around, tugs his trousers down a bit and wiggles his bum for the audience's amusement. The rock'n'roll standard, 'Shout', proves to be just as much of a rave-up, and during the "little bit softer" part of the song, Billie Joe crouches down lower and lower until he's actually laying face down on the stage. A stage hand comes over and puts the fallen crown back on Billie Joe's head, along with a robe, and Billie Joe rolls on his back and begins singing another standard, Ben E. King's 'Stand By Me', before leaping up and continuing with 'Shout'.

The elegiac 'Wake Me Up When September Ends' is dedicated to the victims of Hurricane Katrina, which brought disastrous floods to the American South, decimating the city of New Orleans in particular, in late August. The entire stadium is alight with the flicker of cigarette lighters and glowing cell phones that the crowd holds up, mirrored by the firey sparks raining down over the stage. The main set ends with 'Minority', but considering the wild crowd response, you know there will be an encore and so there is. The band returns and starts up with 'Maria', one of the new tracks recorded for *International Superhits*. 'Boulevard Of Broken Dreams', the group's biggest commercial hit to date, is yet another sing-along, as so much of the set has been for this audience. Most bands would probably be content to end their show on the grandiose note struck by the cover of Queen's 'We Are The Champions', which sees a hail of green, red, and white confetti falling down on the crowd, some of whom pick up the slips of paper as souvenirs. But Green Day has yet another ace up their sleeve. Billie Joe returns to the stage bearing an acoustic guitar and a spotlight picks him out as he sings what's become the signature closing song for the band, 'Good Riddance (Time Of Your Life)'. And to further top things off, at the song's conclusion a spectacular fireworks display fills the sky. The crowd, previously elated, is now utterly ecstatic.

"Thank you for the best fucking night of my life!" says Billie Joe at the show's end. It's a sentiment Robin Paterson comes close to sharing. "Being my very first real concert, I pretty much thought it was the best thing ever," she says. "On a scale of one to ten, I'd say it was a ten."

Seventeen years before, Billie Joe and Mike played their first show to an audience of about 30. There weren't any stage lights, let alone confetti, flame pots, overhead video screens, or giant banners. But the desire to connect with the audience was much the same, along with the passion of the band's delivery and the sheer, unadulterated joy of simply making music. By that standard, perhaps the distance between Rod's Hickory Pit and SBC Park isn't that great after all.

CHAPTER 1

Stranded In Suburbia

"When you were a child, did you know this [performing] was what you were going to do?"

"Either that or be a Safeway truck driver."

— *Billie Joe to the* San Francisco Chronicle, *November 19, 1995*

Across the bay from San Francisco lies a sprawling collection of towns that stretch up and reach around to the southeastern side of San Pablo Bay, from Oakland (a bonafide city, with its population of 400,000), to Berkeley, Albany, El Cerrito, Richmond, San Pablo, El Sobrante, Pinole, Hercules, Rodeo, and Crockett, where the Carquinez Bridge then takes you north to Vallejo. Rodeo (pronounced Ro-DAY-oh), founded in 1890 by the Union Stock Yard Company as a meat-packing centre, has a population of 11,000, a size that no doubt helps the local Chamber of Commerce assure potential residents that "the small-town atmosphere that characterised Rodeo around the turn of the [20th] century still exists today."

And it was here that Billie Joe Armstrong would spend the first 18 years of his life. Born on February 17, 1972, Billie Joe was Andy and Ollie Armstrong's sixth child. He followed Allen (who was 22 years

1

older), David, Marcy, Holly, and Anna. Oil refineries had long since replaced meat-packing as the area's primary industry. "The whole area from Richmond over to about Pittsburg [California] is all oil refinery areas," says John Goar, who taught math and science at the local high school, John Swett, in the Eighties. "That really has an impact on the community. The cancer rate in that corridor is four times the national average. Just about everybody had someone in their family who has cancer. And I learned that it was really inappropriate to breech that subject, at least it was that way when I was there. It was so personal and painful; people know the air that they breathe is giving them cancer, but they didn't want to talk about it, they wanted to shut it out." Years later, Billie Joe would recall how students from his elementary school were often sent home after getting headaches from breathing the fumes of the refineries, which were alarmingly close by.

Andy earned a living as a truck driver. Ollie supplemented the family's income by working as a waitress, especially when Andy and his fellow Teamsters went on strike. "It seemed like he was on strike, holding signs up in front of Safeway every other month," Billie Joe later said. Ollie had dropped out of school to help her family pay the bills. Now, with a family of her own, she continued working to help make ends meet.

Both parents had a strong interest in music. Andy played drums in local jazz bands for 20 years and had a fondness for artists like Frank Sinatra. "That sort of stuff was like the classics to me, where a lot of people thought it was just corny," Billie Joe later told Lawrence Livermore, who founded the label Green Day would first record for, Lookout. "They didn't know what that stuff was about at all... I got asked to do a version of 'Witchcraft' for the *Oceans 11* soundtrack and I was like, 'I know "Witchcraft". I've known it my entire life.'" (Unfortunately, he didn't end up recording the song.) Ollie was a fan of country-and-western in general and Hank Williams and Elvis Presley in particular, which her young son picked up on; Billie Joe's first album purchase was Presley's classic *Sun Sessions*.

Being the youngest of six children also aided in Billie Joe's musical education, as his older siblings had their own tastes, ranging from The Beatles to Bruce Springsteen to R.E.M. So though the first music Billie Joe would play was heavy metal, and then punk, underneath it all he had a solid grounding in the strength of a good, catchy melody. When asked by *Rolling Stone* for a list of his Top 10 albums in 2000, it was evenly split between classic acts like The Beatles, The Rolling Stones, The Doors, and Bob Dylan, and later punk/alternative acts like The Ramones, The Clash, The Sex Pistols, The Replacements, and Nirvana.

Billie Joe's own interest in music and performing was quick to emerge. As a youngster, he would sing along with the performers on TV, using a fireplace poker in place of a mic stand. And at age four he had a stint of formal music education when he began taking piano lessons at the Fiat Music Company, a music store located at the Pinole Valley Shopping Center in nearby Pinole, where Billie Joe's three sisters had also taken lessons.

The music store was run by James Fiatarone and his wife Marie-Louise, who taught piano and voice. The couple was immediately impressed by Billie Joe's potential star quality, aided in no small part by a decided adorability factor. "He has a style of communicating with his hands and head like Al Jolson or Frank Sinatra," James told a local reporter. "I felt he was like a teddy bear and a puppy who could sing like an angel." Marie-Louise was equally enthusiastic. "I've had singers as young as three years old, but none with the charisma and love he has," she said. "To me, he's like a Renaissance angel, like a cherub in a Michelangelo painting."

The Fiatarones were also aspiring songwriters, and eventually took Billie Joe to San Francisco to record a song they'd written, 'Look For Love', accompanied by his sister Holly and some of their other pupils. The 2:11 song starts off with Billie Joe's count-in, then a light-hearted musical backing begins, as Billie Joe chirpily informs the listener that the solution to all of life's woes is — what else? — to look for love, a sentiment echoed by a female back-up chorus who sing the song's title no less than 44 times. When the track was released as a single in 1977 on the Fiatarones own Fiat Records label, the B-side would feature a short interview with the young singer. "How do you like being a recording artist?" a perky female voice prompts. "I love it!" replies Billie Joe. "Would you like to sing to people in other countries?" "Yes. I love people everywhere!" "Well, I'm sure that this song will reach people all over the world through your record, Billie Joe," the interviewer says approvingly. The interview ends with Billie Joe's request for fan mail — "and please send me your picture!" Twenty-four years later, a snippet from the interview would be chosen to open *International Superhits*.

'Look For Love' was promoted on local TV and write-ups appeared in area newspapers. "Billie Joe Armstrong, 5, Might Be On His Way To Top," predicted one writer, who quoted James as saying, "Shirley Temple came at a time of the Depression when our country needed her sweetness. These are almost the same kind of times and I think the world is ready for this kind of feeling." Eight-hundred singles were pressed and packaged in a plain white sleeve. Sheet music was also available, at $1.25 a copy; the pink-tinted cover features a picture of Billie Joe, wearing jeans and a T-shirt emblazoned with the song's title, sitting on a bench in front of a piano. His gaze is that of a child who's been told to smile but won't; his round, slightly pudgy face is framed by a full head of bushy hair. Today the single can be found for sale on line for up to $1,000.

Billie Joe continued performing as a child, singing at veterans hospitals and other community centres. "My parents wanted my time to be occupied and music seemed like the most natural thing that came to me," he explained. Though frustrated in his initial attempts to play the "piece of shit" acoustic guitar laying around the house, that changed when he was given his own guitar, a Fernandes Stratocaster. The Fernandes was a cheap copy of the Fender Stratocaster, and the first-issue of the guitar resulted in Fernandes being sued by Fender, as the copy was too exact. Some accounts have Billie Joe's father buying the instrument for his son; other accounts say it was his mother. However he acquired the guitar, it quickly became his prized possession and he nicknamed it "Blue". The Fernandes remained Billie Joe's signature guitar through the recording of *Insomniac* and he occasionally uses the guitar today ("Though it looks more green than blue now," he told *Guitar World*), and has had a number of replicas of it made as well.

Something else equally life-changing happened to Billie Joe around the same time; Andy Armstrong died of cancer of the esophagus when Billie Joe was 10. Ollie was forced to increase her waitress duties and money became so tight that gift giving at Christmastime was curtailed in the Armstrong household. "We just learned to accept it," he later told

Launch.com. "We just had fun. My family knows how to party, so it was no big deal, you know?"

Ollie's subsequent remarriage to a man none of her children liked added to the unhappy atmosphere that Billie Joe's sister Anna later described to *Rolling Stone* as "dysfunctional". "There was a lot of fighting amongst the siblings, a lot of hitting," she said, a view Billie Joe himself corroborated in other interviews. But it also provided the creative spark for the first song Billie Joe would write, at age 14, the aptly-named 'Why Do You Want Him?' later recorded on Green Day's *Slappy* EP.

But Billie Joe's tenth year was also rounded out by meeting a fellow aspiring musician with whom he formed his longest-lasting artistic collaboration to date: Mike Dirnt. Mike had his own set of challenges to deal with while growing up. He was born Michael Ryan Pritchard on May 4, 1972, to a mother whose use of heroin led to his being put up for adoption six weeks after his birth. He was eventually adopted and moved to Rodeo with his new family, but the family divorced in 1979. Mike first lived with his adoptive father, but eventually returned to his adoptive mother. He later estimated he'd moved seven times by the time he was 15. When his mother remarried, he too would come into conflict with his new stepfather, though ironically the two would become closer when the marriage split up. He was also occasionally bothered by chest pains and panic attacks he was initially told were the result of problems with his heart.

Mike had dabbled in piano at home before moving on to guitar and eventually bass after he realised the instrument would make him stand out more in a group of guitarists. He taught himself to play on "a total piece of shit" his mother acquired from a pawn shop. He also took a few guitar lessons, but preferred to learn on his own, jamming with friends or sitting in anywhere he could, learning a variety of musical styles, including jazz. "I've always been into melody, and the bass seemed like an easier way for me to get to those melodies," he later told *Bass Player*. "I didn't have to finesse it as much as I did when I played guitar." Years later, Mike would design his own signature model bass for Fender, the Mike Dirnt Precision Bass, modeled after Fender's '51 P-Bass.

Despite the poor quality of his first instrument, Mike's bass "made the right sounds," and Billie Joe and Mike soon developed a passion for practise. "Billie and I would just plug into the same amp and play all night," said Mike. "We played and practised because that's all there was to do. We weren't good at sports. I'm not a big guy, so what's my way to look cool and maybe impress some girls? I'm going to play bass! And it was cool. It was something that we could call our own."

Mike later told *Spin* that on first meeting Billie Joe, "we didn't like each other because we were both class clowns," but their joint interest in music quickly led to their forming a fast friendship. And as the two moved into Carquinez Middle School, their musical horizons began broadening as well. Billie Joe made the acquaintance of two brothers, Matt and Eric, who came to Rodeo every weekend to visit their divorced father, who lived on the same street as Billie Joe. The brothers were also keen music fans and introduced him to metal bands like Def Leppard, Ozzy Osbourne, Van Halen, and AC/DC. Years later, Billie Joe would still delight in dropping a signature riff from one of his early idols in between songs at Green Day shows, as at one show in 1998, when 'Welcome To Paradise' led into Black Sabbath's 'Iron Man', which then segued into AC/DC's 'Back In Black'. He quickly shared his new discoveries with Mike. "I remember Billie pulling out Van Halen's *Diver Down* and playing it for me," Mike later recalled. "I'd never heard Van Halen before, and I was like, 'Whoa!'"

When the brothers discovered punk, they again shared the music with Billie Joe, and several of the punk acts would go on to be key influences for both Billie Joe and Green Day. There was Generation X, whose song 'Kiss Me Deadly' Billie Joe later credited with kindling his desire to start a band. There were The Ramones, who Billie Joe first saw in their 1979 cult film *Rock 'n' Roll High School*, later proclaiming them, "the perfect rock band." And then there were The Sex Pistols, whose short career thrust punk fully into the mainstream spotlight for a brief period in the late Seventies. On first hearing 'Holidays In The Sun', Billie Joe recalled to *Rolling Stone* that "the guitar came roaring through like thunder. By the time [lead singer John] Lydon's vocal came in, I definitely wanted to destroy my past and create something new for myself... Anytime that I'm trying to create something, I always refer to The Sex Pistols, because it shows you what the possibilities are as far as music." Of the group's sole album, *Never Mind The Bollocks, Here's The Sex Pistols*, he said, "It punched a huge hole in everything that was bullshit about rock music, and everything that was going wrong with the world, too. No one else has had that kind of impact with one album. . . It's just an amazing thing that no one's been able to live up to."

By now, there were plenty of North American punk acts to discover as well, such as Vancouver, B.C.'s DOA; TSOL, from Long Beach in Southern California; and, closer to home, San Francisco's Dead Kennedys. (Jello Biafra, the outspoken lead singer of The Dead Kennedys had made a memorable bid for mayor of San Francisco in 1979, coming in a surprising fourth.)

So, though both Billie Joe and Mike initially worked hard at perfecting their heavy-metal riffing, they also maintained an active interest in punk and later indie/alternative acts. Billie Joe later credited his sister Anna's interest in "more artsy stuff," as helping to develop his own musical tastes. "That became the biggest influence to me, that bridged that gap from heavy metal to punk," he explained. One group he discovered through his sister was The Replacements, after she brought home the group's debut album, *Sorry Ma, Forgot To Take Out The Trash*. (The Replacements were also one of the first bands Billie Joe saw in concert.) Hüsker Dü also made an impression, and Billie Joe cited their last album *Warehouse: Songs And Stories* as a favourite in *Kerrang!* "For early Green Day, Hüsker Dü is the band we really tried to model ourselves after," he said. Mike also developed broad tastes in music, telling an interviewer in 2001, "I listen to everything from Iggy Pop to Blondie to Etta James."

Originally, metal and punk had been practically warring camps, but as the Eighties progressed, younger, less doctrinaire fans readily conceded there were elements of the music that they liked in both genres. As Nirvana's bassist Krist Novoselic put it in his memoir, *Of Grunge And Government*, "I'd hear punks refuting the old guard — they cast Seventies rock bands away as though they were false prophets. Even though I was a believer in punk, how could I reject the music that gave me so much joy? Where would the world be without Black Sabbath?" Other musical influences Billie Joe and Mike have cited over the years have ranged from Sixties British Invasion groups like The Beatles, The Who, and The

Kinks to Seventies-era Queen and the soundtracks of *The Rocky Horror Picture Show* and *Jesus Christ Superstar.* (Billie Joe would later have the logo from the *Jesus Christ Superstar* album tattooed on his right arm.) In short, music fully consumed the two, and when they weren't practising, they were listening to records or making mix tapes. By eighth grade, before moving on to high school, they decided to get even more serious. They played only original material, meaning that their early shows — when bands most frequently play covers in order to fill out their set — instead featured only their own songs. At first, Billie Joe had fallen into the common trap of simply rewriting songs he'd already heard, but he quickly began finding his own voice. Soon, the two had come up with their first song, the prophetically titled 'Best Thing In Town', which they would finally record in 1990.

In the fall of 1986 Billie Joe entered John Swett High School in nearby Crockett, where enrollment averages around 650 students a year. "Crockett is really the only small town in the Bay Area," says Goar. "It's one of those everybody-knows-everybody type of places. A very old town, a lot of old families. There's a small town feel to the place which you never find anywhere else in the Bay Area, because all the cities are so big."

"Both Crockett and Rodeo are close-knit communities," agrees Ken Leslie, who was Billie Joe's band teacher at Swett. "Especially Crockett. It's smaller and sometimes seems to be right out of the Fifties. The old families of the area include large Italian and Portuguese families. Some families have had up to four generations graduate from the school — the first graduating class was in 1927. The school population was fairly diverse, both ethnically and economically, in the Eighties, and even more so now. The atmosphere has always been pretty good. The school has been a large part of the lives of many people in these towns."

The school itself was "an old three-story brick building," says Goar. "The gym was just a little cracker box. Student enrollment was small for a high school. It was in the single A league in student athletics, and we'd have to travel long distances to find another school that was also a single A league school. I did some coaching, and there were a lot of long bus trips, because every other high school in the Bay Area was larger and we really didn't want to compete with them; we wanted to play against a school that was somewhere near our own size."

Steve Peters, a friend of Billie Joe's older brother David, is today John Swett's principal, and remembers Billie Joe's days at Swett. "The girls adored his blonde curly hair," he says, "and he was actually a very good athlete, in both baseball and football. But he was always interested in music." Goar even remembers Billie Joe being on the junior varsity football team in ninth grade; "For some reason I think that he was number six, but I really don't know where that information is coming from."

Two of Billie Joe's sisters had been involved in the school's band program, and Billie Joe initially followed in their steps by signing up for Beginning Band, as a drummer. Leslie remembers Billie Joe's sister Holly in particular as "quite a good clarinet player," but Billie Joe was less enthusiastic, despite Leslie's insistence that "the band at John Swett had always had a really good reputation of being the organisation to be in. There was no such thing as a band nerd at our school!"

"He was a nice enough kid," Leslie recalls, "but he was one of those kids that never really showed up much. I don't know if he was bored with it, because the kid's obviously a very talented musician, and what we were doing might've just bored him out of his skull. Because you've got a class of 15 or 20 beginning musicians, and especially at the beginning part of the year, you've got to go really slow; 'Three Blind Mice' in the Beginning Band class with the clarinets and the trumpets and one trombone player probably wasn't really exciting to him."

Billie Joe admitted as much himself in later years. "I probably could have done the work if I applied myself," he told Lawrence Livermore in recalling his school days, "but I just was not interested at all." And he told journalist Alec Foege, "I fucking spent the worst years of my life in high school. It held me back from doing what I wanted to do." Mike was also unhappy at his schools. "We went to school in the suburbs," he told *Alter/Native*. "It was really shitty... Then I went to a school that was somewhat more alternative. But there were still a lot of shitheads and everything." He also felt constricted by his immediate environment, coupled with a strong desire to rise above it. "In the Bay Area a lot of people do a lot of speed and a lot of drugs," he said in the same interview. "And they just sit around and they'd rather work shitty nine-to-five jobs and waste out. Instead of actually getting out there and doing what they would rather be doing. Their only limitation is that they're in this suburban subculture." Even as teenagers, for Mike and Billie Joe, music was something they were already firmly dedicated to and determined to stick with, regardless of their chances of success. "People always ask, 'What would you be doing if you weren't playing music right now?'" Mike said in 2001. "Well, we'd probably be playing music right now. We all recognised that this is definitely what we do best and that this is what we want to do."

Nonetheless, even in an environment Billie Joe described as "the most unscenic place on the planet," he managed to find material for future songs. 'Tight Wad Hill', for example, later recorded for *Insomniac*, describes the hillside that overlooks the high school playing field, where those who didn't want to pay to see sporting events could watch for free. It was also a hangout for drug users, "tweakers... crank victims and stuff," fuelled on the locally made methamphetamine.

Billie Joe also ended up in Goar's pre-algebra math class. "It probably wasn't one of his favourite classes," says Goar. "Homework completion was an issue. But he knew where he was going already. I mean, most kids his age are into music or athletics, one of those long-shot type of professions. But I don't think they were as sure about it as Billie Joe probably was. He probably had it in his mind that's what he was going to do, and if you know you're going to be a professional musician, what's pre-algebra?"

Nonetheless, "He and I got along pretty well," Goar says. "I treated him with dignity and respect; I didn't judge him based on his grades or his attendance or anything like that. I kind of do that with students, I think that it's important. He and I liked each other. Not too many kids do I remember from that many years ago. But I do remember Billie Joe. He wasn't goofy. He wasn't a mean guy. He got along with people. It's hard to imagine a 13-year-old version of him, but he had a lot of charisma. I think that's what has made him as big as he is, just the way he can command a crowd. That was evident back then."

Goar also says he remembers Billie Joe's band, then called Sweet Children, performing at the school talent show in the spring of 1987. "It was a competition and his band took second place," Goar says. "The group that beat him was a group of cheerleader girls doing kind of a dance routine. Billie Joe was incredibly upset by that. Didn't think it was fair, thought it was rigged. He felt so deeply about it. He takes a lot of pride in what he does, and to be beat by a bunch of cheerleader dancers wasn't what he liked." If Goar's memory is correct, this would pre-date what's generally been accepted as Sweet Children's first show, in the fall of 1988 at Rod's Hickory Pit.

Billie Joe later invited Goar to see another show. "It was a gig way up a couple of counties north, at somebody's house," he says. "It was a free show type of thing. It would have been a strange thing for me to go to, I wouldn't have known anybody there. It was 50 miles away and my wife was pregnant with our first child at the time, so I didn't go. I kick myself today for that."

Both Leslie and Goar had noticed Billie Joe's increasing number of absences, which usually resulted in a visit to the office of the vice principal, Jack Turner. "If you were a bad kid, Jack Turner was someone you'd have to deal with," says Goar. "He was in charge of discipline at the school. And I suspect that Billie Joe missed school quite often. I bet his attendance wasn't as good as it needed to be. He would be gone for long blocks of time." He'd already stopped coming to band class completely. "I was disappointed," says Leslie, "but it was just one of those things — well, it's not his bag, so, okay fine, go on to the next kid. Though I remembered his sisters and thought, 'They were nice girls, too bad their brother didn't stick with it.'"

Billie Joe ultimately transferred to Pinole Valley High (where Mike was also a student) during his sophomore year, possibly due to recurring attendance problems, and later dropped out of school for good. "I knew he was having problems in other classes and so on," says Leslie. "Then I heard that he had left our school. And when I heard he dropped out of school, I was like, 'Geez, that's too bad. What's gonna happen to him?' Then, boom, here he is, world famous!"

Green Day's breakthrough success in 1994 was as much a surprise to Leslie as it was to many, though from a different perspective. "I was really humbled, to be honest with you," he says. "Here I had been a music educator, and I never saw that in him. It's like, 'Holy smokes, I blew that call.' Knowing how hard it is to make it in professional music, it's heartwarming that he did it because I knew him. But it's also a little embarrassing to me because I didn't realise what there was there. I didn't see it. I don't know what that says about me, but that's a plain fact."

Goar didn't immediately link Green Day with his former student until he saw Billie Joe's name, and, "Finally the connection hit. I saw the name Billie Joe Armstrong, and I said, 'Wait a minute, I know that name!'" Goar had by then moved to Washington state and tried contacting Billie Joe, mailing him Christmas cards. "They probably never made it to him," he admits. "He's got to be a person that hundreds and thousands of people want to see, they all want a piece of him." But he now sees Green Day's shows when they play the Pacific Northwest, first seeing them in October 1995 at the Seattle Center Arena. In a story for *greenday.net*, the official fan website, he wrote of the show, "Someone threw a shoe at Billie Joe and he got pissed off and cut the set short. I liked the *Nimrod* tour a lot more. My wife and I saw Green Day play a small club (DV8) on December 2, 1997 and the show kicked ass. Green Day just wasn't made to play arena shows." And one of his favourite songs is 'Stuart And The Ave.', from *Insomniac*, "because it talks about the neighbourhood where I was when I was in college" — that is, Berkeley.

Goar's youngest daughter is a Green Day fan, and Goar uses his one-time association with Billie Joe to reach out to his students. "Music is a passion of mine," he says. "I've seen more than 450 concerts in my day. There's a lot of music posters up in my room. I've got a couple of Green Day posters. It helps to be able to tell the kids that I taught Billie Joe. That's always a way to kind of get in with them, make a connection. Especially with your hard-core Green Day fans. Which there are a lot of."

And at the end of his piece for *greenday.net*, Goar writes, "Hey, Billie Joe — I bet none of your other teachers have asked for a backstage pass. Next time you come to Seattle — what do you say? I'd like to party with a rock star — and a former student!"

Leslie now teaches journalism at John Swett and students don't hesitate to ask him about his most-famous pupil. His son is also a Green Day fan. "He just loves them," says Leslie. "He's got all their CDs, and so I've heard some of the stuff, and the lyrics are quite good. I'm not into that style of music, but when you just take the lyrics as a form of poetry or something, it's like, 'Wow, that's pretty good!'

"Everybody would tell Billie Joe, 'Geez, you know, if you don't come to school you're not going to amount to anything.' He sure proved a lot of people wrong," Leslie concludes. "You got to hand it to the kid. He did it all on his own, he's a self-made guy. Everybody should be proud of him for that. It's really a success story. And if anybody were to ask me who he could credit with his success, I'd say himself."

CHAPTER 2

Gilman Days

"Thanks for booking Green Day. This is Green Day's first tour and we hope it will be fun."

— *Green Day's first touring contract*

L ess than 15 miles from the halls of John Swett High School, a new venture in Berkeley was coming together that would prove to be remarkably influential in Billie Joe and Mike's musical development: the Gilman Street Project, or as the club is more commonly know, Gilman. The club was well situated to fill a growing need on the part of musicians and music fans in the East Bay, who had been hungering for a different kind of rock venue. For though a college town like Berkeley — home to the University of California, Berkeley (UC Berkeley) — had its share of upstart bands, clubs that regularly catered to new music (and not an endless string of cover bands) were few and far between. Nor were San Francisco clubs necessarily welcoming to groups from what was derisively referred to by the city's residents as "East Berlin", due to the East Bay's perceived drabness.

As a result, young bands constantly on the lookout for places to perform would often find themselves in non-traditional music venues, ranging from abandoned warehouses to art galleries and even pizza joints. "There was this one pizza place where we used to put on shows, Own's Pizza in Berkeley," remembers Frank Portman, better known as "Dr. Frank", guitarist and primary songwriter of the Berkeley-based Mr. T Experience. "That was the kernel of what the Gilman St. thing grew out of. Among the core of the people that would put on shows there, that was the beginning of the idea of, well, we do these shows here, we have to find a venue, a club. Every town has people like that; 'All we need to do is buy this old theatre and then we can run a rock club and book only good bands, it'll be great!' And because of the organisational skills of Tim Yohannan, it actually ended up happening, which I think is kind of unusual. And it's still there."

Yohannan was the founder/editor of the in-your-face punk magazine *MaximumRockNRoll*, and as he explained in a 1996 interview published in the book *924 Gilman*, he had been trying to get an all-ages venue started for some time. "Sometime during 1985, I decided to get serious about putting a club together and started looking for a location," he said. "Then I ran into this lunatic named Victor Hayden, who had a similar idea as well... he was the one who actually found the space at 924 Gilman. I was hesitant, but everyone who looked at it thought it was great, and said, 'We gotta do it.'"

The space, at the corner of 8th St. and Gilman St. — in the back of a building that was also home to The Caning Shop, a caning-and-wicker store — was less than three miles from the more quaint and scenic downtown Berkeley area, and at that time was a largely industrial area. (These days, the district is listed as the "Gilman St. Shopping Area" on visitor's maps, and is home to businesses like REI, Walgreen's, and the Pyramid Alehouse.) A lease was secured in April 1986, and the rest of the year was spent refurbishing the space; a picture of the construction of one of the club's bathrooms later graced the cover of issue "38½" of the local 'zine *Cometbus* that celebrated Gilman's ten year anniversary.

Permits also had to be obtained, though it was decided to make the venue alcohol-free, thus making it easier to do all-ages shows. "Tim wanted to make it an all-ages venue that lasted, that kept going," says Murray Bowles, a computer programmer who had been attending local punk shows and, with Yohannan's encouragement, had started photographing them. "Because there were plenty of bar kind of places that were around, but they were generally only around for a few years, partly because they had underage drinking. I went to the first Berkeley City Council meeting about it, and, oddly, they were arguing about Tim's insistence on their not serving alcohol; the people of the city council were kind of wondering why he was insisting on that since it was perfectly okay with them."

Then there was the matter of how the club would be run. Participation from the community was actively encouraged. "Isn't it time we created a real alternative?" read a flyer promoting the endeavor. "Come and find out for yourself how this project can involve you."

Portman was among those who attended Gilman's planning meetings, as the Mr. T Experience had formed the same year (the band would later record a song about the venue, 'At Gilman Street'). Portman had discovered punk through listening to local radio stations, especially college radio stations, and leaned toward "the kind of punk rock that was more or less pop songs, roughly recorded pop songs... The Ramones, The Buzzcocks, The Undertones, that whole type of punk rock." Since junior high he'd toyed with the idea of setting up a band with his friends. "Three or four guys would be hanging around together, and they were 'in a band', but it was mostly theoretical," he explains. "You design your logo, you come up with a track listing for the first three albums, you chart how the band breaks up when everybody dies in a plane crash, and so forth. The idea that you would try to actually play in front of people was always kind of scary to me in those days. But eventually you acquire instruments and you form a band, then probably 10 years later you learn to play your instruments and then it's all downhill from there!"

Eventually, Portman did start up a real band, the Mr. T Experience (the name being inspired by a character on TV's *The A-Team*, a muscular African-American who sported a mohawk), and welcomed the opportunity to have another local venue to play. "Gilman was a central feature of your life if you were trying to be a band, because you were always looking for places to play and you wanted to be involved," he says. "You had to pay your dues though. In the run up to opening, they had these meetings every week that you felt like you had to go to if you were gonna get booked there, and I cannot even describe to you how tedious they were. It's like they were run by these guys from the Sixties who were drawing from their experience of forming Maoist communes and so forth, so there was a lot of strange bureaucratic nonsense; rarely was someone able to finish a sentence without some kind of crypto-hippie standing up, waving *Robert's Rules Of Order* and saying, 'Point of order! Point of order!' There was a real division between those people, and the 'kids', the people in bands, in their early twenties. The main reason you were there was that you wanted a place to play, not necessarily that you wanted to overthrow the government and remake society on a more egalitarian, smellier basis. That was their trip. We were just like, if they're gonna have a place to play we should be involved in it, 'cause it's a place to play. I went to a lot of meetings, and I'd just sit there; I was in college at the time, so I'd bring my homework, do my Latin while they were arguing about *Robert's Rules Of Order*. It was a real experience."

Portman admits he couldn't resist tweaking the sensibilities of those who took such matters so seriously. "I have kind of a contrarian streak, and I had even more of it back then," he says. "And so I really enjoyed baiting them, I would ridicule their pseudo-leftist pretensions. That was the year of anti-Reagan rock; at that time everyone had to have a anti-Reagan song, and every other song was about El Salvador. So we used to say, 'This is a song about a girl' to introduce practically every song — and most of the songs were love songs or breakup songs, but the reason we started saying that is because it would just drive 'em crazy! And sometimes we would fake 'em out, like say, 'Hey, this one's about El Salvador. . . no, I'm just kidding, this is a song about a girl.'"

"Gilman was sort of like a socialist co-operative grocery store in atmosphere except that it was a punk club," recalls Jesse Michaels, lead singer of Operation Ivy, who would be one of Gilman's most popular bands prior to the arrival of Green Day. Michaels was also involved with Gilman as a volunteer. "It was a collective, a community-organised club, and it was supposed to be a totally democratic situation, but Tim more or less ran it. He was a communist, and tended to infuse everything he did with heavy-handed left-wing rhetoric. For that reason, there was no advertising at Gilman for the first year, no drinking, no racism, etc. It was a good thing in some ways, but very un-rock'n'roll at the same time. Everybody noticed that it was a bit stiff there at times. On the other hand, the organisation was tight, unlike other punk clubs, bands were paid fairly, and security problems — like skinheads — were dealt with instead of just ignored."

And despite his mixed feelings about the organisers, "the most important thing is that it was a place to play," says Portman. "There were places like it all over, but this was the one that was here. I would say that one of the things it did successfully, one of my goals for it which actually did happen, was that it was a place where it was a little bit safer to be a goof-ball, which is all that I knew how to do. Hardcore bands played there, but it was a little bit less alienating. The fact that there was a place to play did mean that the kids who would go had the same experience that a lot of us had; you'd see these people on the stage and think, 'Wow, they're terrible, I could do that,' and so then they'd start to form their own version of it, and that's how the scene developed."

Gilman finally opened on New Year's Eve, 1986, with Impulse Manslaughter, Christ On Parade, Silkworms, AMQA, and Soup — who would have the honour of being the very first band to play on the Gilman stage — on the bill. Shows were held on Fridays, Saturdays, and occasionally Sundays. Initially, the idea was that attendees wouldn't know who they were going to see. "Tim's plan had been that no one would know who was playing," says Bowles. "There would be a music committee, and they would figure out the bands that were good for you to hear. And you would just come to Gilman and see what happened." But audiences were less interested in taking a chance than Yohannan had hoped. "At the beginning, more often than not, there were shows that there were hardly any people at all," Bowles says. "It was only later, especially with OpIvy and Green Day, that there were really big shows. And eventually, the not-knowing-who-was-going-to-play principle wore down, because bands would flyer anyway. And if you were a band enthusiastic enough to flyer, then your friends would know about the show, and then gradually *MaximumRockNRoll* started having their own flyers, and then it was all like a normal club." Aside from one other detail; in the spirit of supporting independent artists, bands affiliated with major labels were not allowed to play the venue.

Membership was required, but the fee was a mere two dollars, and shows themselves were an equally reasonable five; those who didn't want to pay that nominal amount could volunteer to work in some capacity at that evening's show. Though not especially large (the stage itself is wedged into one corner of the room), Gilman exudes a potent atmosphere, with seemingly every inch of wall space covered with graffiti. Bands set up tables on the side to sell their records and T-shirts, there are "free boxes" of used clothing, and a room designated as the "stoar", stocked with candy and soda. Despite the no drink-ing/no smoking policy, attendees slip outside — particularly between sets — to indulge, or, these days, cross the street to go to the Pyramid Ale House for a beer. And though music remained the focus, there was no shortage of other freewheeling hijinks. A 1987 story in *Spin* noted, "Past evenings have been livened by a game of 'Twister', a run-ning battle between two people in mock-FBI mufti armed with auto-matic Uzi waterguns, and a scavenger hunt that turned up everything from 'Garbage Pail Kids' to a picture of someone's mother in a bouf-fant hairdo."

Gilman also had their own documentarian in Murray Bowles, who was there most weekends with his trusty Canon. Taking Tim Yohannan's suggestions, "I learned that you can't just stand in one spot all the time," he says. "You have to move around. I gradually got used to it, going from place to place and getting bumped into and stuff. And eventually I learned how to take pictures holding the camera over my head instead of actually looking through the viewfinder. That was a big plus. My camera, a little Canon range finder, had a 28mm lens, so everything was wide-angled, so you didn't really have to point precisely at what you wanted." Bowles' photos initially appeared in publications like *Ripper*, *Thrasher*, and *MaximumRockNRoll*, then, after Green Day's success, in larger publications like *Rolling Stone*, and the book *Fodor's Rock & Roll Traveler USA*, not to mention countless album covers.

Mr. T Experience played Gilman the first month it was open, on January 10, sharing the bill with Short Dogs Grow, Feederz, and Undesirables; Operation Ivy soon followed on May 17, when MDC (Millions of Dead Cops), Stikky, and Gang Green also played. Both Mr. T and OpIvy would end up on a new local indie label that would also help to launch Green Day: Lookout Records (or, to use its logo'd punctuation, Lookout!).

Some 160 miles north of the East Bay, Lawrence Livermore, then 39 years old, was living on Iron Peak, a remote hillside in the Mendocino mountains, accessible only via Spy Rock Road. The nearest town, Laytonville, was 18 miles away, with a population of 1,000; Willits, the next largest community, was positively robust in comparison, with a population of 4,000. "It's a town full of a lot of artists, free-thinkers, and musicians," says Winston Smith, an artist who lived in the same area, and who would design the cover of Green Day's *Insomniac* album. "People who moved up there from Berkeley or LA during the late Sixties and early Seventies were doing it to leave the big city. It's a precarious balance between redneck cat-hatters and free-thinking, poet, hippie, anarchist weirdoes."

Lawrence had grown up in Detroit, listening to rock'n'roll and doo-wop on local radio in the Fifties, then getting swept up by the city's Motown explosion of the Sixties. "I was inspired not just by the music of Motown, but by the idea that poor and working-class people from the projects could create their own scene instead of waiting for city slickers from New York or Hollywood to do it for them," he explains. "Then after that, I listened to the British Invasion stuff and all the Detroit garage bands that were trying to copy that style."

It didn't take long for Lawrence to become interested in making music himself, though he admits, "I hung around with bands but didn't have the nerve to try playing guitar myself until I discovered Hank Williams and got an acoustic guitar. I had been playing piano, mostly on my own, since I was a little kid, but once I left home I didn't have a piano again until I was in my thirties, so I had to make do with a guitar."

Livermore eventually ended up on Iron Peak as "a kind of 'I'm sick of the city, I'm going back to the land' sort of thing," he says. "Not very logical. My girlfriend and I had a scary adventure in San Francisco one night where this carload of kids wielding two-by-fours chased us halfway across town for no apparent reason, and it was at that point that I said, 'That's it. I've had it with this city. I'm going to go start my own city somewhere else.'" Once relocated, he also finally began trying to put together a band of his own.

A constantly fluctuating membership initially kept the group from getting off the ground, so in lieu of a band, Livermore launched a publication, *Lookout!*, in 1984. "It was named after the fire lookout tower atop Iron Peak, which was the most visible landmark — actually one of the few visible signs of human habitation — in the remote canyon where we lived," he explains. "Originally it was more of a local newsletter for the mountain community where I lived. I occasionally wrote about music, but usually only to make fun of the hippie and reggae music that was popular there, or to further rile up the hippies by claiming that punk rock was better. However, when a delegation of angry pot growers threatened to burn down my house because I was bringing too much attention to the region, I shifted my focus to more regional issues and also started writing a lot more about the punk-rock scene in San Francisco and the Bay Area. And once The Lookouts got going, I of course wrote a lot about them and the other bands we played with, and that sort of grew into covering the Gilman Street scene." Livermore later became a columnist for *MaximumRockNRoll*.

The drummer in Lawrence's on-again/off-again band also happened to be his girlfriend. When the couple split, she conveniently left her drum set behind, and in 1985, a final lineup for Lawrence's band, also called The Lookouts, came together. Livermore played guitar, and, though in his late thirties, drafted in some young neighbours to accompany him. One was 14-year-old Kain Hanschke, soon dubbed "Kain Kong"; the other was an even younger boy, 12-year-old Frank Edwin Wright III, who lived a mile away from Livermore on Spy Rock Road.

The young Wright was born December 9, 1972, in Germany; his father flew helicopters in Vietnam. When his father's tour of duty finished, the family (which also included an older sister) relocated to Mendocino county. His father worked as a truck driver and a bus driver, while his wife Linda was a bookkeeper. The region's isolation left the boy without much to do, which is how he ended up hanging out at Livermore's home, despite the difference in their ages.

Wright already had an interest in music. At age nine, he'd taken up the violin, but as he told *Drum*, "No noise came out that sounded good, so I kind of gave it up." Nor did the music on the only station the family radio picked up ("Hall & Oates, Huey Lewis, all that shit") catch his ear. He was far more interested when Livermore offered him the chance to play on the abandoned drum set. "Even though he'd never played drums in his life and was only 12 years old, I thought he had the right attitude to be in a punk band, and that was more important than musical ability," Livermore says. Frank had already been nicknamed "Tré" by his family, a variation on the Spanish word for "three"; Livermore added the surname "Cool", giving the name an additional meaning, playing on the French word for "very", *tres* (Tré Cool = very cool).

Livermore says the age differences made little difference to the group. "It wasn't that different from playing with people my own age," he says. "I think musicians tend to be fairly juvenile anyway. I know I was. Occasionally I had to be a bit parental, especially with Tré, because as a 12 year old, he just didn't have the attention span for long practises and was hyperactive — still is, apparently. But it didn't take him long to discover that he really enjoyed the drums and was good at them. From then on, the main problem was getting him to stop pounding on them long enough to have a conversation."

The drums proved to be a perfect fit for the energetic pre-teen; as he recalled to *liveDaily.com* about his father's response to his wanting to become a drummer, "He said, 'Well, if you can rub your stomach at the same time as you pat your head, at the same time you're jumping up and down on one leg and kicking the other one out in a circle, and saying 'The Pledge of Allegiance...' And then I did all that just like, bam, you know." Initially, he wasn't allowed to play with the set's full count of cymbals because of the noise he made; as he improved, they were returned to the kit, one by one. Tré's father eventually bought him a kit of his own for his thirteenth birthday.

Tré's practises were described by his mother as "pretty noisy, but a definite improvement on the violin." In fact, Tré improved to the point where he found himself in great demand as one of the area's few drummers. Though still in junior high, he would play with high school and college bands and orchestras, broadening his repertoire by playing a wide variety of music, ranging from classical to big band music to reggae. "A lot of the time they never had drum charts so I would just go off a trumpet chart," he said. "It just got me ready for other things. It just opened my skills." As a result, his influences were equally wide ranging; in one interview he cited both Gene Krupa and Marky Ramone as "drumming heroes".

Meanwhile, The Lookouts were also busy, playing local parties "where all the parents and kids would come," says Livermore. "And we played at a campsite/general store parking lot down by the highway." By 1986 they began getting gigs at the smaller punk venues in the Bay Area, so the opening of a club like Gilman was a welcome development. "Prior to Gilman Street opening, the original San Francisco punk scene had kind of dwindled down to a pretty low ebb," says Livermore. "There were big thrash/metalcore type shows, but the DIY punk stuff was mostly happening in warehouses and garages and really small clubs. It was always a challenge to find somewhere to play, but once Gilman opened, the scene practically exploded, with all these kids starting new bands and their friends coming to see them play and being inspired to start their own bands. I loved just about everything about Gilman. Like it says in the Rancid song ['Journey To The End Of The East Bay'], the place was sacred ground to me. It was a place where all the misfits fit in, where you could make up the rules yourself, and nobody — well, almost nobody — was there to tell you that what you wanted to do was impossible."

Livermore then launched a third venture under the Lookout name, a record label, initially co-owned with David Hayes, then Patrick Hynes, that he started with $4,000. The Lookouts were the first act to release a record on the label, their 1987 album *One Planet, One People* boasting such songs as 'Don't Cry For Me Nicaragua', 'Fourth Reich (Nazi America)', and, in a nod to their roots, 'Mendocino County'. The album's record-release party was held at Gilman (where the group had first played on January 24), Livermore sporting a black eye received from a "local lunkhead" who'd tried to stop the band playing at another show the night before. The other band members used makeup to draw their own black eyes in solidarity.

Livermore was impressed by the quality of the bands playing Gilman, and soon decided to expand Lookout's roster with them. "At the time I thought I'd be lucky to break even and that if I was wildly successful I might be able to sell a thousand 7-inch EPs for each band," he says. One of Lookout's first success stories would be Operation Ivy, whose existence would only span two years and a handful of recordings, but who were a major component of the Gilman scene, an influence on many (including Green Day), and whose sole album, *Energy*, would eventually sell over half a million copies, largely by word-of-mouth alone.

Most of the band's members were all veterans of the East Bay scene. Vocalist Jesse Michaels had performed with Crimpshrine, as well as drumming for a few metal bands in Pennsylvania. Guitarist "Lint" (Tim Armstrong, no relation to Billie Joe) and bassist Matt McCall (whose real surname was Freeman; "McCall" was taken from a character in the TV detective series *The Equalizer*) had played together in Basic Radio; Armstrong had also played bass in Crimpshrine. They brought in Dave Mello to round out the band's lineup, and "basically taught him how to play drums," in the words of OpIvy's online bio. The name, taken from nuclear weapons testing operations of the Forties, had also been previously used by the band Isocracy. After a warm-up show in Mello's garage, OpIvy made their debut at Gilman.

OpIvy's music was a lively ska-punk mix, inspired by an early Eighties Berkeley band called The Uptones. "They were probably the first ska band in America," says Michaels, "and they all went to Berkeley High School. One night the local movie theatre showed the film *Dance Craze* [a 1980 documentary about British ska bands]. It was a very memorable night. The whole theatre erupted, and people were literally dancing in the aisles. So everybody knew about ska here and most of the highschool age rock groups had at least some ska influence. So it was very natural for Tim and I, who were both into ska, to write those type of songs together, in addition to the punk songs. Since we were in an atmosphere of hardcore-type music at that time, we naturally kicked the tempo up until it had a kind of punk-rock energy. Anyway, these things happen naturally and are the result of group energy. All new forms are developed through good luck and magic."

Livermore, a friend of Tim Armstrong's, was overwhelmed on first seeing OpIvy and immediately suggested that the group record for his label. But before that agreement could get off the ground, OpIvy's first recorded appearance came on a double EP compilation

MaximumRockNRoll released later that year, *Turn It Around*. OpIvy's contributions would be the songs 'Officer' and 'I Got No', recorded with engineer Kevin Army, who would go on to work with many other Lookout bands.

"Every punk scene has an engineer that defines its sound," says Michaels. "In LA there was Spot [who produced many artists for the SST label], in D.C. there was Don Zientera, and there were also specific engineers in Boston, Chicago, and New York that recorded everybody's records in the early days. This is because back then, there were fewer qualified engineers who understood punk, so there was often just one guy in town who could really get it right. Another reason is that an influx of energy in an artistic community always co-arises in all fields — in other words, if you suddenly have a bunch of remarkable musicians, you will also suddenly have a remarkable publicist, remarkable writers, remarkable managers, remarkable engineers, etc. This is the nature of group artistic phenomena. Kevin Army was the guy for Berkeley. He had a unique, trashy — in the good sense — sound that seemed to make bad bands sound good and good bands sound great."

On learning the Mr. T Experience had already put out a record themselves, Livermore picked Portman's brain for details. "I knew Larry from this radio show that I did at KALX, the UC Berkeley station," Portman explains, "and he always used to call up and come visit, and I remember him asking, 'How did you do it?' And I said we recorded with this guy, Kevin Army, at this cheap studio, and we told him where the pressing plant was, and then he did his band, The Lookouts, in the same way, and that was what became his first record, Lookout #1. Our second record was on Rough Trade, and we were working on the third one, and Larry was trying to talk me into doing it on his new label instead of Rough Trade, and I remember thinking that there's no way that anything this guy's gonna do is gonna go anywhere, and Rough Trade's a real company. Of course, Rough Trade US went out of business almost as soon as that record was released, so then we basically had to go and say, 'Okay Larry, will you still do our record?' And he did, but it was a little bit embarrassing." The group's first record on the label would be the single 'So Long, Sucker'/'Zero', released in 1989, followed by the album *Making Things With Light* in 1990, which featured the song 'Danny

Partridge Got Busted', about the arrest of Danny Bonaduce, one-time star of TV's *The Partridge Family*, for cocaine possession.

OpIvy had finally put out their own record on Lookout in early 1988, the six-track EP *Hectic*, which was Lookout's third release. (The band initially tried recording at Gilman, but couldn't get the right sound and ended up recording at Oakland studio Dangerous Rhythm, again with Kevin Army.) "Not that many people wanted to put out our albums at the time, mainly just Lookout," says Michaels. "There were less labels back then because at that time, punk records didn't make much money. So it was an obvious choice to go with Lookout. I remember that Matt and Tim had some ambitions of signing with Slash which was an LA punk label that was in bed with the majors. I am really glad that didn't happen because we would have been fucked on that sinking ship."

1988 was also the year Yohannan's group quit running Gilman, and a new group of organisers took over. Gilman survived the transition, and continues today. There were those who felt at that point that the club's best days were behind them, and the glory years were over. But as Frank Portman points out, such views are too limited to encompass the sweep of what Gilman represented. "There's two ways to go in summing up the experience of the Berkeley rock scene and Gilman," he says. "One tack people take is where they describe it as a golden age, where milk and honey were flowing like wine, and there were gold nuggets that you picked up right off the street, and I've heard people do that. And then, I think more in line with how people in bands felt at the time, there's a cynical kind of an attitude, which is I guess what I have.

"But it all boils down to there being something kind of special about San Francisco, the Bay Area, Berkeley in general," he continues. "Irritating as it can be, because everybody's got these crazy pretensions. They started a rock club geared towards a more interesting direction than they sometimes ended up taking, interesting in the fact that there was a little less self-censorship on the part of some of the people involved. There was a time when you could go there, and you wouldn't know what kind of craziness you would see. A lot of it was extremely juvenile and extremely lame, but at least it was happening. And I say that as a positive thing."

Billie Joe later credited his involvement with the music scene swirling around Gilman as having "saved me from living in a refinery town all my life." He first ventured to Gilman with his sister Anna, and soon he and Mike (who later said "Gilman was my high school") were regularly attending shows, and not only at Gilman. "In the late Eighties, there were a lot of shows all over the Bay Area in garages, backyards, clubs such as The Berkeley Square, and also neighbourhood community centres," says Jesse Michaels. "I would say there was about a show a week, although not necessarily in Berkeley." Such low-scale shows were also more likely to be all-ages and cheap (or, in the case of private parties, free), making them all the more accessible to two 15-year-olds. Billie Joe and Mike also ventured into Berkeley, checking out the wealth of record shops, bookshops, and used-clothing stores lining Telegraph Avenue, the busy shopping thoroughfare that runs south from the UC Berkeley campus, beginning across the street from Sproul Plaza (prominently featured in the 1968 film, *The Graduate*), where you can still find vendors hawking tie-dye T-shirts as if it were the height of the Sixties. And Billie Joe got his first close-up look at slam dancing when he went into San Francisco to see a show by Bloodrage and Transgressor at the club On Broadway; though trying to keep out of the way, a skinhead still managed to jump on top of him.

But Gilman would be the primary hangout for the two, and for the first two years of the club's existence, before they began ascending the stage themselves, they received an intense introduction to the burgeoning East Bay music scene and punk culture. "Going to Gilman, and seeing how militant the politics were about racism and sexism, that was the first time I'd thought about some of that stuff," Billie Joe later told Lawrence Livermore.

After making their debut at the club on May 17, OpIvy generally played once a month at Gilman, and the band became particular favourites of Mike and Billie Joe. Crimpshrine (whose bassist, Pete Rypins, was a special favourite of Mike's), Mr. T Experience, Sewer Trout, Neurosis, and Corrupted Morals (whom Billie Joe would later play with) were other bands that caught their eye. And both of their future drummers were in bands that played Gilman regularly; John Kiffmeyer, Jr. from Isocracy and Tré Cool in The Lookouts.

Billie Joe and Mike were becoming even closer as a result of Mike having left his home, and eventually moving in with Billie Joe's family. He got part-time jobs in restaurants to help pay the rent, while still finding time to make music and keep up with his school work (as Billie Joe was becoming less and less interested in his formal education). The two finally took their efforts to the next level by forming a band, Sweet Children, bringing in Kiffmeyer, a few years older than Billie Joe and Mike (and who frequently worked under the name Al Sobrante, a play on the name of his hometown, El Sobrante), on drums. They soon acquired a PA system by pilfering the equipment from a friend known to leave a side door of his house unlocked.

The band even had their own theme song, 'Sweet Children', which would be recorded during the summer of 1990. The song opens with a blast of guitar, then takes off at a brisk pace and ends in just over a minute-and-a-half. The lyric, which looks back in fondness at the antics of the titular children, has a curious nostalgia, given that the group's members hadn't left their own childhoods behind that long ago. And though there are hints of fondness for heavy metal in the guitar and bass interplay, it's the underlying pop catchiness of the song that really captures the attention. The strong pop influence made them stand out from the more hardcore element associated with Gilman, but even so, they managed to land a gig at the club soon after they began playing public shows.

The band made their public debut at the restaurant where Billie Joe's mother worked, Rod's Hickory Pit, located at 199 Lincoln Rd. W. in Vallejo, just across the Carquinez Strait from Rodeo, and accessible via the Carquinez Bridge. The year of that first show has frequently been given as 1987. However, on Green Day's fall tour in 2005, Armstrong told the audience at their October 17 show at Dayton, Ohio's Nutter Center that the date happened to be 17 years to the day since they'd played their first show — which would make it October 17, 1988, when Billie Joe and Mike were in eleventh grade. Livermore also remembers first seeing them in the fall of 1988, "maybe November... [and] they'd only played maybe three or four shows at most before that." Billie Joe had previously appeared at the restaurant on his own, entertaining senior citizens in the banquet room. The restaurant's owner, Richard Cotton, later described him as a "good kid" to *San Francisco* magazine in 2004.

The article also estimated that an audience of about 30 people saw the performance.

And that was a good five or six times the amount of people in attendance when Lawrence Livermore first saw the band, at what he describes as "a fiasco of a highschool party that Tré had organised. It was in some cabin way up in the mountains with no electricity, just a generator. And the kid whose cabin it was didn't even bother showing up, so we had to break in. Sweet Children played by candlelight for five kids, and as I've said many times — because it was the thought that came into my mind at the time — they played as if they were The Beatles at Shea Stadium."

Livermore was not only impressed by the band's charisma and songs, but also by their willingness to make a roundtrip drive of some 300 miles on a stormy night merely to play at a house party for no money. "It was obvious that they just really loved playing music," he says. "And in my experience, that was one of the key ingredients for a successful band. I decided then and there that I wanted to do a record with them. However, at the time, I didn't really expect to sell a lot of records; in fact, I thought I might even lose a bit of money because I guessed that their songs might be a bit too poppy for the punk kids who were Lookout's usual audience. But by that time I'd had enough success with the earlier records I'd put out that I figured I could afford to take a chance on these guys. Punk or not, the songs were so great that they needed to be recorded and heard." Within six months, the band would release their first record.

On November 26, Sweet Children made their debut at Gilman, sharing the bill with Twitch, Raskul, and Altered Ego. Frank Portman believes this may well have been the first time he saw the band. "I thought they were pretty cool," he says. "They were young kids and they were playing in the right place for being young kids. But they were not, at that time, all that exceptional. It's not like you saw them and your head just spun around, and it was like, 'Whoa, this changes everything!' like some people say when they saw The Sex Pistols. Obviously, as they played more and got better, it became clear that people really liked them and that they had something. But the whole point of that scene was people just like that getting on stage and playing music like that, really. I remember thinking, 'oh, this is another pretty cool band of young kids.' But as they started to play more and get more popular, they became a lot of people's favourite local band pretty quickly, because they were good; they put on a fun show, and they had catchy songs, and all the usual reasons why you like to listen to bands."

Murray Bowles recalls Sweet Children as being, "Pretty poppy and happy, and often playing with bands that weren't! That was cool. That made them stand out. If you were going to Gilman shows all the time, or listening to punk rock all the time, it was a large departure. It all sounded so different, but it was real easy to suddenly like it just because it was so different. Because it was good."

In early 1989, Sweet Children entered San Francisco's Art of Ears studio to record their debut release, co-produced with Andy Ernst, who'd previously produced another Lookout band, Corrupted Morals, and would later work with the bands AFI, The Groovie Ghoulies, and Screeching Weasel (whose logo Mike would tattoo on his right arm). "We were excited!" Mike recalled to *Bass Guitar*. "It was like, God, we're going into the studio and we're actually gonna make a record! This is like, unbelievable!" The 4-track 7-inch EP, said to have been recorded in seven hours, was eventually entitled *1,000 Hours*, and released as Lookout #17 that April. The description of the record on the label's website read, perhaps a bit defensively, "These songs are about girls and love, so if either of those subjects make you feel creepy, be warned. This is what got all the kids pogo-dancing to Green Day at the punk rock show. Too pop? So what!" Livermore also admits, "I thought that because the music was so poppy, it might have a hard time finding acceptance with the punk rockers who mostly bought Lookout releases. And it did sell slowly at first; it took six months or so before it seemed to start catching on."

Girls and love were indeed the sole themes of *1,000 Hours*, though "thwarted love" would be a more accurate description, as in three of the four songs the singer is separated from the object of his desire (or, as in 'Only Of You', too tongue-tied to tell her of his feelings). Billie Joe himself later dismissed the title song as being "sappy". The music is an energetic power-pop, delivered almost breathlessly, as if Billie Joe wants to hurry through the numbers before losing his nerve in confessing his love, with Mike's harmonies adding a further melodic edge. If a listener knew nothing about the band, they might not immediately cite punk as one of the group's great loves and influences. The Sixties pop of the British Invasion or the Eighties-style power-pop of groups like The Romantics would be a more likely (and not entirely inaccurate) guess.

The EP's release coincided with the group's decision to change their name from Sweet Children to Green Day, causing Lawrence Livermore some consternation, as the band had already built their reputation under the Sweet Children moniker. But the change made sense, for "Sweet Children" only underscored the band members' youth, and would more likely be a name they'd quickly outgrow (one anecdote claimed an early show was actually interrupted when Billie Joe's mother called and demanded he come home to finish his chores). There also happened to be another local band with the similar-sounding name Sweet Baby. The band's new name was variously attributed to a reference the Muppet Ernie had made in an episode of the children's TV show *Sesame Street* or a slang term for a day spent smoking marijuana, admittedly one of the group's favourite pastimes. (In years to come, numerous articles about the group would bear the headline, "It's Not Easy Being Green," taken from a song sung by another Muppet on *Sesame Street*, Kermit the Frog.) The initial record sleeve was green, with the band's name and the record's title in black, and when Livermore ran out of green paper while xeroxing, he switched to pink paper; the band members themselves helped fold the sleeves.

As was typical of many independent labels, the record was pressed in a variety of colours; according to the website *greendaydiscography.com*, there were 600 copies on green vinyl, 200 each on purple and red, and 100 each on clear and yellow. ("It's also on blue vinyl, but I don't know how many were pressed," says the website.) A second pressing had a sheet of "bilt-in leerics", which noted that while Billie Joe was the primary lyricist, Mike had also contributed lyrics to 'The One I Want'; the music was credited to the entire band. The jokey credits on the back cover identified the band members as "Billy [sic]: Guitar, Hat," "Mike: Bass, Hair," and "John: Drums, Bus." The credits were perhaps in reference to the picture of the band on the back cover (taken by Murray Bowles) which shows Billie Joe's bushy hair barely contained by the baseball cap he's wearing backwards, and Mike hanging upside down by his knees from a railing, his long hair stretching to the pavement. "Thank you! We'll play anywhere," the "leeric" sheet said optimistically.

Sweet Children played their last show under that name on April Fool's Day at Gilman. The next time they played at Gilman, as Green Day, was May 28, the first — and last — time they would open for OpIvy. The members of Green Day had seen OpIvy on a number of occasions by then, and OpIvy was familiar with the band formerly known as Sweet Children. "They used to practise at Gilman Street, I think," says Jesse Michaels, "or maybe they were recording a demo there. Anyway, I saw them playing there on off-hours for some reason. I thought they were a very good pop/college rock band in the spirit of Hüsker Dü and Soul Asylum. They didn't strike me as being a punk band, but I was really into pop at that time and I thought they were really good; I told them, 'You guys are fucking great.' We always got along very well, and still do, although they are out in the stratosphere somewhere these days.

"What has always made them stand out is their musicianship and their superb melodies," Michaels continues. "Billie Joe is an unbelievably solid guitar player. A lot of kids think he is not all that great simply because he avoids solos and plays relatively simple parts. They don't know what they are talking about. He's a machine. He can also play all sorts of flash shit, but he has good taste so he doesn't. He's the salt of the earth. Everybody loves Billie because he is real, and charming, and an all-around nice person. He is troubled at times like every artist, but he never lets it interfere with how he treats the people around him. He loves to have a good time and his sense of humour has never diminished in the slightest." Michaels has equally fond memories of Mike, whom he calls a "very good spirited, nice guy, always had a joke, always clowning around. I mean *always*! Sometimes he drove people crazy. But later, after all the shit they went through, he became a more serious fellow. I think he has really come into himself as a person and is a very good-hearted guy. He knows how to deal with all the shit they deal with and he also knows how to protect his own personal identity. A good bloke."

The May 28 show was especially eventful, as it was the record-release party for OpIvy's album *Energy*. But it was also one of the band's final shows. "I quit the band because at that time we absolutely could not get along and I was living a miserable life of anger and frustration," says

Michaels. "No band is worth waking up pissed off every day. Now I have a healthy relationship with all the members of the old group and I am very glad that I made a decision and moved on with my life before things got really out of hand." The club was packed for the show, which also featured Surrogate Brains, Crimpshrine, and The Lookouts on the bill. Livermore told writer Gina Arnold the show "was like a punk Woodstock — and I was at the real Woodstock, so I should know." Though it's been reported that the Gilman date was the band's last show, Michaels says the real last show was the next day, at a party at the house of a friend known as Eggplant (who also put out the 'zine *Absolute Zippo*, that Billie Joe would later contribute to). "It was a much better show than the Gilman show which was terrifically overcrowded and fucked up," he says. "The Gilman show was good too, but just too hot. The backyard party that followed was much more in the true underground spirit of the band." The later CD release of *Energy* would also feature the tracks from the band's *Hectic* EP, as well as the tracks that had appeared on *Turn It Around*. Each band member went on to play in other groups, Tim Armstrong and Matt Freeman most notably in Rancid.

OpIvy had been something of a house band for Gilman; now that they had vacated the stage, it was Green Day's turn to rise to prominence. Livermore remembers realising the band's potential while watching a show at Gilman "with no more than 100 kids or so, maybe in 1989," he says. "Somebody brought some dry ice to the show and laid it at the band's feet as they played. Then someone put a milk crate onstage and Mike stood on top of it while another kid shone a flashlight up toward his face as if it were a spotlight. They were playing, of course, the song 'Dry Ice' [from *1,000 Hours*] and though it was meant to be a piss-take on the usual arena-rock format, I suddenly thought, 'You know, these guys could be rock stars for real.'"

The group sought out gigs wherever they could find them. On July 15, they made a 50-mile trek to Davis to play a "benefit" show the band Necromancy was holding to raise money to record their album (though the gig was advertised as being free). The show, which also featured the band Phallucy, was held in the city's public Community Park, and the posters conspicuously warned, "NO DRUGS, NO ALCOHOL, NO RACISM, NO VIOLENCE." The number of those in attendance wasn't a huge concern; if a show drew only a few people — as frequently happened, since the band members were under 21 and thus couldn't play the more lucrative bar circuit — the band could still have fun hanging out with their friends. And if they couldn't drink legally, they nonetheless had little difficulty getting their hands on alcohol. On first meeting them, Ben Weasel, lead singer and guitarist of Screeching Weasel, who also recorded for Lookout, initially wrote off Billie Joe and Mike as "idiots" due to their constant indulgence in alcohol and pot. And at an early show in the small town of Garberville, the band members' drunkenness was such that they had difficulty holding on to their instruments — though the show was still considered a success (Billie Joe's fondness for pot had also led to him being nicknamed "Two Dollar Bill" — the price he charged for joints).

But at this stage, Green Day gigs weren't enough to keep the group fully occupied. Billie occasionally could be found playing with Corrupted Morals and Blatz, and Mike joined Crummy Musicians as a vocalist. Mike also moved out of the Armstrong house and lived in a warehouse in Oakland at the corner of 7th Street and Peralta Street, a dreary, industrial area, not far from the West Oakland BART★ station and adjacent to the large Union Pacific Railroad yard. Billie Joe eventually moved in with Mike, and the environment provided the inspiration for the high-spirited, coming-of-age letter home, 'Welcome To Paradise'.

At the end of December, Green Day entered Art of Ears to start recording their debut album, again co-producing with Andy Ernst. The album was a typical quick-and-dirty indie recording, spread over five days (22 hours, according to the album's liner notes), commencing December 29 at 4:30 pm and ending on January 2 at midnight. Recording was mostly live, with a few overdubs; Billie Joe and Mike often recorded their vocals simultaneously, in the interest of saving time. Estimates for the total cost ranged between $600 and $700.

The 10 tracks that made up the album were both tighter and bristled with more confidence than the tracks on *1,000 Hours*, showing how much the band had progressed in a few months. "When the first record came out I thought, 'Pretty good, cute,'" says Jesse Michaels. "When the

★ The region's mass transit system

second one came out I thought, 'I wish I was in this band.'" The primary topic was again unrequited love, most obviously seen in a title like 'Don't Leave Me', and yearning for an unobtainable object of desire was also the focus of songs like 'At The Library', 'Disappearing Boy', and 'The Judge's Daughter'. Yet some other ideas were also poking up through the crunchy guitar riffing. Both 'I Was There' (with lyrics by Kiffmeyer) and '16' take a bittersweet look back at one's youth — again, perhaps surprising statements from a group that could reasonably still be considered "youths" themselves. And 'Road To Acceptance' has the perennial outcast expressing regret about his outsider status. (Billie Joe later said the song's theme was inspired by racism.) And then there's the band's new "theme song", 'Green Day', which Billie Joe identified as being "about staring up at the ceiling thinking of a girl, being stoned."

Aside from the slower tempo'd 'Rest', the album's pace was upbeat; as Lookout's description of the album offered, "Green Day explodes onto the scene with a bright-as-hell burst of pop inspiration. This shit will blow your head off, and your headless corpse will dance nonetheless." Yet the cover, designed by Michaels, struck a curiously solemn note, featuring a soft-focus black-and-white shot of a young woman walking through a graveyard. The back cover had three live shots of the band taken by Murray Bowles at Gilman, and cartoon-style drawings by Michaels of monster faces, safety pins, keys, and a box of matches with "Club 924" on its cover, along with a martini glass — an ironic tweak at Gilman's no alcohol policy. The lyric sheet featured what purported to be a letter from I.R.S. Records expressing interest in the group ("We think you're the hottest group out of the bay area since the Dead Kennedy's! [sic]"), along with two replies, a polite one from Kiffmeyer ("Lawrence Livermore and Lookout Records have treated us very well and even though we are not bound to them legaly [sic] they're our friends and that is pretty important to us") and a more contentious one from Livermore ("You wish you could get somebody as hot as Green Day for your cheesy washed-up label"). But the I.R.S. letter had been fabricated after Kiffmeyer found some of the company's stationery in a dumpster. "About two years later I.R.S. got wind of it and sent threatening letters," says Livermore. "But it was all settled by an apology on our part." When later packaged as a CD, the album also included songs from the *1,000 Hours* and *Slappy* EPs, along with the track 'I Want To Be Alone', which had appeared on the 1990 *Flipside* magazine compilation *The Big One*; it was duly renamed *1,039/Smoothed Out Slappy Hours*. The I.R.S. letter and responses were not reproduced in the artwork.

39/Smooth was released in February 1990, the same month that Billie Joe decided to drop out of high school, a week before the album's release, and two days before his eighteenth birthday. He'd been attending Pinole Valley High where his attendance had been so infrequent, when he went round to his teachers to have them sign his drop-out papers, they didn't know who he was. Music was now his sole focus in life. Mike — determined to graduate — stuck it out and eventually received his high school diploma. (Tré also dropped out of high school during his sophomore year but later received his GED.)

Flush with the excitement of releasing their debut album, Green Day headed back into Art of Ears on April 20 and recorded another batch of tracks for their next record, the EP *Slappy*, which came out soon after. On the record they paid homage to OpIvy by covering 'Knowledge', the opening track on the band's *Energy* album, but where the original had raced along before coming to a halt at 1:42, Green Day's version loped at a relaxed pace, clocking in at 2:20. The EP also included 'Why Do You Want Him?', ostensibly directed toward Billie Joe's mother in response to her marrying his much-disliked step-father, but written broadly enough that anyone could relate to the sentiment. 'Paper Lanterns' is another lament to lost love, while '409 In Your Coffeemaker' finds the narrator contemplating another failed relationship while in a self-confessed daze, perhaps as the result of a "green day." (Billie Joe later said the song was "about how much I hate school.") As usual, the more melancholy sentiments are undercut by the bright, even chipper, musical backing.

In addition to being pressed on the usual assortment of coloured vinyl, the EP was packaged in a sleeve featuring a close-up head shot of a bulldog named Mickey, but who, according to the liner notes written by Aaron Elliott (aka Aaron Cometbus, creator of the *Cometbus* 'zine and a musician himself), had been nicknamed "Slappy" by a friend (Jason Relva, drummer in the band Pennywise). The liner notes, entitled "Green Day Bits", also featured such items of trivia as, "People used to mistake Mike for Axl Rose" and "John has been known to do a naked rain dance when he's drunk too much cheap beer," as well as name-checking various friends and associates.

On May 5, Green Day played Gilman on a bill with Starvation Army, Public Humiliation, Voo Doo Glow Skulls, and Los Angeles band L7, making their first appearance at the venue. L7 was one of a new breed of all-female hard rock/alternative bands (that also included such groups as Babes In Toyland, from Minneapolis; Seven Year Bitch, from Seattle; and The Lunachicks, from New York City), and had previously played in Berkeley. "L7 were no strangers to the Bay Area," says Jennifer Finch, the group's bassist. "The challenge about being in L7 was that LA really didn't have a scene that supported what L7 was doing, so there was a lot of motivation to get out, first to the Bay Area, and then elsewhere. I was always sort of the punk rocker of L7, and I was always really familiar with the DIY scene that was coming out of Oakland and Berkeley through *MaximumRockNRoll* and through what was happening at Gilman."

But Finch has few specific memories of that first show with Green Day. "Musically, I didn't really enjoy three-piece bands," she says. "I grew up with very aggressive, experimental music, and it really wasn't what they were doing at the time. Now, I love it. I think they developed more, and of course I have. At the time, I just thought of them doing a middle-class kind of punk/pop music, doing it in a more sophisticated way — which now, as an adult, I realise was just good songwriting." Four years later, the two bands would be sharing a much bigger stage together, when both were on the 1994 Lollapalooza tour.

Five days after the Gilman show, the band played an outdoor show at Pinole Valley High School. The occasion was Foreign Foods Day, a daylong event at which school clubs sold their versions of foreign foods and local bands played. A video of the event shows Green Day playing on a walkway in front of one of the school's buildings as disinterested students walk behind them. Though the day is sunny, Billie Joe wears a light jacket over his white T-shirt for much of the two-set show, his blonde hair stuffed under a backwards-turned baseball cap; Mike has on a long-sleeved reddish shirt. Despite the scattered applause ("Hey, come up," Billie Joe urges the audience at one point, Mike adding, "Pretend it's

Gilman!"), the performance is enthusiastic. Mike duck-walks, Chuck Berry-style, during the opening number, 'Going To Pasalacqua', and Billie Joe falls on his back, legs akimbo, at the end of 'At The Library' (which they ended up playing twice during the show). 'The Judge's Daughter' was introduced as being "about a chick from this school." Similarly, 'Don't Leave Me' was introduced as being "about a girl who dumped me in the seventh grade," prompting an, "Oh, poor baby!" from the audience. As if wishing to drive the bad memory out of his system, Billie Joe leaps into the air at the song's beginning, and Mike indulges in a furious bit of duck-walking.

The following month the group went on their first US tour, having booked the 45 dates themselves. The contract the band sent out to the venues that had booked them was both deferential in its requests ("We are asking for $100, more if you can spare it. This is not a guarantee, we are only asking") and careful to prioritise ("More important than money is food and a place to stay. We have one vegetarian and four guys who will eat just about anything"), as well as pointing out, "We are not a straightedge band, so don't be afraid to offer us a beer." Still, underlying the surface politeness was the more pointed observation, "You do not have to give us any of these things, of course we don't have to tune before we play either."

The tour, which began on June 19, took the group up the west coast to Canada, back into the US, and across the country to the east coast, down into Florida, up through the Midwest, and finally back to California. Aaron Elliott went on the tour serving as a roadie and wrote a humourous account of the trip in *Cometbus #25*, with dots on a map of the US indicating where specific events had taken place, such as a visit to the Olympia Beer brewery in Tumwater, Washington ("Free samples! Yum!"), a failed attempt to stop at the corner of 53rd Street and 3rd Avenue in New York City (then a notorious pick up spot for male hustlers, immortalised in The Ramones song '53rd and 3rd'), and a stop at the hotel in Washington, D.C. where the so-called "Plumbers" waited prior to burglarising the Democratic National Committee headquarters in the Watergate Hotel across the street. There were also occasional notes on the shows ("Played with skinhead Jimi Hendrix cover band. Not much fun") and informational tidbits like Billie Joe needing medical attention "for really bad poison ivy" and Mike breaking his bass in half (after it fell when his guitar strap broke).

The shows were not always well attended, but the experience was invaluable for a band trying to gain further exposure. With Lookout having little money available for promotion, word about the band's record was largely spread through the few reviews it received in alternative 'zines. The band quickly learned that self-reliance was the key to surviving life on the road. At their first stop in Arcata, California, they arrived to find that a venue hadn't been secured for them to play at; they wound up performing in someone's living room. They boosted their meager income by buying cheap T-shirts at local stores, screen-printing their logo on them in someone's backyard, and then selling them at shows, charging a reduced fee for fans who brought their own shirts. They also adopted a flexible approach to shows that would serve them well over the years; "The day of our first tour we threw away our set lists and said, 'Let's not use them ever again,'" said Mike.

Two other notable events also occurred on the tour. After a show in Minnesota, Billie Joe struck up a conversation with a young woman named Adrienne Nesser, then a manager at a Pier 1 Imports outlet in Mankato. "I was one of only ten people at a Green Day gig and me and Billie ended up hitting it off," she later wrote for a fan website. Nesser eventually moved to California and became Billie Joe's wife.

The other event also took place in Minneapolis, when Green Day was offered the opportunity to record for the St. Paul-based Skene! Records label. Instead of new material, the group decided to record songs from their Sweet Children days; "We just always wanted to be recording," Mike explained to *Guitar Legends*. "Since we were still playing those songs... it was like, 'Hey, we've got studio time — let's record 'em!'" Accordingly, the EP was entitled *Sweet Children*, thus forever confusing fans who have believed this was the first record the band actually recorded. Along with the title track, the EP included 'Best Thing In Town', essentially a love song; the bright 'Strangeland'; and a cover of The Who's 'My Generation', which was the most straight-forward of the bunch; the ending had the band gradually playing faster and faster, before coming to an abrupt halt. The session also marked the first time Mike switched to a Gibson bass (a Grabber G-3) after his Peavey Patriot had broken. He subsequently used that first Gibson for over 700 shows, until "I finally retired it after about the third time its neck broke."

Though the total records pressed didn't exceed a few thousand, the EP ultimately had four separate editions. The first was packaged in a black-and-white sleeve featuring an onstage shot of Mike's legs. The second was packaged in a black-and-white sleeve with a picture of a beat-up Volkswagen and the cryptic caption, "What do you think Mike..." (a third edition, in a red sleeve, featured the same picture). The sleeve also noted that the record had been "reorded" [sic] "in a few hours with Mac at Mac's hole in the ground." The songs were later included on the CD version of the band's second album, *Kerplunk!*, after which the EP was reissued in a white sleeve with a small picture of three children on a dock, one of whom has a sign reading, "Future Feminist". The label was thoughtful enough to put a disclaimer on the cover of the latter edition: "No! This is not a new Green Day 7-inch but the same old SKENE! one that we keep having to repress and hence keep running out of covers for... the music is exactly the same, just in different packaging to keep the people who have to stuff these things into plastic sleeves from getting bored. So keep in mind, catering to collector-scum by paying big $$$ for something because it looks a wee bit different only makes you look like a sap..."

If Green Day returned from their first national tour without much in the way of monetary compensation to show for it, they at least had a sense of accomplishment, especially considering they'd done most of the work themselves. "I didn't have much of anything to do with the tours apart from occasionally advancing them some money or some records to sell," Livermore says. In less than two years they'd managed to put out the equivalent of two albums of material, nearly all of it original. They had a solid core of fans in the East Bay area, providing a sturdy base from which to grow, and they'd begun making inroads outside their home territory on their first national tour.

And then John Kiffmeyer decided to leave the band.

CHAPTER 3

Tour Today, Tour Tomorrow

"We were never concerned about success. We were just looking for places to play."
— *Tré to* Guitar Legends *#81, 2005*

The reason behind John Kiffmeyer's decision to leave Green Day was a perhaps surprising one for a punk-rock band. Instead of the ever-popular "musical differences" excuse, he'd decided to go to college at Humboldt State University in Arcata, a town some 240 miles north of Oakland. What hurt as much as his leaving was that Kiffmeyer's band mates didn't hear the news directly from him. As Billie Joe later told Lawrence Livermore in an interview, he'd been walking around with a few friends, including Aaron Elliott, when Kiffmeyer's departure was mentioned in passing. "And I'm like, 'John's leaving? What do mean, John's leaving?' And Aaron looked at me and goes, 'Oh man, he didn't tell you, did he?' And I'm like 'No, he didn't tell me. Where the fuck is he going?' That's how I found out. And I was hurt. It blew me away."

In addition to their personal disappointment, Kiffmeyer's leaving could also have easily meant the end of the band; "I didn't even know if I wanted Green Day to go on after John quit," Billie Joe told Livermore. Both Billie Joe and Mike had relied on Kiffmeyer's experience, and he'd also handled much of the band's business. And though Green Day was steadily making progress, the band was still at the stage of laying the groundwork for a future career, as opposed to furthering an already flourishing one.

Billie Joe also expressed some doubt over how committed Kiffmeyer had been to the band, pointing out that he had opportunities — such as choosing to go to college — that Billie Joe didn't. As he told Livermore, "I didn't want to feel like anybody's side project." And the "Green Day Bits" insert included with the *Slappy* EP further hinted at some tension between the members, noting, "Band arguments usually center around Billie Joe being irresponsible, Mike being high-strung, and John being overbearing."

'I Was There', on *39/Smooth* has sometimes been read as Kiffmeyer's reflection on being in Green Day, but in fact, the lyrics take a much more general look back at one's past — torn between wanting it to last, but ultimately choosing to look ahead toward tomorrow. Kiffmeyer evidently hoped he'd be able to juggle the responsibilities of both the band and his studies by saying he'd continue to play with Green Day when he was on break from college. Billie Joe and Mike initially agreed, but in the end it would prove to be an unworkable arrangement for a band as anxious to progress as Green Day. It also solidified their determination to keep the band going; lacking the safety nets of higher education or a fulltime job, music was now their best — their only — career option.

The two worked briefly with "Dave EC" (Dave Henwood), a drummer for the band Filth, but there was a more suitable candidate waiting in the wings. Billie Joe and Mike already knew Tré Cool from the Gilman scene (where Billie Joe's first memory of his future drummer was seeing him walk by wearing a plaid suit and a bathing cap), and both their bands shared a record label. Billie Joe had already recorded with Tré Cool the previous July, guesting on guitar and backing vocals on what would be The Lookouts last record, the EP *IV*. Says Livermore, "We didn't exactly break up, just sort of gradually drifted away. The three of us were all living in separate places and I'd gone back to college at Berkeley, so nothing was happening with us, and probably wasn't going to until the next summer at least. Billie invited Tré to jam with them, and they started doing shows together around November. By winter, Tré was officially the new drummer and I guess that was also officially the end of The Lookouts."

In Freudian terms, Tré would most certainly be the "id" of the group, "the source of primitive instinctive impulses and other drives," or, in more prosaic terms, the comic relief element of the band ... the one most likely to come back with a silly answer during an interview or pull some type of goofy stunt. But Tré's essential craziness blended into the band well, and though the group's breakthrough success was still over three years away, the core of the machine that was Green Day was now firmly in place.

Both Billie Joe and Mike were pleased with their new member. "Tré was a better drummer, and he was closer to us in age and mentality," Mike later told *Guitar Legends*. There was also a more practical element: "He had a van!" Others familiar with the band also thought Tré was a good fit. "John's a really great guy, but he used to spend half their set talking," Frank Portman recalls. "He had a microphone, and it would really get in the way of the show, although he was a great guy and he was funny. But I just remember him making speeches, like in Isocracy, making funny speeches was their whole bag. Green Day's shows became more traditional rock shows after switching drummers, and also by that time Tré had turned into quite a good drummer. One of the things that semi-professional bands or grassroots, do-it-yourself bands lack is a drummer that can hit the snare drum hard enough so that it actually works. Most bands, you'll find, have weak drummers, or drummers that are out of control. And that was one thing that set Green Day apart; they were able to sound great because of how hard Tré hit the snare."

Even after Tré was in the band, there was still some lingering tension with Kiffmeyer. Billie Joe remembered Kiffmeyer showing up for a gig in Petaluma Tré was supposed to play and sitting in himself, an incident that in 2001 Billie Joe admitted still made him feel "pretty awful". He also recalled Green Day sharing a bill with one of Kiffmeyer's subsequent bands, the Ne'er Do Wells, and watching Kiffmeyer playing his hardest. "And one thing you can not do to Tré Cool is to out drum him," Billie Joe told Livermore. "One of the first songs we played [that night] was 'Longview', which is like a great drummer's song, and from that point on, it was like, 'Dude, you're so over.'"

"Tré is just a much better drummer," says Eric Yee, who ended up seeing many of Green Day's pre-*Dookie* shows. "They pretty much started really kicking ass after they got Tré. As far as I'm concerned, that era right before *Kerplunk!* is just killer."

Yee, who lived in San Leandro, had become interested in punk in the early Eighties after his brother brought home a Dead Kennedys record. He then began attending shows at now-closed San Francisco venues like On Broadway, Mabuhay Gardens, and The Farm, prior to Gilman's opening. He had first heard about Gilman from Aaron Elliott. "I went to a couple of the early meetings," he says. "I was there one time when they were building it and Tim gave me and my friend some money to go out and buy some sodas for the crew."

When the club opened, Yee became a regular attendee. "I went to Gilman more times than I can count probably," he says. "I went a lot. A lot. It got to a point where I just went to hang out. If I was just bored or whatever, if there was some kind of gig going on there, I'd just go and hang out. The problem with that was when I was a kid. BART closed around 12:30 am, and most shows didn't get over until 2 or 3 am. A lot of times I had to hitch a ride back home."

As a result of his frequent attendance, Yee saw Green Day during their Sweet Children era, but has little memory of their music. "I do remember my initial impression of them was that they all had long hair and I wasn't into that," he says. "I thought they were a bunch of hippies. I wasn't with it. What changed my mind was I was hanging out with my friend Eggplant. He was meeting me at this Mexican place we always ate at, and he was with Billie Joe. So we met up and then we walked over to Gilman. That's the first time I ever met Billie Joe. And I thought, this guy is pretty cool, so I liked them after that. I've always liked Billie Joe, he's a cool guy. But I didn't really start liking them until Tré joined the band, really. They weren't necessarily embraced totally by everybody, because they were kind of like, cutesy, and they sang about girls. You know what I mean?" Nonetheless, he admits *39/Smooth* and *Slappy* are both "kick-ass records."

Yee estimates he might've seen as many as 120 Green Day shows. "They played a lot," he says. "They used to play all the time. If they weren't playing some gig somewhere, they'd be playing at somebody's party, or they'd be playing Gilman. They played quite a bit in the early days. They were definitely the hardest-working band. They paid their dues, you know. It wasn't like they just became instant stars."

As Green Day's reputation continued to grow, they found it easier to get shows, particularly in the now-thriving East Bay area. "In the East Bay scene at that time there were a lot of gigs going on all over the place," says Yee. "There were a lot of parties. Those were some of the best Green Day shows. [A view shared by Murray Bowles, who says, "The shows that Green Day did that stand out for me are when they played parties in people's backyards."] I remember one party I went to, they played in West Oakland at some house. It was somebody's birthday. And me and Eggplant were literally the only people that watched them. It was pretty funny. There was just nobody at that party, it was like a Sunday afternoon. Punk time, people don't get up until 3 or 4 pm or something. They played really early on, and there was just nobody there at this party. They still gave it their all, even to just me and Eggplant. Another time, this friend of mine, Kevin, it was his birthday, so we were sitting around with Jesse Townley [who was also in Blatz]. We were like, 'Damn, what should we do? Let's get Green Day to play Gilman.' And they actually played! Jesse at the time was running Gilman, so he opened up the club and they came.

"Another thing that sticks in my mind, some friends of mine, Eggplant and an ex-girlfriend of mine set up this surprise birthday party for me, and Green Day and Blatz played it," Yee continues. "It was in Eggplant's backyard. They played a lot of funny shows at Eggplant's; Eggplant has had many spectacular parties, legendary, in his backyard. He had this weird hot-tub room, his dad and his stepmom. They played there, next to the hot tub. This really teeny room. It was raining like crazy. I remember the people in Blatz were getting electrocuted, so they didn't like that. That was a very memorable show for me. That was my twenty-first birthday. And I couldn't think of a better way to celebrate than having your two favourite bands play your birthday party. How many people can say their two favourite bands played their birthday party? Not many. I was stoked."

Having fully integrated Tré into the group, the band was now anxious to show off their new drummer on record. Livermore had been urging them to get back into the studio, but they didn't make it until May of 1991, again recording at San Francisco's Art of Ears studio with producer Andy Ernst. But the sessions quickly came to a halt when they finished recording the only six new songs they had; they returned to the studio in September and finally completed the album, *Kerplunk!*, for the princely sum of $2,000.

"That was sort of the secret of Lookout's success," says Frank Portman. "Larry risked nothing in putting these records out, and then when some of them became popular, it was just like an individual winning the lottery. Especially in the context of the kind of albums that people were putting out at the time — which was pretty much just you do an extremely thrown-together, low-budget version of whatever you happen to have lying around — Green Day's records were much better thought-out and more together and more cohesive than practically anything. It was impressive. And they had some pretty great pop songs too, so it's hard to complain about that. Green Day's records were, as albums, better than a lot of what other people were trying to pass off as albums, that's definitely true."

Though Mike later said the band had smoked "a ton of weed" during the sessions ("Note to self: Keep the bong out of the mixing room!"), *Kerplunk!* was by no means a record to bliss out to. It's also the first album that has a recognisable Green Day sound; if *39/Smooth* was an album that depicted a group finding their feet, *Kerplunk!* captures a band that's finding its own distinctive voice. This was apparent from the album's opening track, '2000 Light Years Away', a typically aggressive pop blast said to be about Billie Joe's feelings for Adrienne; though still living in Minnesota, she and Billie Joe had kept in touch. Livermore first heard the album on his way home from Los Angeles, where he'd taken it to be mastered. As his plane raced down the runway, he slipped a cassette copy into his Walkman, and as '2000 Light Years Away' began, with a vibrant cymbal crash before the guitars kick in, "it was so good it was almost scary," he later wrote. "I knew instantly that life was never going to be the same again for Lookout Records or Green Day."

Even stronger was 'Welcome To Paradise', a tongue-in-cheek look at the thrill — and fear — of cutting parental ties for a home of one's own, even as the narrator admits his new environment is a "wasteland", replete with broken sidewalks and gunfire, inspired by the West Oakland warehouse where Billie Joe and Mike lived. ("No place you want to walk around at night," said Billie Joe.) Most exciting was the instrumental break, which featured a descending riff that built in intensity each time it repeated, cracking with all the force of a tightly controlled whip.

Though *Kerplunk!* had its quotient of poppy love songs, the more interesting material displayed a newfound introspection. Songs like 'One Of My Lies', 'Android', and 'No One Knows' all touched on growing old, mortality, and a fear of life passing one by. 'No One Knows' is even uncharacteristically slow, highlighting the pervasive melancholy of the lyrics; it also made Billie Joe and Mike's harmonising on the chorus stand out that much more. 'Christie Road' is another downbeat trip home, the road in question lying a few miles outside Rodeo, next to the railroad tracks. The upbeat tempos returned on 'Who Wrote Holden Caulfield?', which references the protagonist of J.D. Salinger's classic book of adolescent alienation, *The Catcher In The Rye.* As in 'Longview', the main character wrestles with the paralysing combination of having dissatisfaction with his circumstances, but lacking the wherewithal to change them — except that 'Holden Caulfield' is sung from the per-spective of the observer, while 'Longview' is delivered in first person. Screeching Weasel later recorded an answer song, 'I Wrote Holden Caulfield', for their 1993 album *How To Make Enemies And Irritate People*, on which Mike also played. Even Tré had a moment in the spotlight, on his own 'Dominated Love Slave', a ditty in praise of sadomasochism made all the more subversive by casting it as a country-and-western romp. The music was impressive given Mike's later statement that songs like 'Welcome To Paradise', '80', 'No One Knows', and 'One Of My Lies' had all come together in a week.

The cover served up a better reflection of the band's aesthetic than *39/Smooth* had, mixing adolescent jokiness with a darker undercurrent; a cartoon drawing of a young woman, winking and wearing a T-shirt with a smiley-faced flower that would be innocuous were it not for the fact that she's also holding a smoking revolver in her right hand, making her wink that much more sinister. (On the back cover is a young man lying face down, having been shot in the back.) The subversive tone continued in the liner notes, headed "My Adventure With Green Day," written by "Laurie L." (a play on Lawrence Livermore's name), in which a Pinole Valley High teen murders her parents in order to go on tour with the band, a mock celebration of violence that dated back to *The Rolling Stones No. 2* album, whose liner notes (written by the band's manager Andrew Loog Oldham), merely advocated robbing a blind man to get money to purchase the album, "And if you put the boot in, good. Another one sold." Kiffmeyer also received a nod, with 'Al Sobrante' credited as "executive producer." The album's "Thanks" section name checked, among others, the band members' parents, Adrienne Nesser, Murray Bowles, the Fiatarones (spelled "Fiataroni"), Gilman, cities and towns where the band played, The Village People, both John Kiffmeyer and Al Sobrante, and, in a final statement of inclusiveness, "everyone who goes to the shows, and you." The album was dedicated to, Gravy, Mike's late cat.

The initial sessions for the album came to a halt not only because the group ran out of material, but also because they were heading out on the road again. As the band grew in popularity, they began spending more and more time touring. "The story of big rock bands all kind of have similar contours," says Frank Portman. "And those guys toured a lot. That's another measure of how seriously they took their whole deal. 'Cause we were always conscientious of, 'Is there really a point to this?' And we always kinda thought, 'Not really.' But they really did think there was. Talk about paying their dues, they played practically everywhere, and they toured for months and months and months, living like a pack of dogs in a van."

Aaron Elliott wrote a story for *Cometbus #27* that provides a good snapshot of life on the road for an indie band: "Touring is losing things. Losing your clothes, losing your money, losing your mind... Touring is also gaining things. Gaining scars and wounds. Gaining sickness and disease. Definitely increasing your tolerance for both beer and coffee... Touring is cabin fever at 65 miles an hour. No, make that 85." The tedium of driving was broken up by in-jokes, such as keeping track of all the road kill spotted along the highways ("The list is almost up to 10 just from the last two weeks"), getting "stoned as fuck," and keeping in mind the constant need to look for a more comfortable place to sleep, aside

American Idiots: Mike Dirnt, Tré Cool, and Billie Joe Armstrong of Green Day. *(LFI)*

LOOK FOR LOVE

"Billie Joe"

Recorded by "Billie Joe" on Fiat Records

Lyrics by James J. Fiatarone
Music by Marie-Louise Fiatarone

$1.25

Sheet music for Billie Joe's first single, 'Look For Love', recorded when
he was five years old and released in 1977. *(Courtesy of Toxsima)*

A young Tré flexes his drumming muscles, as Lookouts bassist Kain "Kong" Hanschke looks on, circa 1985. *(Larry Livermore)*

An early Lookouts performance. The band was the third project of founder/guitarist Lawrence Livermore to use the "Lookout" name, along with a fanzine and a record label. *(Larry Livermore)*

A flyer advertising the Lookouts' 1989 EP *Mendocino Homeland*, named for the county where the group was formed. *(Larry Livermore)*

The sleeve of Isocracy's 1988 7-inch *Bedtime For Isocracy*. The band's drummer, John Kiffmeyer, aka "Al Sobrante", became Green Day's first drummer. *(Larry Livermore)*

Billie Joe at a show at the Gilman St. Project, Berkeley, September 9, 1989. He later said being involved in the Gilman scene "saved me from living in a refinery town all my life". *(Murray Bowles)*

John Kiffmeyer at Gilman, September 9, 1989 *(Murray Bowles)*

Mike at Gilman, 1989. He said of the club, "Gilman was my high school". *(Murray Bowles)*

Mike, newly shorn, at Gilman, August 31, 1990. Green Day played Gilman more than any other venue. *(Murray Bowles)*

Billie Joe, wearing his baseball cap backwards in trademark fashion, at Gilman, August 31, 1990. *(Murray Bowles)*

Tré at a show in Pinole, California, November 11, 1990, soon after he became Green Day's drummer. Billie Joe and Mike appreciated both his drumming skills and the fact he owned a van. *(Murray Bowles)*

Mike and Tré at Ugene's, Downey, California,
January 26, 1991. *(Murray Bowles)*

Billie Joe at Ugene's, January 26,1991.
(Murray Bowles)

Flyer for Green Day show at The Dome, Boston Arms, London, May 2, 1992. The group steadily
built an overseas following before the release of *Dookie*. *(Courtesy of Jason Funbug)*.

2243 Ashby Avenue, Berkeley; Green Day's HQ during the *Dookie* era. *(Gillian G. Gaar)*

from the van. On one occasion, the traveling party ended up pulling mattresses from a factory dumpster to bed down for the night.

It was often rough living; even having an appreciative audience didn't necessarily translate into a show earning funds sufficient to do little more than buy gas to get to the next town (and T-shirts to sell once they got there). But there was still a sense of community to be found, even among strangers. After playing a show in New Orleans, the band returned to their van to find it had been broken into and most of their possessions, including their tour money, had been stolen. They drove on to their next stop, Auburn, Alabama, anyway, where they played a house party for a group of college students. "It was cool," Tré later told the *Birmingham Post-Herald*. "We didn't have no money or clothes, and everyone was donating clothes and, uh, and basically money."

Years later, Billie Joe looked back with fondness at the romance of the band's early touring days. "There was this certain rock'n'roll underdog thing that we always had," he told *Rip*. "I fuckin' like touring like that — it's like culture shock, really, driving around in a van, setting up my amp when I get there, and playing. That's rock'n'roll, that's what it started out as. A bunch of sweaty pigs in some tiny fuckin' bar having a hootenanny, that's what punk rock was to me." The group handled all tour arrangements themselves. Tré's father even converted an old Mendocino County Library bookmobile into a tour van and served as the band's driver on a few tours. "Frank wanted to be sure they had a good driver," his wife Linda explained (the choice of vehicle also occasionally attracted people who unexpectedly walked inside, thinking it was a real bookmobile). They also made some valuable future contacts, meeting a guitar player named Jason White while playing in Memphis, Tennessee during the summer of '91. White was impressed enough to catch the band at their next stop in Little Rock, Arkansas later that week. After joining the band Monsula the following year, White would later end up in the Bay Area and go on to play with one of Billie Joe's side-project bands, Pinhead Gunpowder, eventually joining Green Day as a second guitarist on the live dates.

When they toured closer to home, dedicated fans like Eric Yee traveled to see them. "The first time I saw them far away I went with Blatz," he recalls. "They were supposed to play three shows together. One was in LA, sort of near Knott's Berry Farm, a place called Eugene's." After seeing Blatz playing at another club the night before the Blatz/Green Day shows, everyone headed for Hollywood. "We were in this camper with these two huge dogs," says Yee. "It was me, my friend Jesse, my friend Kevin, Joey [the drummer for Blatz], and Eggplant's stepmom. We were hanging out on the strip and we ran into Green Day. You remember those magazine covers that you could get your picture on? They got theirs on *High Times*!★ It was really funny. The next night, when we got to the show, we saw Green Day's van there, and we thought, let's go see them. So we open the doors, and there they were, hanging out with a bunch of girls in their van. We ended up going out spray painting. We had this really cheap spray paint, and we just spray painted shit everywhere. We sprayed, 'East Bay, Not LA.'"

At the end of 1991, Green Day made their first trip overseas, leaving in November for the first date of a tour that would eventually run for over three months. Livermore hooked the band up with Christy Colcord and Aidan Taylor, two UK-based promoters who helped organise both this tour and a subsequent one in 1992. In typical fund-it-yourself fashion, they also brought along copies of their own records to sell and a photo negative of their T-shirt artwork so they could continue to print up their own memorabilia in order to raise extra money. The tour took in the Netherlands (where Billie Joe admitted that being able to buy pot legally in Amsterdam took some of the fun out of it), Germany, Spain, Italy, Poland, the Czech Republic (then still known as Czechoslovakia), and the UK. The dates included the usual assortment of venues, from genuine rock clubs to squats. It was an atmosphere they thrived on, no matter how crazy things got, as in Denmark, where they were regularly doused with beer during shows, which wreaked havoc with their instruments and gear. They also played a Halloween show in Denmark, after which they got another surprise when the man who lived in the apartment where they were spending the night decided to introduce them to his friend, "Sleepy" — a human head sealed in a glass jar. Billie Joe also picked up a case of lice during their travels. "I'd love to

---

★ A magazine devoted to marijuana culture and its attendant paraphenalia

say it was crabs, but I wasn't getting laid," he cracked. And they all credited the demanding schedule with tightening them up into a better band.

"I think there should be a rule that any American band that goes to Europe or the UK has to have toured the United States at least twice because they're a bunch of little spoiled brats," Mike later enthused to journalist Ben Myers, proudly adding, "We're not your average American band. We're not shitheads." He also told *Flipside* that while not too many people had heard of the band, "Some people did. There are mail-order punks everywhere. That's rad." The group also managed to hold their own, even at shows where, in Billie Joe's words, "There were five bands on the bill, four of which sounded like Napalm Death. And then there was us."

They made their UK debut in December at London venue The Rails, going on to play in Leeds, Dublin, Belfast, and such exotic-sounding (to American ears) locales like Tunbridge Wells. On December 17, when the group was in Southampton, newly minted copies of *Kerplunk!* arrived, and everyone was so excited they decided to make that evening's show their record-release party, though *Kerplunk!*'s official release date wasn't until January.

As the holidays approached, the group found themselves getting caught up in the spirit of the season, punk-rock style, and during a show at The Cricketers in Wigan, decided to join forces with the other band on the bill, Jail Cell Recipes (who'd been letting the band use their gear, as Green Day's had become increasingly trashed) to stage an impromptu, and decidedly ludicrous, Nativity play.

"We got a little play going on," Mike announced at the beginning, "and we can't seem to get the hang of things unless people sit down. 'Cause it's a real play. So you all got to sit down exactly where you're standing, like it's a hippie festival." The packed room eventually complied, and "Mary" (Tré) came to the mic, wearing a scarf around his head, lipstick, and a huge bulge tucked under his skirt. On squealing, "my water broke!" a midwife appeared to attend to Mary, as a "shepherd", busy defiling a "sheep", suddenly spotted a Christmas tree that heralded the arrival of "the One Wise Punk" (Billie Joe), who "was as smart as Three Wise Men!" said Mike. Various foodstuffs were then pulled from between Mary's legs until a friend with suitably long hair emerged, discreetly wearing a loincloth. "And the King was born!" shouted Mike. "It's a goddamn prophet!" A "placenta" made of rice pudding and tomato sauce was then hurled into the audience. After flooring Mary with a punch, "Jesus" put in a plea to remember the true meaning of Christmas; "Santa Claus gets all the credit, and I think people should think of Jesus Christ more than Santa Claus on Christmas!" Then "Santa" (Mike) turned up to argue with "Jesus", a dispute that ended by the unexpected arrival of the "Easter Bunny" (Sean from Wat Tyler), who knocked the beers out of the hands of Jesus and Santa, shouting "Straight edge! Straight edge!"

After the mayhem, Green Day's set began, Billie Joe without a shirt, but wearing a tie (which he took off after the first song; Tré started out wearing a sleeveless shirt he also took off). The audience was so close to the band, Billie Joe's mic was easily knocked away during the opening number, 'I Was There'. "You guys are making the ceiling fall down," Billie Joe observed afterwards, looking at a banner of cloth tacked on the ceiling that was starting to come down. "Bringing down the house!" said Mike. "You guys are ruthless."

People routinely jumped onto the low stage and leapt back into the packed crowd throughout the show. Though most of the songs were drawn from the group's earlier albums, this particular set also included a number of songs from *Kerplunk!*: 'Welcome To Paradise', 'One For The Razorbacks', '2000 Lights Years Away', 'Dominated Love Slave' (with Tré and Billie Joe swapping instruments), and 'Christie Road'. "It's about a road," Mike offered helpfully about the latter song. "A road in the middle of nowhere," clarified Billie Joe. While playing 'Disappearing Boy', the band suddenly broke off and Tré stepped to the mic to take a vote on who'd been better in Nativity play — Santa Claus or Jesus? The vote seemed to going Santa's way until Mike reminded the audience that the Easter Bunny had also made an appearance, and the resulting cheers had Billie Joe declaring the Bunny to be the winner. The band then played an impromptu version of Lynyrd Skynyrd's 'Sweet Home Alabama' to a seemingly mystified British audience, then finally managed to finish 'Disappearing Boy'. The set ended with an encore performance of 'Dry Ice'.

When the band arrived at Newport, Wales, on December 23, where they were set to do a show at TJ's, they met fellow musician and rock journalist, John Robb. Robb was bassist and vocalist for well-respected punk band The Membranes, who were splitting up at the time he first encountered Green Day. Robb had been interested in music since getting swept up in the punk explosion of late Seventies Britain. "Once punk rock happened, that was everything, really, musically, stylistically, politically," he explains. "The whole thing was just a complete wipeout, it was amazing. It was a really good time to be 16! Things like the music press and John Peel were the lifelines to the music scene."

Throughout the next decade, Robb also followed the US punk scene. "When The Dead Kennedys came along, I was completely knocked out by them because they were such a fantastic band," he says, "and Jello Biafra's lyrics are great, he's a great singer. And they were really interesting songs, like Beefheart speeded up, but it still fit in a punk context 'cause it was really exciting to listen to. Then Black Flag came along and it just seemed to open the doors for loads of American stuff that was really cool. 'Cause there was a time when American punk was looked on as being a bit crap, really. But when these bands came through, people took it more seriously. . . from Black Flag it went to the Sonic Youth, Big Black, Butthole Surfers kind of thing — kind of artsy, all great bands. And then of course Nirvana came along and just completely blew the thing wide open."

Robb knew about Lookout and the East Bay scene because of OpIvy. "A ska-punk band seemed really bizarre then," he says, "because ska was something that had happened a long time before in Britain. That's the good thing about music, it doesn't obey any rules. Just when you think a scene is gone, something just completely spurs it out again. But you need really good bands to make that scene work again, and the great thing about Green Day, Rancid, and Offspring, is they're all really good bands in their own way. If the main bands in that punk scene hadn't been that good, it would never have spurred it back out again."

Robb also knew about Green Day. "You knew the name, and you'd heard a couple of tracks, and you knew what they were about," he says. "The two songs I'd heard sounded good. But you just didn't think this band was going to be filling up stadiums in 10 years time. They just sounded like a good-time band. And they did a good show, but there was no scene for that kind of thing then. The punk scene was at its lowest ebb, in late Eighties/early Nineties Britain. But there were outside pockets of people into more punky kind of music, and TJ's in Newport was one of those kind of places. TJ's is a great venue. It's just basically a drinking club which got turned into a venue. It's a pretty rough-and-ready place, and when the kids turn up it gets wild. It's been a wild kind of punk-rock dive for years and years. But in most of the country, if you played Birmingham for example, in those days you'd probably get about 50 people; there was no one else really into that kind of stuff."

"It was great in Newport 'cause they all seemed to be into American punk, as well as British stuff, and bands I was into," says Jason Funbug, a member of the band Funbug, then living in Newport and a TJ's regular. "Back where I lived in the Midlands, I could've probably counted the people like that on one hand! TJ's is quite an infamous club on the punk scene, everyone has played there. The owner is a Tom Jones lookalike and soundalike when he talks. He and his wife used to cook for the bands in their home above the club — I've had spaghetti bolognaise there with Rancid and Grant Hart [Hüsker Dü's drummer]."

The TJ's gig was also the club's annual Christmas party show, with Knucklehead and Midway sharing the bill. "It was a pretty wild night," says Robb. "That's always a wild night, the Christmas gig. If you're on tour, the first time you come over and people don't you know you well and you get a gig like that, it's always a godsend. The audience didn't tear the place apart; Green Day were pretty unknown the first time they came over. But they were good live, though they were pretty knackered from touring — after about five or six weeks on the road you're like a zombie anyway. I was just a compere for the show, so I probably just asked them how they were, how the tour had gone, and if they wanted me to say anything when I introduced them. There were some drunken hijinks, I remember. And they definitely had a fondness for British beer!"

Funbug was also at the show, having previously heard Green Day on John Peel's radio show on BBC Radio 1; he was also interested in Lookout acts like OpIvy, Sweet Baby, and Screeching Weasel. As the TJ's show also featured a fancy dress competition, Funbug borrowed a nun's costume from his mother. "There were loads of people in fancy dress," he says, and Green Day ended up picking him as the winner, awarding him with a case of lager, which was eagerly consumed that night. A live version of 'At The Library' from the show later appeared on the compilation *Guinea Worm*, put out by *S&M* magazine.

The group spent Christmas Eve and Christmas Day in Bath, where they celebrated by stealing Christmas trees from front porches and Mike made everyone massive veggie omelets, "with everything from hash browns to brussel sprouts in them." It was a rare moment of calm during which everyone could wonder what the new year might bring, a year in which all the band members would finally leave their teens behind and turn 20. Billie Joe later admitted he felt some anxiety during the trip, and experienced a bad case of nerves in Spain. "I don't know if I was having an anxiety attack or what, but I just freaked out! I didn't say anything to anybody. It was weird," he told *Flipside*. "At the time I felt kind of bum-rushed to think about my future," he said to another interviewer. "A lot of it had to do with being in Europe. It was our first time in Europe, we were doing the squats and pub gigs. . . and, you know, it was just kind of scary. I think all of us were scared because we didn't know what our future was going to be at all."

CHAPTER 4

Moving To The Majors

"How do you guys think you'll do in three years?"

"I don't know. You can't always predict what's going to happen three years from now."

— *Billie Joe to* Flipside, 1992

Green Day's European tour was originally scheduled for 50 dates, but it eventually ran to 64, as offers to extend the tour kept coming in. "We were so exhausted we were practically hallucinating, and so we said, 'Sure! We can't think of anything dumber! Let's keep going!'" Billie Joe explained to writer Ian Winwood. By the time they returned to the states, *Kerplunk!* was already out and on its way to becoming one of Lookout's biggest sellers, having sold 10,000 copies on its day of release (January 17, 1992); by the end of '92, sales would reach 50,000. Reviews were positive as well. Writing in the *New Musical Express*, Simon Williams called *Kerplunk!* "storming-but-soothing antidotal cream to smear on the current rash of grunge merchants."

Eric Yee was among the fans who were quickly won over by the album. "My favourite stuff is from *Kerplunk!*" he says. "There was this great show Green Day played right when it came out, and at the show I heard someone from Lookout say, 'Yeah dude, I got the vinyl in.' So after the show we went to Lookout headquarters and I grabbed one, and I was so excited. It's a classic record in my opinion. It's got all the great songs, 'Who Wrote Holden Caulfield?', 'Christie Road', '2000 Light Years Away', 'Welcome to Paradise'. They are all on that album. Pretty amazing album. That's my favourite, at least."

There would be no new Green Day recordings until the band signed with Reprise. And despite Green Day's increasing success, the members still found time to play in various side-project bands. In 1991, Billie Joe had joined Aaron Elliott in Pinhead Gunpowder, a pet project of Elliott's for some time. After one of his stints as Green Day's roadie, Elliott had been dropped off in Arcata, where he tried to get a band going. When the effort proved unsuccessful, he returned to Berkeley, living in a house called "House-O-Toast". Guitarist Mike Kersh (from Fuel) and bassist Bill Schneider (from the band Monsula) practised together at House-O-Toast and invited Elliott, who played drums, to join them. Elliott then brought in Billie Joe and gave the group the name he'd wanted to use for his band in Arcata, taken from a "high-octane green tea" sold at an Arcata co-op.

Due to all the members' involvement in a variety of other bands, Pinhead Gunpowder was never more than a part-time endeavour. In 1991 the group released the 4-track EP *Trundle & Spring* on No Reality Records, followed the next year by the EP *Fahiza* on Lookout. It featured a cover of Joni Mitchell's 'Big Yellow Taxi', along with appearances on the compilations *Very Small World* and Lookout's *Can Of Pork* (the latter of which also featured a song by The Lookouts). In late 1992, Billie Joe also sat in on guitar for one show with Rancid.

Green Day also kept up their rigorous touring schedule, both around the country and overseas. On May 2, 1992, they were at The Dome, Boston Arms, in London, supported by Joeyfat and Funbug. "They turned up really late," says Jason Funbug. "I think they just flew in that day and were jet lagged or something. They didn't really talk much. I remember, thinking I was hilarious, calling them 'Purple Month', 'Blue Year', etc. Then we — I'm a bit embarrassed to say — stole all the cans of lager, which was out of order. A funny thing was, in November they came back to Britain and did a Radio 1 interview and were asked if they had a favourite support band and they said Funbug! Which helped us immensely! I think they might have been joking. But it seems everyone in Britain heard about it. I was in Chicago at the time it aired and my girlfriend even rang me up to tell me." The band's plug might also have been to help Lookout; Funbug was the first non-Californian band to be signed to the label.

The constant touring meant the band was making inroads in unexpected places. In the early Nineties, Lawrence Livermore was on tour in Europe with the Mr. T Experience. On arriving in the city of Bialystok, Poland, Livermore had been thinking they must be the first American punk-rock band to play the region. He then caught sight of the words "Green Day" spray painted on the town's water tower. "They'd been there, done that, months before us," he later wrote.

The touring helped boost the band's records sales — no small consideration — given that Green Day's deal with Lookout had them earning 60% of the profits. For unlike many albums, which sell the most on their initial release, after which sales begin to decline, both *39/Smooth* and *Kerplunk!* continued to sell steadily, which meant the group's popularity also continued to grow. It grew slowly at first, but eventually to the point where it couldn't be ignored. "The shows were getting bigger, the promoters seedier, and the people we stayed with less and less interesting," as Aaron Elliott put it in *Cometbus #41*. "The band was headed toward success but stalled at an awkward impass along the way."

Certainly things had grown to a level the band members themselves could no longer control. In a portent of things to come, shows were having to be cancelled because too many people were turning up at venues that were too small. Sometimes the local fire marshall would shut down the show as a result. Or promoters from the next tier up would take over the show and cheat the band out of their money. The changing character of the audience also brought its own problems. "We were drawing a lot of people who didn't understand punk shows, so there would be fights going on," Mike told *Alter/Native*. "It was all leading to one thing, either quit or go on. So we're going on."

The band's first move, which set them apart from most other bands they'd been playing with in the East Bay scene, was to get professional managers. They went with the team of Elliot Cahn and Jeff Saltzman, who ran the Oakland-based management company Cahn-Man. Cahn got his start in music as a guitarist in the Fifties revival band, Sha Na Na. He left the music business to pursue legal work, then combined his two interests and returned to the music industry as a lawyer and manager. He then met Saltzman, who worked as a litigator but was also a musician, having been a member of the San Francisco band, House of Pants.

The two formed Cahn-Man after Cahn signed a management deal with the heavy-metal band Testament; other bands the two signed included Exodus, Violence, Vicious Rumors, and other metal acts. They were introduced to Green Day by one of their associates, David Hawkins. Like Cahn and Saltzman. he also worked as a musician, playing drums for the local band, Engine.

Green Day's brand of poppy punk was far removed from the metal acts Cahn-Man had been working with, but the two liked the music well enough to decide to take a chance on the group.* For their part, the band felt the managers weren't "a bunch of cigar chewers", in Cahn's words. A contract was duly signed.

Cahn and Saltzman found their new charges to be ambitious, but cautious about making too many changes. Nonetheless, the band had decided that their next step should be a securing a major-label record deal. "We wanted to go from an independent to a major," Billie Joe told *Kerrang!* "We got an offer from Epitaph, but we were like, 'Do we want to be on an independent pretending to be a major, or do we want to be on a real major?' We chose to go to Reprise."

Lawrence Livermore was aware that Green Day was considering its options. "There were occasional rumours that Green Day might go to a major label starting maybe in late 1992/early '93," he says. "I knew that some of their friends and family were encouraging them to do that, but I didn't think too much about it. For one thing they were away a lot on tour, so I didn't see as much of them as I usually did, and besides, things were going so well for both them and the label that I didn't see why

---

* Cahn-Man's roster would later broaden; not only would the company manage The Muffs and Jawbreaker, they would also serve as legal representatives for The Offspring, Rancid, Primus, Mudhoney, and jazz-rock guitarist Charlie Hunter.

they'd want to leave. We'd sold about 50,000 of each album by then, which was phenomenal for a tiny underground label at that time, and things only looked to get better. Still, I knew they might want to leave at some point, and I was fine with that. I did think they should do one more indie record first to solidify their fan base and strengthen their bargaining position, but as it turned out, they didn't need to. They first told me for sure that they were looking to sign with a major sometime in 1993, and it was only a few weeks after that that they did."

Though they would take some heat for this decision later, purists in the community believing that any self-respecting punk rocker that signed with a major label was irrevocably "selling out", others had a far more sympathetic view. The Mr. T Experience had shared stages with Green Day in the past, and would in the future, when the band broke through to the mainstream. But even before that breakthrough, Frank Portman recognised that the band members had always had an air of determination about them.

"My impression is that they always seemed to take their career more seriously," he says. "Almost from when I first encountered them, they seemed like they were pretty serious about being a band, which is very different from my band, and practically all the other bands around here. Even if you had a sort of secret dream that you wanted to be a big star, which I'm sure a lot of people had, you would never admit it to anyone, that would be a real *faux pas*. I know a lot of my friend's bands from LA, you could totally tell how they would talk completely differently; they all had managers and they were all just charting their course to when they'd be getting on the radio and everything. I guess bands up here were doing that too, to an extent, but you had to at least affect an 'I don't care about that stuff' attitude. In our case that was actually more or less genuine, but I think those guys took it a little more seriously. They seemed to put a lot into how they put the band across. They timed their recordings carefully, they didn't overdo it; in the time they did those two albums, some bands could've done five or six low-budget, thrown-together albums. But they seemed to be a little bit more aware of why that would be a mistake.

"I don't think anybody ever imagined that anyone doing this kind of thing was going to become multi-gazillionaire internationally famous rock stars, but I think everybody could tell they were going places," he continues, adding that, at the time, "success" for most rock bands was defined in more modest terms. "When I was a DJ on the college radio station, I did a lot of interviews with some pretty big stars in the college radio world in the mid-Eighties, like The Replacements, that kind of band," he says. "And you would always say, 'Well, what's your ambition, what are you after?' And they would always say, 'I just want to be able to make a living from making music.' And none of them actually would go so far as to say that that's what they were doing; that was the ambition they had in the future, and it always seemed completely out of the question. That was the extent of what you could imagine. If you played a show where you got paid enough, where there was enough money to split up after you had paid off various things, like your practise space rent and so forth, that seemed like a really amazing degree of success. So, somewhere between that and being The Rolling Stones was where you imagined the successful bands would end up. But I think that everyone could tell that there was a potential for these guys to be a lot bigger than this scene."

And instead of seeing signing to a major as "selling out", Portman saw the true risk being that moving to a major was taking a big gamble that more than likely wouldn't pay off. "The complaint that people make about bands signing to a major label is that it's not always a good move," he says. "And in fact it rarely is, in the long run, a good move. If I had been offered a good deal I would've totally taken it, no question, but I made the decision that I didn't want to waste a lot of time chasing after it because I didn't think it would pan out. And I think that was the right decision for me. And most bands that sign big deals that don't pan out are history within a couple of years. When the East Bay pop-punk scene had a buzz about it, and Green Day was starting to get popular — as always happens — a lot of bands got these little deals from big labels just to see what would happen. And it never worked out for any of them, really. And Green Day was smart about how they did it. They didn't spend a lot of money — comparatively speaking — on that first album, they didn't take a huge advance that was impossible to recoup. They were smart about a lot of decisions like that. Some bands just get into a state of delusion where you believe that there's no way to go but up and there's no stopping you, and you make a lot of poor financial decisions. But they didn't do that."

Jon Ginoli, a guitarist with Pansy Division, a band that would also tour with Green Day, also saw both the advantages and disadvantages of signing with a major. Ginoli had moved to the Bay Area in 1989, where he initially worked as a sales rep for Rough Trade Records. "We were selling all these Green Day albums, and that's what got me interested in wanting to check them out," he recalls. "I thought, 'Wow, people are really into this band, they're local and I don't know who they are, so I better get on the case.' They were selling tens of thousands of records as an indie. Then I heard that they signed to a major and I thought, 'They're just gonna get lost in the shuffle. They'll probably make more money selling 50,000 copies on Lookout than they would selling 500,000 copies on a major, so they might as well just stay with the indie.' They were in a real good position, because they were probably making a decent living just off of doing little tours and having these record sales; that was a very enviable position that a lot of people would have wanted to be in. But I think they were kind of overwhelmed trying to deal with the popularity of being on an indie label and people not being able to find the record in stores and that sort of thing; things had sort of gotten out of control by the time they signed with a major. So that a major was actually going to make them more organised. I didn't really have anything against them signing, but I did think that they were one of those bands that probably could've succeeded if they hadn't signed. Like, some bands are going to be unknown unless a major grabs them, but I thought that Green Day still would've gone on to be pretty popular on the underground level, that they would be one of the top underground bands. But the thing is, if you're going to sell 10 million records, of course, then sign with a major, 'cause you're not going to be able to do that on Lookout. But, you know, who would've thought? I mean, I don't think anybody thought that they would be so big."

"I knew there was a lot of interest in them," says Yee. "Because one time we went to see them at the Whisky-A-Go-Go in LA, and there were all kinds of crazy people backstage, A&R types and whatnot. And it didn't surprise me because they were huge at the time. So when they signed [with a major] it wasn't too surprising, really. But they were very sensitive about it, because people were already calling them sell-outs, you know what I mean? They were very sensitive about that situation. I didn't care about the 'sell-out' factor then; now I do, but at the time I didn't. It was more exciting at the time, new territory. A new world. It was pretty cool going along for the ride."

For the previous few years, the band members' living situations had been somewhat erratic. In 1992 Billie Joe told *Flipside*, "I'm not living anywhere, really," and recounted having to leave his possessions at his mother's home while crashing with different friends; Mike added, "Actually, we've moved three times in two months, so we're like, total rock stars." But now, they had a new HQ.

Ashby Avenue is a busy thoroughfare running from west to east through Berkeley, about a mile south of the Berkeley campus. Near the intersection of Ashby and Telegraph, at 2243 Ashby, is an unprepossessing, three-story Victorian house, the mailboxes nailed to the main stairs indicating that the house has been split up into multi-unit dwellings (it's also six blocks from the house where Jann Wenner and Ralph Gleason cooked up the idea for a magazine called *Rolling Stone* in 1967). In 1993, Green Day was hunkered down in the basement, both living there and using it as a rehearsal space. It was here that hopeful A&R reps visited, attracted by the demos Cahn-Man sent out and the band's impressive sales on Lookout. As Megan McLaughlin, editor of college radio tipsheet *CMJ New Music Report* told *Billboard*, "Once people looked at the numbers, it was like, 'Wow — imagine what a little marketing and major-label distribution could do.'"

And the majors were definitely interested: Sony, Geffen, Interscope, and Warner Bros. were among those in the running. In the end, it was Rob Cavallo with Warner Bros. imprint Reprise, who got the nod, despite having never seen the band play live. But Cavallo was impressed by the vigor of the group's music, though even he later admitted, "I never thought it would snowball." And after hanging out in the Ashby house basement with the group, playing instruments together, smoking pot, then going out to dinner, the band decided Cavallo had a down-to-earth attitude that they liked as well. "He's from LA and stuff, but he's married and thinking about having kids," Billie Joe told journalist Gina Arnold, "and that made him seem like more of a genuine person."

Cavallo was originally from Washington, D.C. His father, Bob, was a club owner and, later, a manager, whose roster had included the Lovin' Spoonful; Earth, Wind & Fire; and Prince. The family later relocated to Los Angeles, where Cavallo played guitar in local bands and then began working as a recording engineer, working on sessions by Linda Ronstadt and Fleetwood Mac, among others. He moved into A&R after his father introduced him to Lenny Waronker, president of Warner Bros., working under Michael Ostin (then Warner's head of A&R). From there he moved into production, while continuing to do A&R, co-producing The Muffs' self-titled major-label debut (a record Green Day had liked). In addition to The Muffs, Cavallo went on to produce Jawbreaker, L7, The Goo Goo Dolls, and Chris Isaak. He eventually became a senior vice president of A&R at Reprise.

Green Day's demos included new songs that would be the stand-out tracks on their major-label debut — 'Longview', 'When I Come Around', 'Basket Case' — that had an identifiable Green Day "sound" that the band had perfected; music with enough of an edge to make it alternative, but with appealing melodies and ear-grabbing hooks that were as catchy as anything in the Top 40. "They have all the elements," Cavallo later told *People*. "Great lyrics, great melodies, interesting influences — The Sex Pistols, The Clash, The Kinks, The Beatles." So Green Day signed a five-album contract with Reprise in April 1993, netting an advance of $300,000, though not without some trepidation. "I was struggling so hard even to sign that fucking contract," Billie Joe later recalled. "When I was sitting there, I was contemplating, 'Should I just run outta here right now? Am I making the biggest mistake of my life?'" It was agreed that Cavallo should produce, an unorthodox arrangement with one's A&R rep that raised some eyebrows. But Cavallo stressed it wasn't part of the deal; "It just signified how interested in the project I was. I considered it a gift to spend time in the studio with them," he told Gina Arnold. In a magnanimous gesture, Green Day decided to let Lookout retain the rights to the records they'd recorded for the label. Then Billie Joe used the advance to pay a year's rent on their basement apartment. Tré bought health insurance.

Easing the leap to a major was the decision to record locally, the band members requesting a studio they could ride their bikes to. As it happened, there was an excellent studio about two miles from the house on Ashby Avenue — Berkeley's Fantasy Studios, located just off busy San Pablo Avenue in a quieter, residential area, not far from Berkeley's Aquatic Park. When Fantasy originally opened in 1971, it was primarily used by the artists on Fantasy Records, which then included acts like Creedence Clearwater Revival, Chet Baker, and Sonny Rollins. Over the years a wide variety of other musicians have used the studio, including Santana, Aerosmith, Elton John, Bobby McFerrin, Journey, and Robert Cray, to name a few.

"We have world-class level gear, but mainly what we have is space," says Steve Hart, now Fantasy's chief engineer, but then a freelance engineer who used the studio as his base. "This is an old studio, so there's a lot of real estate," he explains. "It's huge — I think we're 25,000 square feet total. Most newer studios don't have that kind of real estate, so their rooms are small. Here, about half of our bottom floor is all studio complex. So we have state-of-the-art consoles, big rooms, and a lot of vintage gear and a big ol' mic collection, just due to the fact that it's been here since the Seventies."

Hart, who in addition to working with artists like David Bowie, En Vogue, and The White Stripes, has also worked on such films as *Amadeus*, *Titanic*, and Werner Herzog's *Grizzly Man*, says he was one of four engineers considered for the job of working on *Dookie*. "Rob Cavallo wanted to work here because it was local for the band, and he didn't want to bring in a big name LA engineer," he explains. "So he picked four engineers from résumés that the studio gave him. They had a 4-track live cassette and Rob was actually having a sort of contest, where whoever could make that 4-track live recording sound like anything would get the job. Now, at that time, I was pretty busy on an international level; I had been working in Europe for five years and at that moment I was working in Asia, going to and from Hong Kong and Taipei and mixing singles for various artists, and making good money. On the day of the test, I was flying to Taipei in fact, so I just told Rob, 'Look, I can't do your demo, here's my résumé take it or leave it.' But Neill showed up, so he got the job."

"Neill" was Neill King, who recalls his hiring somewhat differently. "The studio manager at the time, Nina [Bombardier], who is a friend of mine, called me up," he recalls. "I was working somewhere else on a Joe Satriani record. I think Rob had talked to her, and said, 'I've got Green Day coming in and we want an engineer, but I don't have anybody.' There may be other stories; they probably did interview other engineers, but I wasn't aware of that. Nina just said, 'Come in and talk to Rob and the guys.' So I came in talked to them, we got on pretty well, and they liked what I'd done in the past. And that was it."

King, originally from London, got his start working with British acts like Madness, Nick Lowe, Elvis Costello, The Undertones, and The Smiths, before moving to Los Angeles and then the Bay Area, producing, engineering, and mixing, depending on the needs of the project. "I prefer producing, but because I'm an engineer and mixer, people kind of get me to do all three, wear all the hats," he says. "In a perfect world, the producer is the artistic liaison between the artist and their songs, their ideas, and he tries to communicate that to the engineer and mixer, whoever they are. And in that perfect world, the producer doesn't do anything with the board, with the sound. He's just involved with the band, with the artistic side of things. And the engineer doesn't usually have very much input with the artistic side of things. But now those have become very blurred. Obviously, I came into engineering and mixing from a musical background; I didn't want to be just an engineer/producer in the old sense of the word. I wanted to be a producer, but engineering was my foot into the door, because I could make the records technically. And the idea was, gradually, not to do all the technical stuff, to have somebody else do it, and just be the producer... the artistic liaison. That's where my main interests lie. But I became a pretty good engineer and mixer, so I worked mainly as that. But in the last 15 years, since my wife and I have moved to the Bay Area, I've done everything. And, in some cases, played on the records as well. And now, there aren't many producers who don't know a little bit about the technical side, and it's very hard to be an engineer if you don't know a little bit about music."

King had never seen Green Day, but knew of their reputation. "The East Bay punk scene was quite a thing," he says. "And I think they liked me because I'd done that kind of scene the first time around in the UK. I think that was one of the draws, they thought they'd like to work with me because I worked with people they'd liked growing up." When he finally did see the band live at Gilman, the knowledge that the group was signing with a major label "was causing a little bit of antagonism among the hard-core punks," says King. "They didn't want that at all, they didn't want them signing to a major label. There was a backlash, so actually it was kind of empty, one of the emptiest times they ever played Gilman. People were kind of boycotting them a little bit. It was ridiculous, but that was what was going on. It was a great show though, terrific show. Probably one of the last times they played there."

Recording began soon after the contract details were finalised. Once in the studio, the band wasted little time in getting down to work, completing the recording and mixing in six weeks. "This was the first time they had a budget," says King. "But still, taking six weeks to record and overdub an album is still 'indie' by today's standards. People seem to take forever in the studio." Work began around midday, with a dinner break at 7 or 8 pm. "We'd go out to eat somewhere," says King, "or at least Rob and I would. The guys would sometimes just go home for dinner. They had no money at all. They were still living hand to mouth.

"Obviously the first two records were done very quickly, so this was more of a production than they'd been used to," says King, comparing the group's earlier work to their major-label debut (it also reportedly marked the first time they used a guitar tuner in the studio). But one common factor among all three albums was that the songs had largely been worked out prior to recording, so little time was needed to work out arrangements, as listening to the demos reveals. "The songs were pretty much worked out," King agrees. "Billie is extremely talented. He's a great singer, and he knew those songs really well. He would just nail the takes, each take. And they usually were complete takes, no punching in. We were doing it from beginning to end. A lot of singers today can't do that; they don't have what it takes. But on that record, it was just so together. He gave me three, four good takes of each song, and I compiled the best of each take. Then Billie and Rob would listen and they'd say, 'This is great. . . try something else with this line. . .'

"Mike's bass parts were terrific," King continues. "I did edit a lot though. I did a lot of editing on Tré's drum tracks — not that they weren't good, but again, we just wanted to get the best of the best. I did

70

a lot of tape editing — it was before Pro Tools and computer editing. I would tape edit two or three drum tracks and stick those together and make the 24-track master. And then we'd put Mike's bass on, which didn't take too long. And then Billie went for his guitar tracks. Rob had a great guitar rig, a Marshall stack I think, that really sounded good. Rob was very good with guitars, that was his main thing; he was a great one with guitar sounds, so the guitar sounds were fantastic. Billie had his trusty Fernandes, we used that a lot. And then on the solos, we tried a bunch of guitars, we rented a bunch of different Telecasters just to give a different sound on the solo bits. In retrospect, we kind of introduced that 'produced punk' sound, if you like. Everybody else seemed to take it up after that. It was still punk, but obviously you'd spent a little bit of time working on it. I think everybody after that copied that… you know, Blink-182 and all those bands. It had the same energy, the same production techniques, but I think we were the first to come up with that."

Steve Hart also dropped in on the sessions. "Neill's a friend of mine, so I went in a few times and sat in," he says. "It wasn't like a big deal thing, 'cause they were just another local band, you know. But I checked it out; I like Neill and since I also had been called on the job, I was interested to see what he ended up doing. If you're an engineer dropping in on another engineer's session, you don't want to get in the way, so usually what my MO would be, and still remains to this day, when they're playing it's fine, you can sit there and listen and be a fly on the wall. But I would not hang out when all the band members would come in the control room or anything, because that's their moment. They don't need distractions.

"What I remember is that it was very straightforward, very live," Hart continues. "There wasn't a lot of messing around with tons of overdubs and stuff, and nothing excessive in any way with the amount of mics or gear or anything. Rob was trying to make it cheaply, so the simpler, the faster. But it sounded great and I really liked the band; I remember being totally impressed with how short and to the point the songs were, which is not always the case. The band were cool, straight-ahead working. By no means was it painful at all, and it didn't seem like any party on the other hand, either. I don't remember any copious amounts of booze or anything, it was work."

The few visitors helped keep distractions down to a minimum. "It wasn't like the place was full of people coming in," says King. "It was just the band Rob, me, and the managers would show up maybe once a week to check out the stuff we were doing. I don't think they even had any roadies. Rob, apart from being the producer, also represented the record label, so there weren't any other label people coming in. And he had the American Express card! It was great. He did his part, I did my part, and the band was great. They played great and they had great songs. It was all just facilitated really well. It was just first class, from beginning to end."

For his part, Cavallo wanted to have an atmosphere where ideas could be freely shared. "When you go in with a band, you want to make sure nobody feels that they should be embarrassed or ashamed to throw out any kind of an idea," he told *Taxi.com*. "I think that's one of the most important things you can do — to create that open kind of environment. Because then what you end up doing is truly getting the best out of the artists that are in that room." In the same interview he added he wanted to have the kind of relationship with Green Day that The Beatles had enjoyed with their producer, George Martin.

The album opened with 'Burnout', a song Billie Joe had written on the way home from Laytonville one night, while in an altered state himself. The song that would introduce Green Day to a major-label audience was a fast-paced ode about a stereotypical stoner loser who, after one too many highs, finds himself "amongst the dead". 'Having A Blast', with its references to blowing oneself up in a rage, sounds disturbingly like the tale of a suicide bomber, though later verses seem to point to the singer's anger being motivated by yet more romantic complications, as opposed to political complaints. 'Chump' is a diatribe against a rival, and, in a nice touch, the musical assault at the end segues neatly into the introductory loping drum beat of 'Longview', which would become the album's first single.

The song is ostensibly about another loser, stuck at home, whose boredom with his usual pursuits (watching TV, masturbating), has him caught in an apathetic slump. Billie Joe later said it was drawn from his own feelings about having to live back at his mother's house on occasion, when he had nowhere else to go. "I felt really pathetic," he told

Rolling Stone. "For a time I was wallowing in my own misery and liking it. The lyrics wrote themselves."

Somewhat at odds with the listless sentiments is the fierce power of the music during the chorus; also ironic was the fact that this slacker anthem, with its refrain of "no motivation" was performed by a group that, despite their image, was the antithesis of slackerdom, given the hard work, drive, and ambition they'd poured into advancing their careers. Chief among the song's many strengths is how the smooth glide of Tré's drums and Mike's bass line (which he told *Rolling Stone* he came up with while "flying on acid. . . later, it took me a long time to be able to play it, but it made sense when I was on drugs") have fully captured your attention before Billie Joe's vocal even begins.

Eric Yee and Eggplant were at the session when the song was recorded. When seeing the song performed live, Eggplant had been in the habit of shouting "You will!" following Billie Joe's line about being called pathetic, and the group had him shout the phrase during the session. "Listen closely and you'll hear someone in the background go 'You will,'" says Yee. "That was Eggplant! He used to do it at shows, that's how it came about. We'd always be just hanging out in the pit, messing around, and Eggplant would just yell it during the song."

Along with the new songs, a few previously recorded songs were re-recorded, including 'Welcome To Paradise'. The arrangement was the same as that on *Kerplunk!* (though *Dookie*'s version runs slightly longer), but comparing the two offers a clear way to assess what the band gained by stepping up to major-label production. The sound is fuller, gutsier, and the extraneous guitar noises during the instrumental break are more subdued, meaning that when the descending riff begins, the force with which it builds is far more powerful and exciting — at the end of sequence, you have the impression that the song is literally about to jump the track. "It's gonna get its fair shake now," Mike explained. "We thought [the song] fit this album really well lyrically, content-wise, and we just wanted to show what a strong song it was."

'Pulling Teeth' is a black-humoured "love song" about domestic violence, though in this case it's the woman, not the man, who's the abuser; the bittersweet mood is perfectly enhanced by the skillful vocal harmonising. Then comes 'Basket Case', which would go on to be another

Green Day classic. This portrait of another hapless soul on the verge of a mental breakdown starts out quietly, but with an unmistakable intensity in the vocal delivery. The music, which initially seems to lurk in the background, bursts forth — as if freed from its cage — on the words "cracking up". From then on, the song goes full throttle, before crashing to a stop. In a neat lyrical twist, which could easily be missed if you didn't read the lyrics, the gender of the prostitute patronised by the narrator changes gender in one line. Billie Joe later admitted there was an autobiographical element to the song, inspired by his own bouts with anxiety.

'She', 'Sassafras Roots', and 'When I Come Around' all deal with people trapped in unhappy circumstances — the woman in 'She' who feels suffocated by her pre-arranged life, and the dissatisfied couples in the latter two songs (though at least 'When I Come Around' ends on a more conciliatory note). 'Coming Clean' tackled a more unusual topic — at least in rock songs — of coming to terms with one's sexuality. "I still struggle with that too," Billie Joe said in the Warner Bros. bio. "It's part of adolescence and growing up." To the gay/lesbian magazine *The Advocate* he said, "I think everybody kind of fantasises about the same sex. I think people are born bisexual, and it's just that our parents and society kind of veer us off into this feeling of, 'Oh, I can't.'"

Unhappy relationships were also the focus of the next two songs. 'Emenius Sleepus' — with lyrics by Mike — has the narrator running into an old friend, and realising with sadness how much each has changed. 'In The End' is a seemingly bitter critique of another romantic rival, though Billie Joe revealed that the song, like 'Why Do You Want Him?', was again directed at his step-father. The closing track starts off deceptively like a folk song, with Billie Joe singing the initial two verses and choruses accompanied by an acoustic guitar. Then the instruments come charging in and the song's title becomes clear — 'F.O.D.' stands for "Fuck Off and Die." Then comes a further surprise; after around 1:20 of silence, comes the "hidden" track, Tré's 'All By Myself', a lovelorn tune recorded at a friend's house, whose lyrics consist mostly of the title, and which Tré sings in a style that wouldn't be out of place on a children's record.

Some of the tracks that didn't make the album later appeared as

B-sides: 'On The Wagon' as a B-side of 'Longview', and a cover of The Kinks' 'Tired Of Waiting For You' and a re-recording '409 In Your Coffeemaker' as B-sides of 'Basket Case'. And there was another song Billie Joe wrote at the time that the group elected not to record; a softer ballad called 'Good Riddance', which they'd keep under wraps for another four years. The song, in addition to 'She' and 'Sassafrass Roots', was inspired by a breakup with a young woman Billie Joe had been seeing in Berkeley, "a total, raving punk rocker who didn't approve of me being on a major label," he told *Spin*. "She moved down to Ecuador, saying she couldn't live in a world with McDonald's and such." The album itself was called *Dookie*, slang for excrement, a word chosen to "keep in touch with the child within," as Mike said in the Warner Bros. biography (though perhaps less childish than the purported original title: *Liquid Dookie*).

"We really wanted to make our records sound like us, but a bigger version of it," Billie Joe told writer Dan Epstein. "If a punk band signed to a major label, it always seemed like they compromised their sound, and we didn't want to do that." Indeed, comparing *Dookie* with *Kerplunk!*, the biggest difference was only in the quality of the production. The band had welcomed the chance to have more time to work on a recording, "to actually pay attention to what we were doing," as Mike put it. "The whole album sounds bigger... I think we obtained the same sound that we would have obtained if the other ones had been on a major label."

By the end of the sessions, King had a feeling the record was going to hit. "I knew Green Day was special," he says. "Any time I worked with Elvis Costello, I knew it was going to be huge. When I did the first A-Ha record, I knew it was going to be huge. When I did the first Smiths record I did, I knew... you can just tell. What they had, and what you have to have for those records, is a huge self-confidence. Not in a cocky way, but they just knew that their stuff was *it*. They knew it was their time. They knew they were going to be big. To get to that point, you have to have that. There's plenty of people that have the attitude, but they just don't have the songs or they don't have it. Whereas they knew they had it, all three of them. They knew it was all there, this was a special record. And I've worked on some great records and I can always spot when something great, something special, is going on. And it was just their time. They had this bunch of songs, they were all great players, and it just went really well. I knew it, they knew it, the producer knew it.

"Nobody could tell how many it's going to sell," King qualifies. "That's something altogether different. I would never have thought that. The other thing was that the timing was so good. In some ways, they'd been the leaders of the new punk revival, and that happened to become the popular thing at the time. And they were ready with the best record of that genre when that genre was exploding. It's possible — and that's part of it being so good — that the timing was perfect. If we had done that record three years earlier, it would still have been a great record, but it might have sold 50,000 copies. But all the ducks were in a row. Everything was right with that record. The timing was right for that kind of band. The kids were getting into new punk, second time around. Green Day had the best songs and the best record of that style."

And King certainly didn't expect the record to go on to sell over 14-million copies. "Not bad for a record that cost less than $100,000 to make!" he says. "Which may seem a lot, but you don't make demos for that anymore. You get baby bands that come in and they spend half a million on a record, on a band that just doesn't have half the quality that they had. You couldn't make a record for what they made *Dookie* now.

"Of course I was thrilled by *Dookie*'s success," King continues. "I got a lot of calls on the back of that record, which was terrific. It was great to know that you were vindicated, because it was such a great record, and it was received as such. And it's quite amazing how people still refer to that record. I go around to studios and I have a handful of CDs I use when I go into a new control room; I put them on so I can tune the room to those songs, because I know they sound good and they sound good in certain ways. Reference discs, I use them as reference discs. And a lot of people have *Dookie* as a reference disc for their control room sound. So I think, from a technical point of view, all the frequencies are there in the right proportions, the drums really punch very well, the bass is great. That kind of thing. The proportions are right. So if you're doing a band, they can look at that and say, 'These proportions are *right*, let's refer to that'. Then they can look at that and see, for instance, where the vocals sit in the mix. They can try and do a representation of that, and say, 'Well, I know that record sounds great outside, so I'll use that as my point of reference to where I want my vocal to sit.'"

"For me personally, it was, 'Wow, I messed up,'" says Hart of the job he missed out on. "'I guess Neill's got good luck, and he's gonna have a good run ahead of him.' And he did, too. He definitely got a ride for a few years off of that success, which is cool. From a musical standpoint, I don't think I was terribly surprised at the record's success, because I thought they were very good. But you never know. I've been doing this for 30 years and have only twice ever called a hit. You just never know, honestly; you think it's one and it's not, or the vice versa."

After finishing work on the album, Green Day joined Bad Religion's Recipe For Hate tour. After the tour, they also ended up going back into the studio in LA to remix the album and re-record 'Longview' so Tré could re-do his drum part, and because the band felt they were playing it better after two months on the road (though it retained Eggplant's "You will!" from the Fantasy recording). And though the album was a good six months from being released, signs of the punk realm's discontent continued to poke up. A show at the Phoenix Theater in Petaluma, California was picketed by punks asking fans to boycott Green Day's major-label album on its release. Gina Arnold's book *Kiss This: Punk In The Present Tense* recounts a more vocal outburst during a show at San Francisco's Warfield Theater, when a detractor in the audience yelled the inevitable, "Sell outs!" Quick as a flash, Mike responded, "Takes one to know one!" "This is about you, buddy," Billie Joe chimed in, introducing 'Chump'.

"I went to a bunch of shows when they first started that tour with Bad Religion," says Eric Yee. "I saw a lot of those shows, Santa Cruz, LA, Tijuana. That was a killer show, actually, the one in Tijuana." Due to his friendship with the band, Yee "would just hang out until I would see them arriving for a show and they would just get me in — that was the strategy. But as they got more popular, that got harder and harder. At one particular show, me and my friend Kevin went down to see them in LA, at the Hollywood Palladium with The Muffs. I decided just on a whim to go down there, check it out. We were trying to sneak our way in, as usual. But we couldn't get in. At one point I had to go to the store to go get a sandwich because I was starving. And Kevin stayed in the car, and they went in, Kevin didn't seem them, and we didn't get in. So I was like, screw this. I'm just going to go and buy a ticket.

"But Kevin was like, 'No, hold on a second. There's Mike D, from The Beastie Boys.' I'm like, 'Who? Who's that?' I was totally oblivious to stuff like that. But Kevin walks right up to Mike D and he's like, 'Hey, Mike!' Mike D kind of looks at him like, 'Do I know this guy?' Kevin said, 'Mike, if you go inside, tell Billie Joe that Eric and Kevin are outside and they can't get in, and they came all the way down from the Bay Area.' Mike D goes, 'Eric and Kevin. I'm going to tell him.' I was like, 'You gotta be kidding me, that guy isn't going to do shit for us.' So I bought a ticket, then we went in. Green Day had just played their first song when I got in, and Billie Joe said, 'Hey, is Eric Yee here?' I'm like, oh shit, I can't believe it, like Mike D told him! Billie Joe goes, 'Eric, raise your hand!' He had the crowd chanting my name, which was one of the coolest things ever. That's the first and last time that's ever going to happen. So we hooked up with him and then he got us into the show the next night."

The size of the shows tipped Yee off to the fact that Green Day wasn't going to remain just an East Bay success much longer. "Those big gigs in LA were massive," he says. "There were kids there with their moms and dads! I was freaking out. It was crazy. And after that they were always touring. You couldn't even just go to a show like the Palladium; if I could just find them, they'd let me in, but by then, it was impossible."

It was decided that the album's first single and video would be 'Longview', mutually chosen by the label and the band, though Mike admitted the band was "a little more hesitant" about the choice than the label was. The video marked the first time the group worked with Mark Kohr, with whom they would make a total of nine videos. "They've always been great," Kohr says. "We've always had a really good working relationship. There's always been a good balance in terms of Billie, Mike, Tré, and me working it out together. Billie's the main, creative force there, though Tré and Mike would come up with things. But Billie's always the final say. He wouldn't be difficult about it. But you just knew that when he spoke, he was setting the tone."

Kohr was originally from the Los Angeles area and moved to San Francisco in 1982 to attend San Francisco State, majoring in Fine Arts with a minor in business advertising. After graduation, he worked at Colossal Pictures. "They did TV commercials, credit sequences, cartoons," he says. "I did some film effects, like *Ghostbusters*, that's one I worked on. All kinds of different things. Then in late '89, a friend of mine said, 'Why don't we make a video? I'll produce it and you direct it. We'll use our own money.' And I said, 'Sure. That'd be great.' Because everyone always says, 'I want to be a director,' and I thought, I'm not going to talk about it, I'm just going to do it."

Kohr's first video was with the local band Buck Naked And The Bare-Bottom Boys, on the equally colourfully titled 'Teenage Pussy From Outer Space'. He then began working with Primus, for whom he made a number of videos. "It was a great relationship, because we did artistic, really cool videos," he says. "But they just didn't show that much on MTV."

In late '93, he was contacted by Cahn-Man and went to meet Green Day at their office. Kohr was not familiar with the group. "I didn't do the whole East Bay scene," he says. "I didn't know Green Day and I didn't know Rancid or those guys. I didn't know that Gilman Street thing. Because Primus wasn't really a part of that scene. If I did go to punk shows, it would be in the city, like at the Mabuhay Gardens and stuff, but that was before Green Day. I would go and see bands all the time, but I wouldn't see bands like a nut. I wasn't like, 'I want to be in this band thing, in this band culture.' For me, it was all about making images and all about working with emotions and being creative. That was my background, it was a visual background."

What struck Kohr on first meeting the group was how young they were. "They were just like kids," he says. "Billie had these sort of dreadlocks. They were just so young. And they were a little nervous, because they hadn't done a video. I think why they came to me was because I was the guy who was doing the Primus videos, and at the time, we were doing a lot of fun work. And they really respected those guys.

"The meeting was kind of like, 'Let's see if we get along,'" Kohr continues, "but at the same time, I think I had the job, unless it completely didn't work at all. And so I went and I talked to them. And I've always been really open to the artist expressing themselves; I'm a really good listener, because I'm an artist myself, and I know where they're coming from. I've always known that when an artistic person talks, you really need to listen; they're actually telling the truth, but they're nervous, because you are a new person in their environment, and so they're not fully expressing their meaning, but it's all there. I remember going in and saying, 'Do you guys have anything in mind?' And Billie said, 'I was thinking maybe you'd just shoot us watching TV in our apartment.' I took that and I went and listened to the song, and I was like, 'Yeah, this is like watching TV, beating off, and not having anything to do, being bored and stuff.' So I submitted a treatment, because the way music videos are dealt with, you get a song, then you get a number — how much they want to spend — and you write a treatment. And so I wrote a treatment that was pretty close to what they ended up doing. And the budget was approved real quickly. During that time, Billie would call me, or I'd call him and ask if they wanted anything else, and he'd throw in, 'Well, can we have a monkey?' and I was like 'Sure, let me see if I can...' and then we'd find a monkey."

The video was shot over two days at the Ashby Avenue house. "It's always easier shooting on a set," Kohr says. "But what was great was that it had all these things, like it had a real low ceiling, and visually it would really feel like it was pushing down on them, oppressive and claustro-phobic." The video cuts between Billie Joe, lounging around the messy living room on his couch watching television and the band performing in even smaller spaces like the bathroom. Underscoring the seediness of the environment, the band members themselves look somewhat grimy. At the end, Billie Joe stabs the couch in frustration, then sits back in boredom as the couch's stuffing falls silently around him. At one point, the TV screen shows an animated sequence of a dog throwing a handful of "dookie", making a visual link to the album's cover.

Kohr put in a few other touches. "I had the mirror panels put in there behind Billie's head," he explains, "so he's watching TV, but you also see the TV in the same shot. Just stuff like that, so the story's clear. Because if you just have a shot of him, a shot of the TV, then you just have more shots of him but you never see another TV, in terms of the story, or if the viewer comes in at the middle of the video, they might not get what's going on."

Kohr says the band also wanted to make the song's references to self-gratification more explicit. "They wanted to somehow imply that there was a guy who was masturbating in there, and they wanted to use this friend of theirs," he says. "And so I had a PA run out to this vintage store where they have stuff from the Fifties, because I was like, 'I need to get something that doesn't have a copyright on it so that we don't have to pay for it, and where we can fuzz out the naughty bits, so it's not so risqué that TV won't show it.' When he came back the guy was like, 'I went to this place, and I've never gone to a place like that before!' and he had *Gent* or something. And we shot this thing where there was a guy pretending to masturbate. And it was kind of funny and awkward and stuff. But it didn't make it in the video."

Despite Gilman's ostensible ban on bands on major labels, Green Day did manage to play the club again. Livermore remembers an unannounced show around Christmas in 1993, when they played under an assumed name. He later wrote of the gig, "We were all dancing and singing along together, and it was all warm and festive and family-like, but there was also this bittersweet feeling that came from knowing that things would never be like this again, that this was the last time we'd all be together this way."

"Green Day played at Gilman until they got too big for it," Jesse Michaels says. "There was never an intentional 'final show', but people may have called it that after the fact. When they were really huge they showed up once or twice and played shows. I'm sure it was a confusing mess. The best shows were when they were the house band and it was another day in the neighbourhood."

But those days would soon be behind them. Though no one realised it, *Dookie* was about to turn their lives upside down. In retrospect, people like Frank Portman say that shouldn't have been a surprise. "There's no mystery why *Dookie* was such a runaway hit, because it's so well recorded and the songs are so well constructed and catchy," he says. "It's obvious when you hear it. I mean, it was like that with *Nevermind*; I remember first hearing 'Smells Like Teen Spirit', and when somebody told me it was Nirvana I was kind of surprised, but then it was like, 'Okay, alright, they take this chord progression and have made it into this thing that's going to be the biggest deal in the world.' I mean, the second you heard it, you knew that. And there's something of the same thing about the sound of *Dookie*; when you first heard it, you just knew it was destined for big things."

It was also destined to change the main thrust of the alternative rock scene. As Simon R. Barry wrote after *Dookie*'s release in the UK magazine *e.p.*: "Grunge is dead, long live Green Day."

CHAPTER 5

The Dookie Hits The Fan

"I still scratch my head and say, 'How in the hell did they make it?'"
— *Tré Cool's dad to* Rolling Stone, *January 26, 1995*

*D*ookie was released in the US on February 1, 1994. The cover art featured a cartoon illustration of the East Bay in the process of being bombed. UC Berkeley's Sather Tower — more popularly known locally as the Campanile, after the tower of the same name in Venice — is on the right, and a cluster of factories emitting fumes next to a drawing of a skull and crossbones can easily be read as the oil refineries of Rodeo. Some of the band's friends cavort among the people in the foreground; Murray Bowles can be seen holding a camera up to snap a picture in his trademark fashion. A BART train snakes through the scene and the blue-and-white striped awning of a Telegraph Avenue hangout, Café Mediterranean — here labeled "Da Med" — can be seen. Dogs on the rooftops hurl fistfuls of excrement down on those below; one also pilots the plane that's dropping bombs labeled "DOOKIE". Green Day's name rises out of the resulting blast, while a monkey sits in the lower left corner, looking at his own handful of poop, thinking, "Throw?" The illustration was by Richie Bucher, a member of East Bay group Sweet

Baby, and whose artwork on a record by the band Raooul (another Lookout act) had favourably impressed Billie Joe.

The in-jokes continued throughout the accompanying booklet. Among the illustrations are a sign reading, "Now Entering OAKLAND," a flyer under the lyrics for "Having A Blast" reading, "Having A Blatz," and, on the last page, one of San Francisco's bridges being blown up (as the drawing is in black and white, you can't tell if it's meant to be the grey San Francisco-Oakland Bay Bridge, or the more well-known orange Golden Gate Bridge). The back cover featured a photograph of a mosh pit. On the original version, a hand puppet of Ernie, from *Sesame Street*, can be seen emerging from the middle. On later pressings, the Muppet was airbrushed out, supposedly because of possible copyright infringement, though the original booklet did note that the character was copyrighted by "Jim Henson Productions, Inc." [sic]. Billie Joe later said that the complaints of an "old woman", who'd bought the record for her kids and been "horrified" at the album's content had led to Ernie's removal.

The album (which was also available in a limited edition on green vinyl) sold a modest 9,000 copies in its first week of release. Sales were initially slow; it wasn't until the following year that *Dookie* would peak in the US charts at number two. And for all Mark Kohr knew, the 'Longview' video wasn't about to take off immediately either. "When we were working on the video, we had no notion of whether it would turn into anything at all," he says. "It could have shown once on MTV as far as I knew, because that's what I had done up to that point. We would do these incredibly cool videos for Primus; I mean visually, they were amazing, and really innovative, stylistically. And they would show once, and it was always really disappointing to us. I'd later hear, 'Oh yeah, when that "Mr. Crinkle" video came out, it blew me away, and so-and-so brought it in and showed it to everybody...' I wish we knew that, because we felt like we were doing them and just throwing them out there and they were having *no* impact. So with 'Longview' I felt like, 'This video isn't really going to do much of anything.'"

But 'Longview' generated strong interest as soon as MTV added it to its playlist on February 22 (it reached the station's "Buzz Bin" on March 28). "Oh yeah," says Kohr. "It became huge! Later, when I'd pass the house where it was filmed on the way to my chiropractor's, I'd blow it a kiss. I'm serious. Every time. Because my career just — boom! — took off huge after that." And three days before the video reached MTV, *Dookie* entered the *Billboard* Top Pop Albums chart at number 127. It would stay on the charts for 113 weeks. The singles charts in the magazine had long since been split into far more categories than simply Pop, R&B, and Country. There were now charts for Modern Rock, Mainstream Rock, Airplay Chart-only, Sales Chart-only, Heatseekers, and more, reflecting the ever-more niche-driven US radio markets. Songs also charted if they were simply serviced to radio and not sold to consumers. So, while 'Longview' didn't appear on the Pop Top 40, it did top the Modern Rock chart, peaked at number 13 in the Mainstream Rock chart, and reached 36 in the Airplay chart.

As the album, single and video wended their way up the various charts, Green Day was busy promoting their album on the road. March was full of TV appearances: *Late Night With Conan O'Brien* on March 16 (Mike later told *Entertainment Weekly* he'd been so mortified at how he looked and sounded that he trashed his hotel room), *The Jon Stewart Show* on March 17, and MTV's *120 Minutes* on March 20.

By the time the band briefly came off the road in April, *Dookie* had sold 65,000 copies and the band began working on their second video, 'Basket Case'. "'Longview' took off immediately," says Kohr, "like — boom! — it exploded. We were all really taken aback by it, and then they wanted us to start talking about the second video really quickly. So I went to meet with the band, and Billie was like, 'I'm just getting freaked out; every time I turn on MTV, there's my face.' He was a little bit nervous about it. So I said, 'What do you guys want to do?' And Billie said, 'Well, I was thinking we could shoot in an insane asylum, and I'd be surrounded by crazy people'. . . maybe reflecting the situation he felt he was going through. And of course the people in the meeting were just like — I could just see the hair go up on their heads — 'Are you out of your mind?' Again, I just try to be calm with the artist and not say, 'No,' because that's not the way to go; there are ways to deal with things where everybody gets what they want."

Aside from the unusual setting, 'Basket Case' was essentially a straightforward performance video. "I felt that if I had them to act too much, they might be uncomfortable," Kohr explains. "I mean, they've grown more comfortable with that in time, but I just really tried to be easy with them in terms of that stuff at the beginning. The great thing is that Billie, he's just a natural, a natural entertainer. And you basically build the environment around him, and you put everything in place, and then he knows what to do; he just feels it and he goes with it. It's very easy with him, if you set everything up right. But at that time, if I over-directed him and Mike and Tré. . . well, Mike would get stressed out. Not Tré. Tré is always a big ham. But they might get stressed out and it might be really wooden and unnatural and they might feel they were doing something that they shouldn't quote unquote 'be doing.'

"At the time I also had them take care of their own clothes," Kohr continues, "because I just really wanted them to feel the most comfortable. We were in the Bay Area at the time, and they really had an idea of what they wanted to do stylistically. Whereas, when you come down to LA, everyone needs a stylist and the stylist goes and picks stuff out. But if it can happen naturally from those individuals, it's so much more expressive and appropriate." (In fact, it looks like Billie Joe is wearing the same T-shirt he had on in the 'Longview' video.)

Kohr located an actual insane asylum in the Bay Area, where the video was shot over the course of two days in an empty wing. "It was creepy," he recalls. "It was haunted, it felt like. It was so rich, full of vibes. And of course part of it was a functioning insane asylum, so we'd go by the places where the insane people were, and it was pretty heavy." The video starts with Billie Joe being handed his guitar by an aide. Tré is wheeled up to his kit in a wheelchair, and Mike is wheeled in on a stretcher, as if coming from a bout of shock therapy (disoriented, he is led to the mic stand and has to have someone help him strap on his bass). As the band plays, other "patients" meander around them; most were friends of the band, many of them (including Tré's father) wearing Kabuki theatre masks that Kohr had picked up. The music conveys a joyous sense of release, but at the video's end, the band is securely locked inside the ward. As the single wasn't going to be released until the summer, Kohr had time to shoot in black and white, and then have the film colourised.

"I shot it all on 16mm, so it'd have kind of a rough look," he explains. "But it would also have this really strong colour on top of it. At the time, people would shoot in 35mm, so it'd be smooth, and then put the colour on it. But I wanted it to be kind of gritty, because it's a punk thing, so I shot in 16mm. And then it was all hand-painted. It worked out well, because the colours are really unusual."

The shoot occurred in early April — coinciding, Kohr recalls, with the shocking announcement that Nirvana's lead singer, guitarist, and creative force, Kurt Cobain, had been found dead in his Seattle home of a self-inflicted gunshot wound. Green Day had just played in Seattle at the all-ages club Oz on April 5, and returned home after playing Vancouver, B.C., on April 6. "I remember going to their home, Billie was just like, 'Oh my God, did you hear. . .?' He was sitting on the same sofa that we shot him on [in 'Longview']. And I was like, 'I know.' It was just wild. He was really taken aback by the whole thing, of course, he was really affected by it." (In a slight variation, Billie Joe remembers hearing about Cobain's death when ideas for 'Basket Case' were still under discussion.)

Nirvana had been credited with kicking the door open for alternative rock, when their landmark album *Nevermind* was released in September 1991 and the hitherto little-known band ended up topping the US charts four months later. In retrospect, 1991 had been dubbed "the year punk broke" (ultimately the title of Dave Markey's documentary of Sonic Youth's summer '91 tour of European rock festivals, which also featured Nirvana), when the underground/alternative music scene that had been percolating beneath the surface over the previous decade finally breeched the mainstream arena. Observers such as Dean Carlson, a DJ who'd worked at several radio stations in Washington state during the Eighties and Nineties, notes that the dearth of compelling music in the American Top 40 meant that the listening audience was ready for something new and different — like Nirvana — and, later, Green Day.

"In the early Nineties, I think pop ran out of new ideas," he says. "That was kind of a stinky time. You had bands like INXS that kept releasing records. You had very average-sounding hip-hop/R&B that wasn't really hip-hop because it was before it was really political. You had Michael Jackson releasing his umpteenth album, and you had MTV and VH1 churning out so much sound-alike music. That was also the early stage of when boy-bands were exploding and New Kids On The Block segued into Backstreet Boys, and there was just so much sugar and sac-charine out there that punk was refreshing. And that's really when 'alter-native,' to use a term that I loathe so much, because no one really called the music that unless you were in the industry — the chart was alterna-tive, but if you bought the music, you never really called it that. Anyway, that's why alternative was so refreshing at the time when all that other music was just boring everyone to death. And not only the tastemakers were hungry for something new, I think the masses were hungry for something new. Sometimes that's all it takes. It's almost like all the planets have to be aligned at once. It's more than having the right thing at the right time; when you say 'the right time,' that means, 'What else is out there?' And sometimes if what's really popular is just boring everyone to tears, then it's time for everybody to gravitate toward something new."

For the next few years, that something new was grunge, as Nirvana, Pearl Jam, Soundgarden, and Alice In Chains all hit the top of the charts. Similar Pacific Northwest acts like Screaming Trees, Mudhoney, Tad, and the original grungemeisters, The Melvins (who had by then relocated to California), also secured major-label deals. Major record companies quickly set up "alternative" music departments, and contracts began giving the new crop of bands more leeway as far as artistic control over their work. The mania for all things "grunge" soon surpassed the musical realm into a celebration of all accoutrements of the supposed grunge "lifestyle," from coffee and micro-brewed beer to "grunge fashion." (In perhaps the best example of the media utterly missing the point, *Vogue*'s December 1992 "Grunge & Glory" fashion spread featured "designer grunge" knockoffs of thrift-store wear priced at $500.)

Yet the underlying tone of grunge music, steeped in melancholy (some would say negativity) also meant it would perhaps be harder to maintain substantial interest in the genre over the long run. "There was a point where grunge was so big, and there were so many bands, and it was so heavy, and they were so down, that you could only deal with so much," says Carlson. "It really was a downer. It just was so *heavy*, espe-cially when we started losing the musicians; that kind of brought it all home, especially when they took their own life. You're just like, 'Wow, this isn't a fashion statement. They're really living this life.' Punk was very expressive and grunge was, not intuitive, but it just was. . . what spoke to so many people was that it was so personal. I mean, Kurt's lyrics were incredibly touching. He was a sensitive guy, and he felt a lot of pain, and he shared that. Punk was more like the reaction from the pain. Punk is 'hurt you' and grunge is 'hurt me.' Or, 'I am hurt.' It's almost like grunge turned inward and punk turned outward.

"And maybe that just had to happen," he continues. "I think, in some ways, the people listening to grunge were ready for something a little more positive. They just wanted to crawl out of the pit, if that makes sense. I even remember the gathering that happened at the Seattle Center after Cobain died [a public memorial held on April 10], and you could literally feel that we were ready to write a new chapter, that this would give way to something else. It's not like the Seattle sound went away, but there was a shift."

And it was a shift brought around, in part, because of Cobain's unexpected departure from the music scene. "I think that happening kind of created this space for Green Day," says Kohr, expressing a view shared by many. "After Nirvana, there was a weird kind of vacuum really," says UK musician/journalist John Robb. "And I don't think anybody expected poppy-punk to fill that vacuum at all. It was a real shock. And I felt that when Green Day came over, that vacuum was getting filled; there were a few poppy-punk bands around at the time, like The Descendants, and a few other bands, even Bad Religion, to a certain extent. Green Day seemed like a younger version of all that, like an extension of that thing. I thought *Dookie* was a fantastic record. It was really big in England, In every little town in Britain you'd sce loads of Green Day T-shirts; they definitely made an impact. The kids that had just missed Nirvana now had their own band. Even though they weren't as heavy or intense a band as Nirvana, they touched the same topics, alienation and those kind of things. I remember seeing The Offspring and Green Day both being Top 10 in America. It seemed really weird to see punk bands names in the American Top 10, 'cause it's always really crap, the American Top 10; it's always R&B or really middle-of-the-road music, like The Dave Matthews Band or something like that. It was great to see some exciting bands in there; it was a complete regeneration of what punk was about."

A regeneration to some, but for much of Green Day's new audience, *Dookie* provided an introduction to a musical genre — and history — they hadn't previously been aware of. "My knee-jerk reaction to *Dookie* at the time, being a jaded 30-year-old, was, 'Oh great, they've repackaged The Buzzcocks,'" says Carlson. "But then, once I calmed down, I realised that this represented a whole new resurgence of bands. Yeah, of course it sounded like 1977, but the lyrics were different. The lyrics were more timely. They had taken the — template is too technical of a term to use — but they had taken the idea of punk rock and made it a little more relevant to what was going on in those times. So even though there were these little two minute, 15 second songs that were filled with melody and a barrage of guitars, it was updated, and it didn't take very long before I could tell that this wasn't just another hyped thing from the record labels — 'Look, we've reinvented punk rock!' What this was, was a whole slew of bands that were taking a sound and making it available to a whole generation of kids that weren't even born when punk rock was being created. But I think that's okay, it's perfectly okay for bands to reinvent things from the past. I mean, follow it back, it's been going on from the beginning; everyone's guilty of it."

Green Day had no time for such analysis. At the end of April, the band headed out again on a 40-date European tour. At an advance marketing meeting, Warner Bros. European executives had been given an introductory "kit" about the group with a copy of *Dookie*, a 'Longview' video, and other promotional items packed inside individual lunchboxes. Their June 3 show in Madrid was recorded for broadcast on Spain's Radio Nacional, and select tracks also appeared later as B-sides (a March date in Florida had been recorded for the same purpose; tracks from that show also appeared on a six-track CD released in Japan, *Live Tracks*). In London, they taped a session for the BBC's Radio 1.

They also met up with Lawrence Livermore in London, who was invited to attend the band's June 6 show at the Astoria II. He went backstage to see his friends, but soon left as "the celebrities and TV lights were getting on my nerves." But while walking home, the band's tour bus pulled up, and Tré stuck his head out the window, yelling for Livermore to come aboard. While drinking together in a bar, the band was shown a copy of *Billboard* that had a full-page ad Reprise had taken out in the band's honor. The ad read "*Dookie* Is Gold."

As a joke, the band later gave a gold record award to *MaximumRockNRoll*, feeling the magazine had regularly slighted them. "Green Day has always felt that *MaximumRockNRoll* was out to get them," agrees Eric Yee. "But if you look at the record reviews, up to the major-label records they always got great reviews. It was mainly because of the people writing letters complaining about them that they got this idea that *Maximum* was anti-them. I don't think Tim [Yohannan] was ever out to get Green Day. Though he was anti-corporate rock, that's for sure."

Meanwhile, in the charts, 'Basket Case' spent five weeks at number one on the Modern Rock chart, reached number nine on the Mainstream Rock chart, and number 26 on the Airplay chart. 'Welcome To Paradise' also released as a single, reached number seven on the Modern Rock chart. Kohr says there was no video for the latter song. "Billie never wanted a video for 'Welcome To Paradise'," he says. "My understanding, though I could be wrong, is that Billie never wanted to do a video for it because it was essentially about the way that they lived when they were a poor band, when they didn't have any money, and they and all their friends were in the East Bay and they were living this particular lifestyle. And 'Welcome To Paradise' kind of means welcome to this world, with a bunch of kids who don't have very much money, who're all friends. And Billie didn't want to be singing from the position of being a popular entertainer or rock star, someone who's making money, and singing this song that's taking the piss a little bit about the way he and his friends used to live, because he obviously wasn't living that way any more. He wanted to be respectful of his friends who lived that lifestyle, and respectful, I guess, of what living that way gave him.

"There's one song in the new White Stripes album [*Get Behind Me Satan*] that talks about being in your little room," he continues. "And then the next verse is about when you get a bigger room; you get a bigger room and you try to think of something good, but you can't, and so you have to think about what you were thinking about in your little room. Whenever I hear that song, I think of Billie and 'Welcome to Paradise', how the little room is what made him big, but once you get big, you can't go back to the little room."

(According to Bob Sarles though, who'd edited the first two Green Day videos, a performance video was made of the song, shot during a sound check before a gig at San Francisco venue Slim's, and directed by Robert Caruso.)

Back in the states on another short break, Billie Joe and Adrienne Nesser (who'd moved to California earlier in the year) got married on July 2. The ceremony, held in the backyard of Billie Joe's house, was "pieced together," he said, from texts drawn from the Catholic, Protestant, and Jewish religions, in order to cover all the bases. The couple spent their honeymoon at Berkeley's posh Claremont Resort & Spa, a locale later used for band interviews over the years. The next day, on picking up a home-pregnancy kit, the two learned that Adrienne was pregnant.

Just six months previously, Green Day had been largely unknown outside the punk rock underground, the band members living in a cramped basement. Now they were well on their way to becoming household names and selling their first million records, if not yet earning their first million in dollars. But there was scarcely time to take in all the changes in their personal and professional lives, for the band was heading out on the road yet again, touring the US and Canada on their own tour in July, and then joining the 1994 Lollapalooza bill in August. The Lollapalooza festival was a traveling rock show that had begun in 1991, co-founded by Perry Ferrell of Jane's Addiction, spotlighting the emerging alternative scene and providing a platform for what was then Jane's Addiction's farewell tour. (The word "lollapalooza" is defined by the *American Heritage Dictionary* as, "Something outstanding of its kind.") The first tour featured Jane's Addiction as headliners, along with Nine Inch Nails, Violent Femmes, Ice-T, and more off-the-wall performers like The Jim Rose Circus Sideshow. Nirvana had been the original headliner for the 1994 festival; after Cobain's death, Smashing Pumpkins was chosen to fill the slot. Other bands on the bill included The Beastie Boys, Cypress Hill, Nick Cave & The Bad Seeds, The Breeders, The Flaming Lips, Guided By Voices, and L7. Green Day was only scheduled to play part of the festival, replacing The Boredoms. "We were conned into it by our management," Mike later joked — presumably — to *Spin*.

Green Day was also booked in the opening slot, having signed on to the festival prior to *Dookie's* having made much of an impact. "They were opening to nobody at the beginning of the tour," says Jennifer Finch of L7, who had made a point of listening to *Dookie* once she learned Green Day would be sharing the bill with them. "But then the awareness of the band really skyrocketed through the rest of the tour. They didn't show any attitude; they operated with a lot of grace and dignity about it. They were very sweet, very humble. Just fun to be with. And they had a real sense of family, those three were really like a family together — all for one and one for all — which you really can't buy in a band. They say a musician only gets one band like that in their lives... where everyone is just really into it because they're into the other band members and into being together."

Nonetheless, Finch and L7 couldn't resist teasing the members of this hot "new" band they'd known since Green Day's members were still in high school. "We made fun of them intensely," says Finch, "because they deserved it! They were like our lost little brothers. There's those famous photos from Lollapalooza of L7 holding up signs that said, 'Punk Rock For Sale,' 'Grunge For Rent,' 'Get Your Punk Here,' during Green Day's set. But it was with them, not against them. It was about the marketing of punk, the sales of it. Not the band creating it. In my perception, 1994 was the year that punk rock became a commodity in the open major-label market. I think in the Eighties is when labels shifted from having a love of music to being run by people with law degrees. And those people with law degrees did a great job of hiring people that could give the illusion that it was still about the music. The Nineties is when everything went real sharehold, that's when things started to get sold, and companies went public, and things like that. All that sort of thing happened that year. That was the same year that L7 wrote 'Punk Rock Broke My Heart'."

After playing Atlanta, Green Day left Lollapalooza for a few days to play an even higher profile event: Woodstock '94. The original Woodstock, held August 15 to 17, 1969, had become a landmark event for the Sixties generation, "Three days of peace and music" that had featured such iconic acts as The Who, Janis Joplin, The Grateful Dead, Santana, and Jimi Hendrix, whose elegiac rendition of 'The Star

Spangled Banner' was seen as a bittersweet commentary on the turmoil then going on in Vietnam. (Elliott Cahn, then in Sha Na Na, had also performed at the festival.)

Now, 25 years later, the original promoters came together to present "Three more days of peace and music" (as the subsequent documentary was subtitled), mixing together baby-boomer faves like Santana, Crosby, Stills & Nash, and Bob Dylan with newer acts like Nine Inch Nails, Melissa Etheridge, Salt 'n' Pepa, and Green Day. The festival was held August 12 to 14 at the 840-acre Winston Farm, in Saugerties, New York. At the time, the event was somewhat derided for being a cynical exploitation of boomer nostalgia (despite the presence of contemporary acts), further tainted by the heavy-handed touch of corporate marketing: Pepsi had paid $5 million to be the 'Official Soft Drink' of the festival, tickets were $135, and a live broadcast of the show was offered via pay-per-view at $50 a pop (though the fuss over Woodstock 2's commercialisation would seem remarkably genteel after the havoc caused at the 1999 event, when the last day of the festival degenerated into rioting, resulting in extensive vandalism, property destruction, and reports of numerous sexual assaults. "The first Woodstock was peace and love, the second chaos and confusion, and the last one was just stupidity," Mike told *Entertainment Weekly*).

Still, it was a chance to perform before their largest audience to date, a reported 350,000, not to mention the additional exposure obtained through pay-per-view, and future video and record sales. "Despite the scale of it though, it was just another gig for us really," Billie Joe later told journalist Ben Myers. "We were asked, 'Do you want to play in front of 300,000 people?' and we said, 'Sure, why not?'"

Ironically, as the group arrived for their slot on August 14, Billie Joe carefully navigated his way to the stage, anxious to keep his new Converse sneakers clean; clean shoes would be the least of his worries by the end of the set, which ranks as one of the most raucous, chaotic — and legendary — in Green Day's history. The rest of Billie Joe's outfit was not dissimilar to what he'd wear on the later *American Idiot* tours: black trousers and shirt, with a red tie sporting a large black question mark. Mike wore a Screeching Weasel T-shirt. Tré had green hair; Billie Joe's was dyed bright blue.

The incessant rain during the day hadn't dampened the crowd's spirits, though they had become restive during the lengthy set by acts from the touring WOMAD world music festival that preceded Green Day's arrival. As a result, the audience was wound up to the breaking point, and when Green Day's set finally kicked off with a rousing version of 'Welcome To Paradise', a mosh pit erupted instantaneously. "Don't smoke the brown weed!" Mike crowed afterwards, a reference to a stage announcement during the first Woodstock warning the audience to avoid the brown acid that had been circulating (in a jab at Woodstock '94's corporate sponsorship, singer John Popper had told the crowd to stay away from the "brown Pepsi" during the Blues Traveler's set). "Look at you fuckin' dirty mother fuckers!" said Billie Joe, before asking them to do "the wave," over Mike's protest, "This ain't a fuckin' baseball game! What the hell!" "This is off one of our records that no one has," Billie Joe continued, introducing 'One Of My Lies', keenly aware the audience probably didn't even realise the group had released any records prior to *Dookie*.

And then the mud began to fly, as some in the crowd, seeking excitement beyond simply moshing, started hurling mud clods around. "Yeah, we suggest that you throw mud. That's fun!" said Mike in response, adding, "I said [at] each other! Come on!" a moment later, when mud began flying in Green Day's direction. Prior to starting 'When I Come Around', Billie Joe grabbing a flying mud clod and smeared it on his face to the crowd's cheers (this performance ended up on the soundtrack album and video of the event). Eventually, a torrent of mud and clothing was being thrown at the stage. 'F.O.D.' finally lit a fire under the fans, who began leaping onto the stage in a steady stream, as a plastic tarp was hurriedly pulled over the large camera rolling on a dolly in front of the stage to protect it from flying mud. As 'F.O.D.' segued into 'Paper Lanterns', the mayhem increased, with the crew coming on stage trying in vain to block in-flight mud clods.

Eventually, as Mike and Tré vamped on their instruments, Billie Joe dropped his guitar in favour of picking up mud clods and hurling them back at the audience. Though stopping momentarily to shout, "This isn't love and peace, it's fucking anarchy!" he couldn't resist in indulging in a little more anarchy himself, going back to throwing mud. Mike lay on his back on the now mud-soaked stage, still playing his bass, then getting up to avoid Billie Joe, who slid across the stage on his stomach. Billie Joe then leaped up, shouted, "Hey, look at me, I'm a fuckin' idiot!" grabbed his mic, and pounded it into smithereens on the stage. Grabbing another mic, he split the crowd into rival shouts of "Rock'n'roll!" and "Shut the fuck up!" before leading them in a brief singalong of Twisted Sister's 'We're Not Gonna Take It', then grabbed a young stage diver and hauled him back to centre stage, encouraging him to recite the title of The Beastie Boys classic '(You've Gotta) Fight For Your Right (To Party!)'. "Future idiot!" Billie Joe said proudly as the boy ran off stage.

Perhaps sensing there was no other way to end things, Billie Joe finally announced, "Hey, everybody, say, 'Shut the fuck up' and we'll stop playing." When the crowd duly complied, he said, "Okay, we're gone! Goodbye!" though even on exiting, he couldn't resist running back to leap around with some fans who'd just jumped on the stage. Mike wasn't so lucky; when he tried to exit the stage, the bouncers, mistaking him for a fan, caught him in a full body tackle and slammed him down, knocking some of his teeth out. The mud-drenched band finally escaped in a helicopter. It was, Billie Joe said of the experience, "the closest thing to total chaos I've ever seen in my whole life." He later received an admonishing letter from his mother, who'd watched the show on pay-per-view and been highly displeased with what she called a "disrespectful and indecent" performance, adding how disappointed his father would have been with him over his antics.

In August, *Dookie* was certified Platinum. After their Woodstock appearance, it leapt back up the charts to number five, and by September had been certified double Platinum. On September 8, the band attended the MTV Video Music Awards, held at Radio City Music Hall in New York, but despite being nominated for three awards — Best Group Video, Best Alternative Video (for 'Longview'), and Best Newcomer — they walked away empty handed. Still, the band used their appearance to unveil a new song, turning in a high-powered performance of 'Armitage Shanks'.

The next night there was further chaos at a free outdoor concert at the Hatch Shell, an outdoor venue located in a large park along the banks of the Charles River in Boston known as the Esplanade. Throughout the day, fans had arrived to secure a good spot for the show, resulting in a crowd that swelled to an estimated 65,000 by show time, 15,000 greater than had been expected. The *Boston Globe* quoted Andy Govatsas of Reprise saying, "The [expletive] place is going to explode" as people continued to pack themselves into the area, and after an opening set by The Meices, the barricades in front of the stage were reinforced. Even before Green Day came on, fans were being crushed against the barriers, resulting in several pleas for the crowd to "mellow out" and step back, "or else Green Day won't come on."

Green Day came on shortly after 8 pm. Billie Joe, unwisely in retrospect, further worked up the audience by cheering their efforts at tearing down a balloon emblazoned with the name of two of the sponsors, WFNX-FM and alternative newspaper, the *Boston Phoenix*. On seeing the size of the crowd, Mike gasped, "Oh my God!" then sounded a more cautionary note, telling the audience, "If you fall down, pick each other up," a comment Billie Joe would echo later in the show. But fans broke through barriers during the first song, and during the seventh number, 'F.O.D.', it was decided to stop the show. "It was getting pretty out of hand," the *Globe* quoted Elliot Cahn (himself a former resident of Boston suburb Brookline) as saying. "It's horrible — bottles flying, people getting hurt. We thought it was a pretty good idea to end the show."

But fans refused to disperse, shouting, "Hell no, we won't go! Pigs suck!" at the police, throwing mud, rocks, and bottles, then rampaging along the Esplanade, tearing up flower beds. Fifty state troopers and an additional 70 employees from Wizard Security had been on hand initially; now additional police squads, including K-9 units, were called in. More than 100 people were treated for injuries and 40 arrests were made.

The event provoked a controversy in Boston, especially as the show was the first big rock event that had been held at the Esplanade since 1973. "Arthur Fiedler is probably turning over in his grave," remarked Angelo Tilas, a district supervisor with the Metropolitan District Commission (MDC), referring to the conductor of the Boston Pops Orchestra, who'd held annual Fourth of July concerts at the same location. WFNX/*Phoenix* president Barry Morris claimed the band was in "relative obscurity" at the time they had been booked and that, "It would have been difficult for the MDC to know as much as seven days ago to have a sense of what would happen" (perhaps they should have watched the Woodstock performance on pay-per-view). An editorial in the *Globe* even denounced the double standard in both the media coverage and police response: "Had a stream of African-American kids leaving a rap concert flung bottles and cursed drivers in a predominately white neighbourhood, the night would be cobalt blue with squad car lights... But the responsibility for the violence that did occur bounced off white kids like Teflon, while for black kids, it would have stuck like a criminal record." Backstage after the show, Billie Joe admitted, "A band like us is basically a disaster waiting to happen a lot of times," but added, "If things were run more properly, I think we could have completed our set."

Again, there was no time to reflect further on their escalating fame and increasing chaos at concerts, for after a quick visit to Europe, the band headed out across the US once again. For opening acts, they enlisted Germany's Die Toten Hosen (whom Green Day had opened for in Germany the previous spring) and Pansy Division (whom they'd also toured with in July).

Pansy Division had been formed in San Francisco in 1991 by Jon Ginoli. Ginoli, originally from Peoria, Illinois ("A town that is a national joke," he says, "a place without culture"), spent his childhood glued to his radio. "I really liked Sixties pop radio," he says. "The last half of the Sixties is probably the high point of Top 40 radio, ever." He later became interested in the punk and new wave acts of the late Seventies, like The Ramones, The Au Pairs, and The Buzzcocks, and formed his first band, The Outnumbered. The band released some albums on Homestead Records, but eventually broke up.

Ginoli had been open about being gay in The Outnumbered, but still felt he couldn't address the topic in song. "I thought, 'If I ever have another band, it's going to be a band where I can be totally open and not write songs that make people read between the lines,'" he says. "But I also thought, 'Nobody's going to want to hear a gay rock band.' I just couldn't think of anything that was less commercially viable."

But inspiration came from three unlikely sources. Ginoli had been greatly impressed after seeing a show by controversial performance artist Karen Finley. "I had so much admiration for the fact that she seemed fearless and just would say anything," he says. "She just really didn't give a fuck." He was equally struck by the outspokenness of NWA's *Straight Outta Compton*. "That made me realise you could probably do anything in music now except be gay," he says. "There's anti-gay references on that record; they don't go out of there way to do it, it's just part of the life they were leading where they grew up. But it made me think, 'Okay, you can talk about how many people you've killed, you can talk about murdering people, but you can't talk about being gay. It seemed like it was the last taboo. It was like the last frontier."

By 1989, Ginoli had moved to San Francisco and was working for Rough Trade Records during the time the label released albums by the lesbian folk-rock band Two Nice Girls. "They weren't really a punky band, but they had this song called 'The Queer Song', which was really funny and really blunt," he says. "And I thought, 'Why aren't guys doing anything like this?' And after attending a Two Nice Girls show where he was invited by the group to be one of their go-go dancers for the night, Ginoli began writing songs for a group he already had a name for — Pansy Division.

Chris Freeman became the other founding member of the group, which was primarily a three piece (a second guitarist joined in 1997). In 1992, they put out their first record, a single, on Lookout. "And the thing about going with Lookout that turned out to be so advantageous was because of the Green Day connection," Ginoli says. "The funny thing is, I'd never seen Green Day before we ended up going on tour with them. They always used to book shows in San Francisco and then cancel them, so there were a couple times they were supposed to play a club two blocks by my house, and both times I went to the club and they had canceled the show. I thought their Lookout records were pretty good, which is why I wanted to go see them. I thought, 'If they're this good live, they could be great.' So I was interested in them."

Ginoli had liked *Dookie* ("I thought *Dookie* was great," he says, "*Dookie* and *Warning* are my favourite albums of theirs"), and had received an unexpected offer to tour with Green Day in May 1994, the fortunate result of running into Tré while riding a BART train with Chris Appelgren, who worked at Lookout and later became a co-owner of the label. "We were changing trains," Ginoli recalls, "and there was Tré. And it was like, 'Oh hey, hi, how are you doing? Hey, nice to meet you. Hey, I gotta get on this train, bye.' And Chris said to me, 'You know, Green Day are fans of yours.' (Billie Joe told MTV Pansy Division was "the future of what's going to happen in rock-'n'roll music.") And I said, 'Really? I didn't know that, that's cool to know. I'd like to open for them.' And Chris says, 'Well, I think they might be looking for an opening band.' So he gave me Tré's number and I called him up, and left a message. He called me back and he says, 'Hey, so, do you guys have a van?' That was basically all he said. And I said, 'Yeah, we've got our own van.' And he goes, 'Okay. Then I didn't hear anything, and I thought, 'Well, I guess we're not going to go on tour with Green Day.' Then about six weeks later he calls back and says, 'Hey, we're going on tour, do you want to come open for us?' And I said, 'Hell, yeah!'"

In contrast to those who thought signing with a major inevitably meant "selling out", Ginoli says, "One of the things I admired about Green Day was that they signed to a major label and didn't do anything different. I think selling out is when you change your sound in order to make money, and they've never done that. So I have tremendous admiration for the way that they've conducted themselves, and conducted their career, both when they were on an indie and when they were on a major. I felt really lucky that not only did we have this chance to tour with a big band, it was also somebody whose music I enjoyed and that we could really support. And who didn't act like rock stars, just acted like cool people who were musicians."

Though in between drummers, Pansy Division having a perennial drummer problem ("Between the first show we played with Green Day and the last show we played with them in early '95, they saw us play with four different drummers"), a suitable player was secured in time for the tour. "We got along really well with Green Day, they were really nice people," Ginoli says. "And they liked us, but one of the main reasons they wanted us along, why they asked us instead of the other bands they could've asked, was that they were having growing pains. They were finding themselves face to face with a pretty mainstream audience who were not like the more informed indie punk audiences that they had had before. So they were getting people at the shows who were being jerks and doing stupid things and it really irritated them. (In the wake of Hatch Shell melee, Billie Joe had made a similar observation: "Punk rock has become mainstream again and a lot of the people in the public don't know how to grasp it.") So they thought, 'Huh, let's get Pansy Division. That'll show 'em!'"

Their first tour with Green Day took in "secondary, second tier, middle-sized cities," says Ginoli. "There were a bunch in Canada. I think Philadelphia was the biggest city we played." There were several challenges for the band, not least of which was adjusting to playing on a larger stage, something Ginoli noted Green Day was now able to do with ease. "We were used to communicating with a hundred people who we could all see," he says. "And suddenly you've got 9,000 people in the Philadelphia arena. I remember at one show Chris said something about what was going on down front, and I was just like, 'Chris, shut up. Ninety-eight percent of the people here have no idea what you're talking about.' You have to make your gestures bigger, you have to change how you communicate with the audience. So we were trying to do our best to keep people's attention. And Green Day were great at it, they were big, big ol' hams. And we could be too, but we had to learn how to do it."

Then there was the fact that the audience was impatiently waiting to see the headliners. "It wasn't just a band that people were going to see," Ginoli says. "It was a band that people had discovered recently and were fanatical about. So we knew that whatever band was going to be there opening was going to have an uphill struggle. But we did okay. I mean, we had a really mixed reaction, but we always would sell T-shirts and CDs at the end of the night. And the audience was real young; I mean, we were expecting when we started our band that people would be in their twenties, thirties, and forties, not teenagers, and certainly not 13-year-olds or 11-year-olds. So it was pretty eye-opening."

Especially as this youthful audience was confronted with songs like 'Groovy Underwear', 'Rachbottomoff', and 'A Song Of Remembrance

For Old Boyfriends'. "We didn't set out to be an educational band," Ginoli says. "We set out to document things that people like us hadn't had documented in songs. And we were playing for an audience that already got it. Suddenly we were playing for an audience that had no idea what we're talking about, and it really scared kids, but it also really awakened kids. What was great about it was it got kids talking; here's teenagers hearing somebody just talking about being gay, and it's real matter of fact. We thought, 'Suddenly we have access to all these young ears, and what are we going to tell them? We're going to tell them that gay is okay in a non-preachy, really enjoyable way.' And we're funny and we're playing music in a style that they can identify with. So we really kinda blew their minds; they knew they shouldn't react against us, but they couldn't react for us either. And then there were some times where it was pretty successful, where the audience seemed to genuinely enjoy it."

One advantage was that many of the venues had general admission, enabling the crowd to always be jockeying for a better viewing position. "Pretty much the places we were playing were sold out," says Ginoli. "They were packed. People wanted to see Green Day and they wanted to get as close as they could, so they would grab their places and then stay put. But we always had a certain amount of rancour. It wasn't violent, it was just, you know, like being heckled. There were very few times where it was really tilted one way for us or against us." One of those times when the crowd was definitely tilted against them was in Detroit, when the band was pelted with coins, though Ginoli adds, "They threw some coins at Green Day, too." Ginoli ended up picking up $40-worth of coins from the stage after Pansy Division's set.

"And if the crowd didn't react too well toward us that night, Green Day would say something about it during their set, like, 'What's wrong with you idiots? Pansy Division are great, what's your problem?'" he says. Once, Ginoli saw Tré slam-dancing in the mosh pit during their set. "And they'd always mention us during their set, and we were always so grateful for that, that they were truly supportive," he says. "I had wanted at one point to contrive some pictures of me and Billie Joe making out, to start spreading rumours [especially in the wake of the interview Billie

Joe would do with *The Advocate* in 1995, where he expressed his support for gay rights, not to mention the band's penchant for wearing women's clothing on stage]. And he consented to do it, but then my camera ran out of film, so I only have one picture and it's not too lascivious, unfortunately. The moment was there, then the moment passed; I wished I had more film!

"And the Lookout connection turned out to be really important," he adds. "After we stopped touring with them, they brought all these other Lookout bands on tour opening for them. So it said something about trying to keep a connection to the indie world instead of going off and having whatever major-label unknown band open for you. I think it made a comment about — and I kind of hesitate to throw around this word — a kind of community."

Another way of demonstrating their support to the indie community they sprang from was Green Day's endeavouring to keep ticket and merchandise prices down. 1994 was the year members of Pearl Jam had testified before US House Subcommittee hearings about the practises of the nation's largest ticket vendor, Ticketmaster, claiming the company had a monopoly in the industry and that the service charges tacked on to ticket sales were too high. Conversely, Green Day was able to keep their ticket prices low by reducing their cut of the ticket sale, sleeping on their tour bus instead of in a hotel, and employing a small crew. The cost of a number of shows in '94 was less than ten dollars, a strategy one booker told *Billboard* was "a brilliant move... Who's not going to go for $7.50?" One reason the group had played Woodstock '94 was, in fact, because of what they were offered to do the show, a fee which helped offset the loss they took by keeping their ticket prices so low the rest of the year. As Billie Joe later told the *Boston Globe*, "It's what we think we're worth... We sleep on the bus. We're all fairly young, so we can still take some bumps and bruises on the road."

On November 4, Green Day won the first awards of their career, when the 'Longview' video received both the Maximum Vision award (given to the video clip that's judged to have done the most in advancing an artist's career) and the Best New Artist award in the Alternative/Modern Rock category at the 16th annual *Billboard* Music

Video Awards, held at the Loews Santa Monica Hotel in LA. The awards were accepted by Wendy Griffiths, Warner Bros' director of national video promotion, as the band was, of course, onstage that night at the Olympic Velodrome, in Carson, California.

In December, the band arrived in New York City. On the second, they performed at the Nassau Coliseum in Uniondale on Long Island, where they came on "like an atomic bomb, sending a capacity crowd into a body-surfing, clothes-throwing pop-star frenzy furious enough to suggest a Saturday-morning cartoon show might be in Green Day's future," in the words of *Newsday*. Those who made donations for radio-station sponsor WBAB-FM's annual food drive were also entered in a drawing to win backstage passes for the show. The next day, the band members could be found behind the counters of J & R Music World and Sam Goody record stores in Manhattan as part of Counter AID, an event organised by the AIDS charity group LIFEbeat, which enlisted well-known personalities to serve as shop clerks for a day. That evening they made their debut on *Saturday Night Live*, where they performed 'When I Come Around' (a performance that later appeared on Volume 2 of the CD *Saturday Night Live: The Musical Performances*), along with a new song, 'Geek Stink Breath'.

They wound up their stay in the Big Apple with another notable appearance by headlining radio station Z-100's Acoustic Christmas Concert. The show, which also featured Bon Jovi, The Indigo Girls, Weezer, Sheryl Crow, Toad The Wet Sprocket, Melissa Etheridge, Hole, and Pansy Division on the bill, benefited both LIFEbeat and the American Suicide Foundation. Despite the show's name, most acts didn't play acoustic sets, and the number of artists on the bill had the show running over six hours, into the wee hours of the morning. But Billie Joe managed to jolt the crowd awake by returning to play the group's encore, 'She', completely naked, save for his guitar. "His impulsive need to be noticed turned a musical endurance test into what will be one of the most talked about concerts of the year," said the *New York Post*. The next year, 'She' would reach number five on the Modern Rock chart and number 18 on the Mainstream Rock chart.

December also saw the release of the band's next single, 'When I Come Around'. The song topped the Modern Rock charts for seven weeks, and turned up at number two on the Mainstream Rock chart and number six on the Hot 100 Airplay chart. For the first time, the band was so busy that Mark Kohr's initial discussions about the video were held with the management, not the group. "The band was out on the road, and I couldn't get in contact with them," he explains. "And the management said, 'Well, Billie says it's about voyeurism. He wants it to be about voyeurism.' And I was like, 'Okay.' And then they said, 'Why don't we make it about this girl, and there's this guy, like this evil kid, and he's like looking at the girl. . .' And I was like, 'Oh God! We don't need to put out any more images like that!' Because the band was so incredibly popular, and I didn't want to be communicating that kind of message.

"What I try to do in my music videos is I always try to work with different ideas, different visual themes and emotional themes and different stories, ideas, philosophies," Kohr continues. "'Longview' was a sort of realistic presentation of these guys and their house, their apartment — it had theatrical elements, but still, they were not overly theatrical; it was cool, it was their environment. Then we had this colourised insane asylum. So I thought about 'When I Come Around' and thought well, why don't I make it about this concept of the beautiful stranger, or the stranger you fear."

Kohr's idea was to have a chain of people looking from one to the other. "But the thing is, it really took a lot of finesse to communicate that," Kohr says, "Because when I went to talk to Billie about what we were going to do, I had to do that in front of the managers. And they didn't want my idea. But I told Billie and he liked it, and I was like, 'Thank God.' Because I know it sounds funny, but television is an incredibly powerful medium. It really shapes the way people think and view their world, and so I was just trying to be responsible."

Kohr's underlying intention was to put the viewer in the shoes of the video's varied cast of characters, as they look from person to person and get their own ideas of who they think that other person is. "There's the first guy and he looks out his window and sees a woman in the window opposite," he explains. "And then we go to the woman, but she's this old lady and she gets kind of dressed up. And she looks out the window and she sees like a mom and her little girl, and she's like the old pretty lady who never had any kids. And she has her idea about them. And then we go to the little girl, and she looks out the window and she sees the 'bad man' and then the bad man looks and he sees the couple that are kissing, and thinks about how, 'Gosh, that's what I would like' — the girl thinks he's a bad man, but he wants to be a lover. And then the lovers walk and they look, and they see the old man in the wheelchair and they fear death, or whatever. It's like that, it goes around in a circle. It's sort of that idea that we all judge each other, but really we all are in that same situation of thinking that everyone else might be in a better situation — or a worse one, or whatever — than yourself, but really we're all kind of experiencing the same thing. And what's great is that people have told me that they interpreted it as exactly that, and I was like, 'Thank God, I did my job.'"

For the first time in one of their videos, the band isn't seen performing. Instead, they are shown walking around the streets of San Francisco (and, in some shots, a BART station; the other scenes were shot in the Ambassador Hotel in Los Angeles), making them, or at least Billie Joe, the singer, something of a Greek chorus, commenting on the action. The video premiered on MTV on December 11.

What had been the busiest year in Green Day's career finally began winding down with a December 13 show at Chicago's Aragon Ballroom filmed for later broadcast on MTV. It was final proof of their surging popularity. Even with their prodigious touring schedule, they still couldn't be everywhere at once; a filmed performance would help them reach fans all over the world . The cameras also caught the band singing Pansy Division's 'Groovy Underwear' in their van after the show. "But it's not credited, so people who didn't know us have no idea what it is that they're doing," says Ginoli. A New Year's Eve show had also been set at the Cow Palace in San Francisco, with Pansy Division and Dinosaur Jr. opening. "And I was like, 'That's going to be the *greatest!*'" says Ginoli. "But Tré's wife [the couple actually married in March 1995] was about to have her kid, so they cancelled out. I was like, 'Oh no, they can't cancel it!' She had her baby like a week later"

The show may also have been cancelled because the group was just worn out. Billie Joe told *Entertainment Weekly,* he was "Exhausted... I'll probably sleep for the rest of the year." It had perhaps not yet sunk in that the band was now firmly on the major-label album-tour/album-tour treadmill, and the current respite would only be momentary. With demands for more touring and the all-important necessity of releasing a follow-up album while the band's profile was still high, Green Day's schedule would be just as hectic the next year.

CHAPTER 6

Rolling With The Punches

"Before Dookie *everything was really fun, and after that, everything was angrier and more diverse."*

— *Mike to* Bass Player *September 2004*

As 1995 began, Green Day was still reaping accolades for *Dookie*, which had now sold over five million copies. *Billboard* named them number two Modern Rock Artists of 1994, with 'Longview' coming in at number three on the year-end Modern Rock chart, 'Basket Case' number four on the same chart, and *Dookie* twenty-fourth best-selling album. 'Basket Case' was MTV's number one video for 1994, with 'Longview' coming in at number 18, and a clip of 'When I Come Around' from their Woodstock performance, number 70. *Time* was one of many magazines that called *Dookie* the best rock album of the year, writing, "While the raucous, cathartic songs of this Berkeley-based punk band are adolescent and snotty, they're always laughing with you, not at you, or are they?" In February, *Dookie* had finally peaked in the US at number two, a year after its release. A reissue of 'Basket Case' reached number seven in the UK (on its first release it had stalled at 55), soon followed by 'Longview', which reached number 30, and 'When I Come Around', which reached number 27; *Dookie* had reached number 13.

Green Day's success also paid off handsomely for Lookout Records, at least initially, as sales of both *1,039/Smoothed Out Slappy Hours* and *Kerplunk!* soared; *Kerplunk!* topped *Billboard*'s Catalog chart (so-named as it reported sales of back-catalogue albums), *1,039/Smoothed Out Slappy Out* reached number four. Both albums were certified Gold; *Kerplunk!* was later certified Platinum.

On January 26, the group made the cover of *Rolling Stone* for the first time, having come out on top in the magazine's annual Music Awards. Readers voted them Best New Band, Billie Joe as Best New Male Singer, and *Dookie* as Best Album and Best Album Cover, while the magazine's critics also chose them as Best New Band. The accompanying article, "Green Daze: It's Official, Green Day are the Best New Band in Rock," by Chris Mundy, was the first in-depth profile of the band, and has since been quoted in innumerable books (including this one), fan websites, and other magazine articles.

"Like every great cartoon, the band has it all: exaggerated insanity; video images in brilliant, primary colours; and an underlying, unexplainable innocence," Mundy wrote, succinctly summarising their appeal. In addition to detailing the band's history and background, Mundy also caught the group at a crossroads, coping with pressures they hadn't anticipated having to deal with. "I'm not going to say that I don't want to be a rock star," said Billie Joe, trying to find his way after a year in which Kurt Cobain's suicide sent a sobering message about the price one can pay for fame. "If you don't want to be a rock star, then quit. That's your best answer. Don't be one... I want to try and make some sense of all this and not become a parody of myself."

Nor had the band anticipated the hostility they would face from those in the punk community for whom "selling out" to a major label was a cardinal sin. *MaximumRockNRoll* had driven this point home in the illustration on the cover of their June 1994 issue, which had pictured just such a "sell-out" pointing a gun in his mouth, captioned, "Major labels: Some of your friends are already this fucked." Commenting on flyers that discontented punkers had passed out accusing Green Day of tarnishing their world by "bringing MTV into our scene." Mike told

Mundy, "I've never seen one TV in the punk clubs we've played. I think your mother and father need to take your cable away is what they need to do." One disgruntled patron went so far as to scrawl, "Billie Joe must die" on the wall at Gilman.

Lawrence Livermore's last column for *MaximumRockNRoll*, which also ran in the June '94 issue, was a defense of Green Day. "Is there anything still to be said on the subject of major labels?" he began. "I can't help thinking of the preacher who, every Sunday, year in and year out, has to come up with new ways to denounce Satan." He then pointed out the economic realities of signing to a major, namely, that most bands that do sign don't go on to make huge amounts of money, either through record sales or touring. As such, Green Day's signing to a major had less to do with money and more to do with taking advantage of the clout a major offered *vis a vis* promotion and distribution. "If you don't like what Green Day or Jawbox or Samiam or Shudder To Think or god knows who else signed this month are doing, don't buy their major-label records and stop worrying about them," he concluded. "They're big boys and girls and can take care of themselves. The only place you have in the decision-making process is in whether or not you want to go along with it."

"My main point was that Green Day was playing exactly the same music they'd always played and that they were entitled to do whatever they wanted with their music," Livermore says today. "I also pointed out that they'd been more of a DIY band — touring in their own van, playing basements and free shows everywhere — than most supposedly indie bands I knew. I don't think other bands on the label had a problem with Green Day doing what they did. If there was a problem, it might have been that some bands began thinking, 'If Green Day can become big rock stars, we should be able to,' and unfortunately, not every band gets to become big rock stars. So when they didn't, sometimes they might try to blame the label for that. But that was the exception; most of the bands were very happy about Green Day's success, not only because they liked the band and the music, but also because the attention Green Day drew to the label and the scene was beneficial for us all."

More opened-minded music listeners also grew tired of the backlash.

One longtime Bay Area music fan, who calls himself Toxsima, was not initially interested in the band's music, especially after hearing their first two EPs. "At that time, I was all about harder, louder, faster, or at least musically obscene and outrageously weird," he says. "If you weren't as hard as say, The Offenders or early Black Flag; as obscene as Scratch Acid, Big Black, or later-period Black Flag; or as weird as early Butthole Surfers, then I thought you were *weak*, and therefore not capital 'p' punk, in sound or spirit."

Yet Toxsima admitted he enjoyed *Dookie* ("I thought it was pretty catchy, kind of like how Social Distortion can be kind of catchy") and the 'Basket Case' video. He'd also been familiar with what he calls, "the Green Day equals Great Music/Punk Savior vs. Green Day equals WeakLammoWannabeCrap" debate that went on in the Letters page of *MaximumRockNRoll* during Green Day's pre-fame years, and, after spending some time out of state, returned to the Bay Area post-*Dookie* surprised to find the same debate still raging.

"The majority consensus amongst the 'underground' was that 'Green Day sold out the scene, man!'" he says. "That was 99.9% of what one heard from the mouths of the East Bay punkeratti; if you were 'cool', it was definitely 'uncool' to like Green Day. But most capital 'p' punks are a little too conformist in their nonconformity for me — very similar to any group where there is a party line that people are supposed to follow. And the more they moaned about how much they hated and disowned Green Day for 'selling-out' the scene, the more I *liked* Green Day, because I thought they were being narrowly and unfairly judged by these 'alternative dictators.' It made no sense to me that people were not happy for the three little local stoner boys done good. Why was it necessary to hate widespread approval beyond a certain level, when deep-down it's all that any creative type hopes for?"

In the end, for every group like Creedle, who released a single entitled 'It's Not Cool To Like Green Day Anymore', there were old friends like the band Wat Tyler, who released a five-track EP on Lookout called *I Wanna Be Billie Joe* (though it was only the title of the record, and lacked a song of that name). Years later, Billie Joe said he wished he'd been able to not obsess on the backlash so much. "I should have taken that time and reflected a little more," he told Livermore. Or, as Mike told the *New Musical Express*, "You've gotta put the blinders on sometimes and go forward and say, 'To hell with what anyone says.' You've just got to move forward and I think, at the end of the day, I'm glad we're here."

The band's sudden fame also had other unexpected consequences: Billie Joe and Adrienne had moved into their first new home together, but were forced to move again when a local radio station read the address over the air. A happier development was the birth of their first child, Joseph Marciano Armstrong, in March; Billie Joe had his son's name tattooed on his right arm. Tré's girlfriend Lisea had also given birth to their child, Ramona, in January and the couple subsequently married in March. And the band members went out of their way to show that they weren't just proud of becoming new fathers, they also understood the difficulties of raising children — and who was usually stuck with that burden. "Mothers have got the worst jobs in the whole world," Billie Joe would tell Craig Marks in *Spin*. "And I never realised that until I had a kid. I don't care what you do, or what job you complain about. Try to be a mother. You won't last a fucking day."

"It takes so much more than physical strength," Mike added. "It takes an emotional and mental strength that I don't think guys possess." These were not the kind of statements usually made by A-list rock stars — and certainly not expected from a band often written off as "snot-nosed punks" themselves.

On March 1, the band won their first Grammy award. The ceremony was held at LA's Shrine Auditorium, and the group had been nominated for four awards, including Best New Artist (they lost to Sheryl Crow), Best Rock Performance By a Duo or Group with Vocal for 'Basket Case' (they lost to Aerosmith's 'Crazy'), and Best Hard Rock Performance for 'Longview' (they lost to Soundgarden's 'Black Hole Sun'). They finally won Best Alternative Music Performance with *Dookie*. They were also honoured the same month closer to home at that year's Bay Area Music Awards ceremony, sponsored by *BAM* (Bay Area Music) magazine, held at San Francisco's Warfield Theater on March 11. *Dookie* won Outstanding Album, Mike won Outstanding Bassist, Tré won Outstanding Drummer, and Green Day won Outstanding Group.

On May 27 and 28 the group played their first Bay Area shows in some months, two concerts held at the Henry J. Kaiser Auditorium in

Oakland, benefits for the Berkeley Free Clinic, the Haight-Ashbury Free Clinic, Food Not Bombs, and the San Francisco Coalition on Homelessness. Pansy Division opened. "It was an 8,000 seat place," Jon Ginoli recalls. "And Food Not Bombs was a radical group, so I thought, 'That is so great.' So we finally got to play in front of all the people here who had been hearing about us playing with Green Day but hadn't had a chance to see us. So that was very satisfying, that was fun."

In fact, Pansy Division got somewhat better notices than the headliners. Barry Walters wrote in the *San Francisco Examiner*, "While Green Day struggled to retain its rebellious edge while enjoying MTV saturation, Pansy Division celebrated the true meaning of punk." Green Day he found to be "...unfocused. Unless you surrendered yourself to the moshing hordes, the bad acoustics ate away at your attention. After an hour of speedy tunes and bratty catcalls, everything sounded too much alike." However, he did note the band's skill in subverting their new-found popularity: "Although Green Day's speedy strummed sing-alongs have become frat-party staples, the evening was enlivened by a running parody and critique of traditional college-age masculinity that went beyond Billie Joe's brashly thoughtful lyrics. Like Nirvana before them, the members of Green Day flaunt contempt for the bonehead element of their massive mainstream audience."

The band's main task for the year was completing a new album, again using Cavallo as co-producer. The arrival of children in the Green Day family had an impact on how the songs were written — Billie Joe later said he had to retire to his basement to find a suitably quiet environment — but not necessarily on the subject matter. The bigger issue was, of course, the pressure to follow up an album that had not just been wildly successful, but something of a phenomenon. The band tried to ignore it as best they could, though Billie Joe later said that emotions had occasionally run high in the studio, and that Cavallo, among others, had even cried. When a reporter from the Dutch magazine *Oor* spoke to the group toward the end of the sessions and asked, "Are there any big bosses from the record company who have been watching here now and then?" Tré jokingly replied, "There's someone waiting outside for me with a gun."

After rehearsing the songs in their Oakland practise space, the album was recorded at Hyde Street Studios in San Francisco during the summer; though the group had 22 songs ready, only 14 made it to the album (the first studio version of 'Good Riddance' was also said to have been recorded during the sessions). Though *Dookie* was undeniably laced with moments of apathy, alienation, and even despair — not always immediately apparent due to the brightness of the music — on *Insomniac* such feelings were at the forefront, and readily seen in the song titles themselves: 'No Pride', 'Jaded', and 'Panic Song' (the latter with words by Billie Joe and Mike, based, as they later said, on personal experience). The album opens with the self-loathing of 'Armatage Shanks' and closes with a song that seems to sum up the group's feelings about their unexpected success — 'Walking Contradiction'.

Musically, the album is punishing — a tightly wound, non-stop barrage of noise from start to finish (the album runs just under 33 minutes — "Actually, it's an hour's worth of songs, but we played them so fast it cut them in half," Billie Joe joked). The beginning of 'Panic Song' is particularly aggressive, with an opening musical assault that goes on for almost two minutes, readily depicting the out-of-control feeling of a panic attack (something the narrator of 'Bab's Uvula Who?' — a line taken from a *Saturday Night Live* skit — also suffers from). Illness and disease are recurrent themes throughout the album — even the album's title evokes a disorder, insomnia, that's also the subject of 'Brain Stew'. 'Geek Stink Breath' is about the pleasures and perils (rotten teeth, bad skin) of over-indulging in methamphetamine, aptly described by Billie Joe as, "an ugly song for an ugly drug," and drug abuse is also the subject of 'Tight Wad Hill', with its "white trash mannequin" left rotting on the hillside after his excursions with drugs.

Songs about unhappy relationships suited the album's pessimistic mood perfectly, as in the dominated love slave of 'Stuck With You', or the failed romance of 'Stuart And The Ave' (the intersection of Stuart St. and Telegraph Avenue in Berkeley). 'No Pride' serves up more self-laceration, but the most bitter observations came in '86', Billie Joe's comment on not being welcome at old haunts like Gilman, which begins with some serious riffing that wouldn't be out of place in a Sex Pistols song — a punk rock "you can't go home again," a song that's equally tinged with sadness and burning with rage. Billie Joe would disingenuously tell *Rolling Stone* that *Insomniac* "sounds angrier than the last record but not really on purpose," but later qualify that by saying in the same interview, "I always thought anger was a lot more interesting than feeling good about yourself." Mike would be more blunt in *Oor*, saying, "The album leaves a trail of black burned rubber behind."

Its striking cover art was designed by Winston Smith, who had known Tré back when they were both living in Mendocino County. Smith was originally from Oklahoma, though "I left there as soon as my two feet could carry me," he says. "I was 17 when I finally left. About 16 years too late!" He'd developed an interest in art at an early age, in part because his mother was an artist, and, finding no encouragement in his immediate environment, dropped out of high school to attend the Academy of Fine Arts in Florence, Italy, where he lived from the late Sixties to the mid-Seventies. On returning to the states, he had offers to stay with friends in Boston and San Francisco, settling on the latter city "after realising that Boston was too cold."

Smith then worked as "a rent-a-roadie at an outfit that rented studios and equipment. Everyone came in: Santana; Crosby, Stills & Nash; Journey — I liked a couple of guys in that band, but couldn't really groove to their music." But eventually he relocated to the same mountainous area where Tré and Lawrence Livermore were based. "All my neighbours gave their land names, like Sunrise Ranch or Shangri-La Ranch or Fairy Dust Ranch," he says. "Kind of half-assed hippie names. Pretty Kitties Ranch." In response, Smith called his home "Ground Zero." "I said, in America, it's all ground zero. There's no getting away from it," he explains. He'd also taken on the name "Winston Smith", after the character in George Orwell's grim futuristic novel *1984*.

"Larry had a place just like mine," Smith says. "In fact, he was much more advanced, he had solar power. Kerosene lamps they used sometimes, but usually they would power up a generator. One of the first performances on his ranch had some dinky generator powering the amp, then kerosene lamps on the front of the thing. I thought great, blending the 19th and 21st centuries." Oddly, Smith never saw The Lookouts or Green Day perform, though he did spend a lot of time with Livermore. "Mainly we used to hang out in San Francisco because we would be at friend's clubs," he says. "I recall one time going down 18th Street trying to figure out who was the oldest guy in the scene, him or me, he was a year older than me. Then we realised, no, no! Tim Yohannan [founder/editor of *MaximumRockNRoll*] is older than both of us! Good, we're not the oldest geezers." Smith also frequented Gilman, which was around the corner from where he'd previously lived in Berkeley.

Smith's interest in the music scene led to his designing posters for local shows. Eventually a mutual friend introduced him to the Dead Kennedys' Jello Biafra. "A friend of mine that I worked with at the time kept saying, 'You've got to meet these friends of mine, they have this band,'" he recalls. "'You think just like my friend Biafra. Here's a record they put out, *California Uber Alles*.'" Smith was impressed; "They actually had something valid to say," he says. "Some bands are just screaming weirdoes, and entertaining, but not very deep. Dead Kennedys actually had some substance to them." On finally meeting Biafra, Smith learned that the singer had been equally impressed by an image Smith had created: a crucifix wrapped in dollar bills, complete with a bar code. "I was thinking of people making money off of religion," he explains. "Like Jerry Falwell, and all these right-wing guys, shows like *The 700 Club*, which I called *The 666 Club*. Biafra said, 'This is dangerous! We need to use this.' Years later he wrote in an introduction in my second book, 'I didn't have a record in mind, but when I saw the piece I had to think of a record to go with the artwork.'"

Smith went on to do a lot of design work for the Dead Kennedys, including the group's logo, a circle with a "D" and "K" emerging from the middle like the spokes of a wheel. Tré had previously asked Smith if he'd design something for The Lookouts, and though Smith agreed, nothing came of the offer. Now Smith received another call from the drummer. "He said, 'Hey, remember when you said you could do a thing for our band? I'm in this different band now, can we come over and check out your stuff?'" says Smith. "I'm like, 'Yeah, come by, I live in North Beach.' So he, Bill, and Rob Cavallo came over — I think Mike was out of town. We spent two or three hours going over piles of pictures that I had. They were saying, 'How do you do it?' I said, 'Well, it's not easy, but you just cut it out.' 'It's all done with computers?' 'No, no it's just a razor blade and glue.' I can't work a computer."

Smith showed them one image from the Forties he'd clipped out of an ad of a woman in a striped dress holding a flower up to the nose of her husband, sleeping in a hammock. "And I had a picture of an armadillo and said, 'Look, we can put an armadillo in her hands, that's pretty weird, check it out,'" says Smith. "And Tré picks up this little revolver that I had just cut out a few hours before, and he goes, 'Oh, how about this? She can blow his head off!'" Smith would base the rest of his design on that "spark of inspiration."

Smith had not yet realised Green Day was no longer "a squirrelly little band." "We went down the block to grab a pizza at an old beatnik café called Caffe Trieste, which has been there since 1956 or '57", he says. "It's one of my favourite hangouts in North Beach. We were sitting there going over more pictures and I said to Tré, 'How's your band doing? Are you getting gigs? Do you have a day job?' He said, 'Let's see, the last album we sold about nine million records.' I nearly fell on the floor. Son of a bitch! I am literally so completely out of it, I am probably the least connected to contemporary culture of anyone I know — for me, Madonna was a religious painting. I just thought they were still gigging around, just one out of 4,000 other dinky little bands. It was really gratifying to know that they were successful."

Smith calls his work on *Insomniac* "probably the most satisfying art project I've even worked on. Usually people say they'd like to use a picture I'd already done, and that's fine. But these guys wanted something original. I kept saying, is there a particular scene or image you want, like gorillas or aardvarks? Biafra would be quite literal with a lot of things, he'd want to spell it out artistically. The Green lads were very open-minded; they said, 'We just want you to do whatever you want to do. Just do your thing. It's your record. We'll do the music, you do everything else.'"

At that point, the album was provisionally called *Tight Wad Hill*, a title Smith admits "didn't make much of an impression on me." Instead, using Tré's suggestion of having the woman pointing a gun at her husband, Smith decided to "build this swirl of madness" around the image. The pictures that Smith ultimately utilised, clipped from books and magazines, included two chimpanzees performing circus tricks; a violinist, somberly attired in a black robe, undergoing a chest x-ray while having his vision tested; a man trapped in "dental hell"; and Uncle Sam, praying on his knees, "taken from an old Fifties ad basically promoting McCarthyism, saying America is on her knees, and the Communist threat is going to take over the world. He's earnestly praying, begging the Red Overlord in Moscow to let us survive." An armadillo lurks in a corner, and flames threaten to engulf the entire scene. In a final touch, the woman lovingly pointing the gun at her husband holds Billie Joe's guitar, "Blue", in her left hand.

Smith designed an equally macabre collage for the back cover, of an ostensibly innocuous domestic scene; one woman sleeps in her bed, while another takes a bottle of milk from the refrigerator. But the soldier standing by the fridge is casually handing his rifle to an infant in a high chair, who in turn is busy feeding a monkey. Another man embraces an oversized bush baby, while through a window the fiery explosion of a PT boat can be seen. In the foreground, a woman applies her makeup, ignoring the mayhem around her. Behind the CD's tray is a collage Smith had designed to be printed on the CD, a circular collage drawn from the front cover's images. "It's before I knew what a CD was," he says. "I thought CDs got put on like records, you watch them spin around. Then someone said, 'No, you can't really watch them spin.' I'd thought, 'And on side two they could have...' 'No, no Winston, CDs don't have side two, they only have side one.'" Ultimately a close-up of the man hugging the bush baby, (an image originally from "some insurance ad from the Thirties") was used on the CD. "I guess the art director who slapped it all together in LA just changed his mind about what I'd done."

Smith brought the finished work for the band to see, while they were working at Hyde Street Studios. "I used to go there all the time as a roadie," he says. "And when I walked in there were two pieces of mine on the wall, hung in the room where the pool table was. It was kind of a shock. I said, 'Hey, do you want me to sign that?' They said, 'No, no, no, that's done by Winston Smith.' So I pulled out my ID, and then they were like, 'Oh yeah, will you sign it?' I should have said, 'That'll be a dollar, please.'"

The group was equally impressed with both Smith's work, and how he'd managed to complete it. "Bill asked me, 'How long did it take you to do this?' I said, 'I've been awake for 38 hours now.' I couldn't stop working on it. It was like I was on this adrenaline high. He said, 'You're kidding me, didn't you sleep?' I said, 'No, I don't sleep, I'm an insomniac.' About a month later when the record came out it was called *Insomniac*. I asked Billie one time, 'Did you name it that because of what I said?' He said, 'No, it was something else.' Then, a couple years ago I saw this teeny-bopper unauthorised DVD on Green Day, that interviewed a bunch of friends and people who knew them. And one guy who was being interviewed, his nickname was 'Insomniac.' Apparently that was why they named the album that."

Smith had given the front cover collage the title, "God Told Me To Skin You Alive" ("At one point Bill said he was sorry he didn't use that as the title for the album!"), the opening line from the first song on the Dead Kennedys' *Fresh Fruit For Rotting Vegetables* album. The back cover was titled, "Long Ago And Far Away." The front cover art was also oversized for a CD, at 18″ × 18″. Instead of reducing the image to fit a CD's 5″ × 5″ space, the image was only slightly reduced to 14″ × 14″, then folded to fit in the CD. "I wouldn't do it again, because people fold and unfold the picture so many times that there are little holes in the corners where the creases intersect, like a road map that's been stashed in the backseat of your car for years," says Smith. Yet the folding also adds to the underlying horror; what at first just seems surreal imagery becomes sinister when the unwary unfold the picture to reveal that the woman's holding a gun.

Prior to the release of *Insomniac*, a new Green Day song arrived with the inclusion of 'J.A.R.' on the soundtrack of the film, *Angus*. Ginoli remembers Green Day being shown a film script for the movie when he was on tour with them. "One of the things that they liked about the script is that it was based on a short story where the main character has a gay father and a lesbian mother," he says. "And they filmed the movie that way and then apparently it didn't test well, so all of the gay references were excised. Though there's a couple of odd things that are in there that don't really make much sense — there's a few lines of dialogue that would make more sense if you knew that the parents were supposed to be gay. I heard through the grapevine that Green Day weren't too happy about the way the movie turned out, but I've never really talked to them about it."

The sudden death of a friend of the group had inspired both the song, and its title, 'J.A.R.' standing for Jason Andrew Relva, who died in a car crash, which gives the song a decided poignancy. (Mike got a tattoo matching one of Jason's in his memory.) The song had been demoed during the *Dookie* era, but the arrangement of the officially released version is similar, if more polished. The song again topped the Modern Rock chart, reached number 17 on the Mainstream Rock chart, and number 22 on the Airplay chart.

At Green Day's request, Pansy Division also appeared on the *Angus* soundtrack, contributing the song 'Deep Water', which had originally appeared on their album *Deflowered*. (Lookout acts Tilt and Ben Weasel's new band The Riverdales, both of whom had toured with Green Day, also appeared on the soundtrack; Billie Joe had The Riverdales' logo tattooed on his right arm.) "We got $10,000 for being on the soundtrack," says Ginoli. "We don't get royalties on the record sales, they just gave us a flat fee up front. It bought us a new van and we really needed one. And because that damn movie, which was not a big hit, has been shown in cable systems virtually everywhere in the world, it's 10 years later and I'm still getting BMI royalty statements for airplay. Twenty-four dollars from Spain, $16 from Singapore, it just keeps trickling in. I get a few hundred dollars a year from *Angus*. It's real nice. So whenever we get another check, Chris Freeman says, 'Green Day — the gift that keeps on giving.'"

But the song 'J.A.R.' also reportedly played a role in Green Day's sudden split with their management, Cahn-Man. Earlier in 1995, Cahn and Saltzman had formed their own label, (510) Records (funded by MCA and named after Oakland's area code, and a nod to San Francisco label 415 Records, named after San Francisco's area code). Their first signing was Berkeley band Dance Hall Crashers, though Saltzman told *Billboard*, "We will have a couple of punk-pop bands, but we certainly don't intend to fill our entire roster with that kind of music." When Green Day unexpectedly fired their managers in July, rumours spread that the reason was because Cahn and Saltzman had leaked 'J.A.R.' to Los Angeles radio station KROQ in return for gaining exposure for bands on 510. Cahn and Saltzman denied being responsible, but the song had indeed leaked somehow, and soon bootleg copies were circulating, causing Reprise to rush out official promo copies.

On August 29, Cahn and Saltzman sued the band, claiming they had reneged on their contract and owed Cahn-Man substantial monies. The band's contract with Cahn-Man said they were entitled to 20% of Green Day's earnings, and Cahn-Man's lawyer, David Phillips, claimed the band paid less than that. Conversely, Green Day's lawyer, Bernard Burk, said the percentage had previously been renegotiated. "The parties had their differences," he told the *San Francisco Chronicle*. "One of the differences had to do with what the manager was being paid. Other differences remained and it was those differences that resulted in the severance of the management contract." He added, "If [Cahn] didn't see the road signs [of the impending break-up], he was driving with his eyes closed." The case was later settled. Both sides have remained tight-lipped about the dispute. In one of his few comments, Billie Joe simply told *Rolling Stone*, "We felt like we weren't being treated like people anymore but as assets."

Going into the release of a follow-up to a wildly successful record was not the best time to be without management. For the moment, the band opted to manage themselves, utilising one of their guitar techs (and future tour manager), Randy Steffes, as their liaison. They did few interviews, and debated whether *Insomniac*'s release would even be accompanied by any videos. Eric Yee also recalls the band saying "they were never going to do a video ever again" around the time of the Oakland benefit shows in May.

At the time they were sued by Cahn-Man, the band was overseas, playing the Reading Festival in the UK on August 25, then touring Europe. As a result, their appearance on that year's MTV Music Video Awards was live via satellite from Stockholm, the group performing 'Stuck With Me'. 'Basket Case' had been nominated for nine awards, including Video of the Year, but lost in every category.

Insomniac was released the next month, on October 10 in the US, selling 177,000 copies in its first week and debuting at number two in the *Billboard* charts, ultimately kept out of the top spot by Mariah Carey's *Daydream* (it was released October 21 in the UK, peaking at number eight). The reviews were generally positive, but with some caveats, as in this review by *Entertainment Weekly*, which stated, "The songs are new-generation-punk formula, but there's no denying the band's ear for a hook. Green Day sound exactly the same as on their first album, albeit with crisper production and, ominously, a palpable degeneration in their sense of humour."

The dark themes of the album were what struck many listeners. "*Insomniac* felt like such a sad and painful record at points that I found it difficult to listen to it all the way through," says Lawrence Livermore. "I always thought of it as their *In Utero* [Nirvana's third album]." A decided black humour certainly pervaded the video accompanying the album's first single, 'Geek Stink Breath' (a single which in the US reached number three Modern Rock, number nine Mainstream Rock, and number 27 Airplay, and number 16 in the UK), which quickly became notorious for its depiction of a tooth pulling. Yet it aired nonetheless because, in the words of director Mark Kohr, "Green Day went through a phase where they couldn't do anything wrong. It was really amazing to witness that. I'd never had an understanding of that, really, that there's a phase in an entertainers' career where they literally cannot do anything wrong. It's wild.

"What was interesting, Billie had said he didn't want to do any videos for the second album," Kohr continues. "I was doing a lot of videos for a lot of other people at the time, and I was really busy, so I was like, 'Okay,' because I'm really good at letting things go and not being clingy. And I remember I was at my apartment in San Francisco, I was moving actually, and my sister was there, and she was helping me pack up boxes, and the phone rings and my sister yells out the window, 'Mark, it's Billie,' and I'm like, 'Really?' Because at that time they were off, they were out there in the world.

"And so I went and talked to him and he was like, 'Hey, how you doing, blah blah. . . what are you up to?' And then he says, 'Well Mark, a friend of mine is about to get all his teeth taken out. He was a meth addict and he's got all these rotten teeth, and I was wondering if you could film it. Maybe we could put it in a video.' And I was like, 'Sure.' And he was like 'Cool.'"

The more he thought about it, the more excited Kohr became over the visual possibilities of the procedure. "I was going to use these optics, so I could get into the guy's mouth," he says. "So I could shoot on film, not on video, on 35mm. We'll make this really cool, I thought, so we're really *in* there. Billie's friend only ended up getting one tooth pulled, but that was okay. We shot in this place in San Francisco, and I remember the dentist's last name was Lipscomb and I just thought, 'How on earth can you have a dentist named Lipscomb?' Because it's like 'lip scum.' And he had a lisp. . . oh my God, a dentist named Lip Scum and he had a lisp! It was terrible.

"Anyway, we shot it, and it went real well. Billie showed up with his wife, and they brought their boy, little Joey, and I had to have a picture of them, with Billie holding this wrench in his hand, pretending to work on the dolly. It all went good, and then we talked later and Billie was like, 'Well, come up with an idea for the rest of it.' And so I came up with what you see, which is this very visual, textual, vibe-related band footage."

The final video mixed footage of the tooth pulling and the band performing, cutting between the two with a near-frantic intensity. "I made it that way because the song is about somebody who eats sweets and does crystal meth, and so I tried to do a visual representation of the anxiety one might feel as a meth addict," Kohr explains. "And so there's all this flashing. The film we processed in tubs as opposed to in a regular film machine, so that it touched itself and got all this speckle on it. And we shot the band with a video camera, a little tiny one, like a pen on a pole. And then we put that [footage] on a TV, and we shot the TV with a camera, and then as we're shooting it we had this magnet that we turned on and off to have the lines in the TV bend and distort; we shut off the TV so the image would drift off the TV and it would just be black on occasion. And I said to my editor, 'I want you to edit this thing like you're so anxious that you're like a meth guy. You're so anxious that you can't do things at the right time. You're always trying to do things too early. Make it so the edits are too early, they're arriving too fast.' Not just fast in frequency, but they're arriving before they should in terms of from a musical edit standpoint." Hence the raw look and jerky feel of the video, which ends with a close-up of the bloody, extracted tooth sitting on the dentist's tray. "Isn't that great?" Kohr says proudly. "That's the real deal!" He estimates the final budget "wasn't much, it was like seven or eight grand."

There was some consternation about the graphic nature of the tooth pulling, but Kohr says, "What was so nice was that Green Day was so popular that they *had* to show it! But when they'd show it they would always give this disclaimer with it, like, 'This is someone who did too much crystal meth, and that tells you, kids, don't do drugs!' They showed it for about two or three weeks, and what was so great was that I remember walking down the street in San Francisco and hearing people say, 'Oh my God, did you see that Green Day video with that tooth pull? That was disgusting!' And I remember thinking, wow, how great that it had that kind of impact. But they only showed it for short time."

The band also began a US tour in October that continued to the end of the year. On November 11 they appeared on the *Late Show With David Letterman*, performing '86'. "The first time they were on our program, they scared the hell out of me," host David Letterman admitted, though he also said, "I'm very fond of these guys and I'm hoping to adopt them." It was an unusual song choice, given that the song wasn't released as a single. Billie Joe and Mike were now using a distinctive "concert stance" on TV appearances like this one, a visually strong look that had the left leg forward, and right leg back, with the body of the guitar or bass resting on the right thigh and the neck pointing forward, like a weapon. At the song's conclusion, Tré ran to the back of the stage and lay down in a pool that was part of the set.

On October 17, when the group played the Seattle Center Arena (now the Mercer Arts Arena), Billie Joe's old math teacher, John Goar, decided to check them out. "It took me a while to warm up to *Dookie,*" he says. "But I was really thrilled for their success. And the show rocked! I was blown away by Billie Joe's stage presence and charisma." Goar wrote down the setlist for this and every subsequent Green Day show he attended. This show, though dominated by songs from *Insomniac* and *Dookie*, also featured songs from their first two albums and during the encore, Tré performed his two signature numbers, 'All By Myself' and 'Dominated Love Slave'.

There was more unexpected excitement when Billie Joe was arrested for indecent exposure following at a concert at Milwaukee's MECCA

Arena on November 21. Security was tighter than usual at the show. While items like cameras and outside food and beverage were routinely prohibited, binoculars were also banned at the concert, in an attempt to restrict the kinds of items being thrown onstage at the band. As a result, the crowd resorted to throwing toilet paper rolls onstage, presumably taken from the venue's public restrooms.

"Bad behaviour is one of the band's signatures," noted the *Milwaukee Journal Sentinel* of the show, at which, "Armstrong playfully baited fans to yell profanities back at the stage" as he had during the band's last show in the city a year before, at the Eagles Ballroom. Halfway through the show Billie Joe capped one such exchange — perhaps he was just inspired by all the toilet paper — by turning around, dropping his pants and "mooning" the audience. Later, he shared the advice, "Don't smoke marijuana... Listen to your parents. Listen to Hootie & The Blowfish!" and simulated masturbation.

It was perhaps the wrong place to try such a stunt, as Milwaukee has a proud tradition of arresting performers who flout public convention. In 1972, comedian George Carlin was arrested for using obscenities during his show; in 1981, punk rocker Wendy O. Williams was arrested for making "obscene gestures" during her concert; in 1989, G.G. Allin and his band, The Toilet Rockers, were arrested "for reportedly defecating on the stage of the Odd Rock Cafe and allegedly performing other lewd acts on stage."

The police wisely decided to wait until after the show to make their move, thus not disrupting the concert and risking the wrath of the audience. Instead, when Billie Joe left the Arena about a half hour after the concert ended, he was surrounded by police, handcuffed, and taken a few blocks away to the Police Administration Building. Photographer Jeremy Prach, who shot pictures of the arrest, later said police tried to confiscate his camera. "The problem was he exposed himself to a crowd of about 6,000 people," said Lt. Thomas Christopher at the time. "Including people as young as ten. That was our main reason for taking the action."

Billie Joe was kept in a holding cell until a bond of $141.85 was posted ("I wasn't in the bullpen," he said later. "I was in with the other ones, the not-so-bad ones. They made me take all my jewelry out. And my shoestrings, so I wouldn't hang myself or something."). He faced a maximum fine of $250, but the city attorney's office declined to prosecute, so charges were dropped and the $141.85 returned to Billie Joe. It had been decided that the case would be hard to prove, as Green Day was known for such frisky behaviour, though the *Sentinel* added that, "The city intends to warn concert promoters that such actions in the future probably will be prosecuted."

On December 14, there was another Bay Area show at the Oakland Coliseum where their reviews were much better than their previous concerts. "For one scant but exhausting hour, singer Billie Joe, bassist Mike Dirnt, and drummer Tré Cool screamed through an astonishing 16 songs plus encores, at speeds that ranged from merely fast to suicidally revved," wrote the *San Francisco Examiner*. "It was like being witness to one huge, raw nerve onstage, and the effect was intoxicating... if you didn't stand up and dance, you had to be near death." The paper concluded, "They are no flash in the punk pan. Green Day is here to stay."

The year ended with Green Day topping *Billboard*'s year-end chart-toppers list as Top Modern Rock Artist. Billie Joe spent New Year's Eve at a friend's house, where the bands Juke and The Tantrums played in the backyard, like the old days. The same month, 'Stuck With Me' was released as a single overseas (reaching number 24 in the UK), and, with a European tour pending, a video was needed. "We did it in a hurry," says Kohr. "Billie said, 'Could you work with Winston Smith, and come up with some animation that we could weave a performance in and out of?' So it wasn't like we worked really hard at that one, other than that we had two animators to animate this cutout artwork. We tried to come up with little sequences of action for each setup. We shot the band down in LA on this reversal 35mm stock that felt really beautiful and did some swing and tilt optic stuff. It wasn't that we didn't work hard on it, but we didn't lose a lot of sleep over that one — except for the animators, who got no sleep."

"Two other artists and I toiled for two full weeks on that," Smith agrees. "Twelve hours a day, cutting pictures out and making little paper puppets out of them, making them all move; they move like four times a second. There was a camera suspended over five layers of glass to get the effect. It was painstaking, with capital pain. To get it all done in time, it was really a horse race. Fortunately, the song only lasted like two minutes. It was blissfully short, otherwise it would have taken us another five years. We didn't do it on computers.

"The best part about that was, we had a couple of meetings with Mark and a couple other production guys," Smith continues. "A friend of ours, Rob Shapiro, he had a company called Satellite Productions, was working on it. He said, 'We can't show guns on MTV; no nudity, no guns, no religion.' And we had just about all of that in there! Instead, he said, 'We can have the woman pull out a circular saw and cut the guy in half, then his skin will fall off and there'll be like the *Gray's Anatomy* pictures of the muscles.' I thought, that's even more gruesome than a gun! I asked him, 'Did someone tell you that the original title for this is "God Told Me to Skin You Alive"'? And he said, 'No, that's amazing!' She actually is skinning him alive on the cartoon.

"Mike came up to me later and said, 'That was really, really great computer work you did on our video.' I said, 'Computer? Hell no, that was all done by hand!' That was done like early turn-of-the-century cartoons. He said, 'It cost so much, I thought it was done on computers.' So apparently the production of it was extremely expensive, just the camera work and all the people working on it."

In January 1996, Green Day headed back overseas, first to Japan, then Thailand, Indonesia, Australia, and New Zealand. Following a quick stop in Hawaii, they made an appearance on *The Tonight Show With Jay Leno*, performing 'Brain Stew'. Tré ran off again after the song's conclusion. At the end of the show, as the group sat in chairs next to host Jay Leno, he promptly tipped himself backwards. The band then retired to their dressing room, which they reportedly trashed, smearing a couch with peanut butter. Then the band headed overseas for another European tour (during which they recorded a session for MTV Europe). This time they brought along the Mr. T Experience as an opening act, the first time the band had played stadiums.

"It's weird," says Frank Portman of the experience. "It's a very strange thing, especially when you're not used to it. We would just do our own tours, and they were small, but they were on our own terms. The difference between doing a tour in clubs and something like that is... they just have nothing to do with each other. It's like a military campaign. In fact, it was very military in the fact that their management was always calling our tour manager; every morning we were late or we did something else, and he would get chewed out by those guys. It was this huge organisation; those three guys were just like us, sort of shlumping around, but they had a whole organisation behind them, which included their road crew and their management, and then all of the people who had administered these hockey stadiums or soccer rinks in Europe. So it was a lot different. There was something very cool in a bizarre, surreal way about standing on a stage with 8,000 people; not too many people get a chance to do that. But it was very weird, and it was not like any rock tour experience that I ever had, it was completely something unto itself."

Also along on the trip was filmmaker Lance Bangs. Bangs had started making films at age 11, shooting on "a little Super-8 camera." As he got older he began shooting experimental films, "just filming empty places at night, like the bathrooms of gas stations or 24-hour laundromats, and doing tape-recorded narration over them. Like journal entry-type things. They weren't made for the purpose of being sold or publicly exhibited. More like a diary type of thing."

While staffing a Greenpeace booth at an R.E.M. show in Philadelphia in 1988, Bangs met R.E.M.'s lead singer, Michael Stipe, and passed on a tape of his films. Stipe was interested in Bangs' work, and brought him to Athens, Georgia, where R.E.M. was based. Bangs started up a monthly screening night of Super-8 films at Athens club the 40 Watt, and began shooting visual material for R.E.M. to use during their live shows. Soon other bands were asking him to do the same thing, which led to his directing music videos. "I never intended or set out to direct music videos," he says. "It's just that bands that would come to the Super-8 screenings started asking me." He also ended up filming bands both when they came through town and touring with them on the road. "I just kind of ended up in that world of indie rock bands," he says. "Documenting a lot of shows and touring with different bands and shooting footage." Before working with Green Day, Bangs had directed videos for R.E.M. ('How The West Was Won And Where It Got Us'), Sonic Youth ('The Diamond Sea'), and Pavement ('Spit On A Stranger').

In the spring of 1995, R.E.M. was on tour supporting their album

Monster. Bangs and Chris Bilheimer, who worked for R.E.M. as a graphic designer, came out to see the band's show at the Shoreline Amphitheater in Mountain View, near San Francisco. Billie Joe was going to attend the show with his wife and other friends, "and Chris and I were going to meet them, help them find their seats, make sure they were taken care of. Something along those lines," says Bangs. Bangs had seen Green Day over the years, "but at the time I was really not into the bouncier California pop thing," he says. "I was into more sad, singer/songwriter type music. But they were really good at what they did. And I saw them at Lollapalooza; they were coming out and doing, like, 'We Will Rock You', and 'Eye Of The Tiger' by Survivor. All the kids were going nuts."

Backstage, Bilheimer remembers Billie Joe making an attempt to disguise himself. "We saw this guy sitting in the corner," he says. "He was wearing a stocking cap, and he had all these really bizarre dread-locks hanging out of his hat. We looked really closely at him and realised it was Billie Joe. Adrienne had just recently cut off all her dreads, so as a disguise he put on a cap and shoved all the dreadlocks inside it and became pretty unrecognisable. He was just sitting there by himself and we were like, 'Who's that dude? Oh, that's Billie Joe.' He was just sitting by himself, so Lance and I went over and just started talking to him. That's how Lance and I both met him and struck up a friendship with him."

"Billie and Adrienne were in a goofy mood and being funny and enjoying coming to a big rock show," says Bangs. "Chris and I had a really good time hanging out with them. Then we took them to meet Michael. Took a bunch of Polaroids and goofed around and stuff. I don't remember how we kept in touch, I think they gave me their address or phone number. They asked to see some of the other films that I had made. I made a tape and sent a copy of *Jesus Of Suburbia*, a film I did when I was a teenager, then a bunch of other short films and things I'd done for bands." Soon after, Bangs was asked to accompany the band when they next went on tour.

Bangs remembers the European tour as being "really amazing at first. It was a lot of places I had never been before, like a lot of Eastern Europe. Slovenia, Poland, and places like that. It was a pretty amazing opportunity to go over there." The shows were also deliberately geared toward a younger audience. "In Europe, they call it Kinderpunk," says Frank Portman. "The headliner would go on at 8 pm, and the show would be over by 9. We played at 7 or 7:30, something like that. And then there was a totally grueling schedule where a lot of times you had to leave for the next show immediately after or you wouldn't make it by the next day, so it was a little bit of a challenge."

Portman also says the initial dates went well. "They had a chef who had all of his cooking equipment in anvil cases, and he made these very kind of nouvelle cuisine fancy dinners and everything," he says. "And the whole crew, us included, we'd all eat this crazy food, like sautéed flowers, and stuff like that in the back room of these stadiums. And Green Day was nice. I was conscious of a kind of a wall separating us, though. I mean, it's just like when anyone gets a lot of money or becomes really successful, it's just a little different. So they were really nice and they were really friendly, but it wasn't the same as hanging around with them at a party, definitely. They were like our employers. And they didn't care, but their tour manager really didn't let us get away with any nonsense. I wouldn't trade that experience for anything, but if it had actually gone for the full three months, I don't know what would've happened, 'cause it was rough."

And as the tour went on Green Day's efforts to be accommodating began to overwhelm them. "Their popularity had blown up so huge that there was this crushing demand for them," says Bangs, "and they were still trying to be really cool and deal with that. They were making time for all these people every day; well, here's the Italian version of *Rolling Stone* magazine, and here's the local music paper, and here's 20 kids that have these *Sniffing Glue*-type fanzines and wanted to do these hour-long interviews. It was kind of crazy how they were trying to overly accommodate everybody."

Their efforts to keep ticket prices low also backfired among local promoters. "My sense of it was that it was important to them to keep ticket prices really low, and yet the size of the audiences that would want to come would mean that you would need to be in a bigger venue," Bangs says. "And those venues were normally controlled by the people that are doing more expensive ticket sales for their shows. The promoter there isn't going to want to deal with security and staff if they're only making this lesser amount.

"And the impression I got from the shows was that they were being booked by people who weren't regular concert promoters," Bangs continues. "And they weren't always in venues necessarily that were ideal venues to be in. We'd be in, like, a former Russian Eastern bloc hockey practise space rather than a regular concert venue. Some sketchy promoter would claim he could put on a show and have a proper PA, and do it for $7 a kid, then he'd run away with a bunch of the money and we wouldn't really have security or a PA. There'd be holes in the floor and no electricity in the dressing rooms. No heat. A lot of the venues seemed like buildings that hadn't really been finished yet, or they were like old abandoned buildings that weren't really used anymore."

The strain eventually began to take its toll on the everyone. "It was this weirdly stressful tour driving to all these bizarre places," says Bangs. "It was cold and miserable. I ended up feeling sick. It was right after one of the early pre-SARS kind of things, there was some respiratory thing going around. It really seemed to effect Mike, he was wearing one of those breathing protection masks a lot. Trying to avoid getting sick from everyone else and so on." Mike and Billie Joe later said they'd both suffered from serious bouts of anxiety during the tour.

And though Billie Joe also said the group had disliked making the jump to large venues ("We were becoming the things we hated, playing those big arenas") the problem may also have that the spaces weren't suitable to begin with. In a January 1996 interview with *Amusement Business* magazine, the band's production manager, Mitch Cramer, stressed the lengths the band and crew went to in order to ensure everyone's safety and comfort at shows. Set-up time was four hours, and the doors would be opened at least two hours prior to showtime, to allow a more relaxed entry. Cramer had also prepared security guidelines that he handed out to the local staff at a venue, and met repeatedly with them throughout the day. "What we're trying to do is head off problems before they start," he said. "That is why I'm so security-minded and so into making sure these kids have a good time."

But the condition of the European venues used on the tour threw those kind of carefully laid plans into disarray, and the tour's end came when the band arrived on March 28 at a particularly shoddy "venue" in Germany. "That one was grim," Bangs recalls. "There were broken bottles and holes in the floor and rocks. Holes in the walls. No dressing rooms. Again, there was this local sketchy promoter dude. We're like, 'Where's the stage?' and he's like, 'Oh, we're going to put one in.' Well, we're here to load in our gear, what do you mean there's no stage and you're going to make one? Where can we put our stuff now? And there's a broken staircase with missing stairs — at the top of that, there's a place to put our bags. I believe it was on the Eastern side of Berlin, and they were demolishing all the buildings around it. This was my impression of it, that it was some warehouse space that some dude had claimed he could put on a show in.

"I was outside trying to film some of the building and how fucked up it was," he continues. "Then some guy speaking German comes up in a demolition hat and the orange vest with little stripes and everything and he's like, 'Move the bus, move the bus' — whatever German it was, I could make out he was telling me to move the bus. I was sort of exaggerating that I didn't know what he was saying; it certainly wasn't up to me to go and move the tour bus. He was just like some guy who was bummed that we had parked back there. I said, 'I don't know, I'm not the person to go to with that.' He was really intent, 'You must move the bus,' I was like, 'I don't drive the bus, someone else does.' Just trying not to deal with it.

"Then he's like, 'No, the boom, the boom,' and making explosion noises. I'm like, 'Do you mean there's a bomb in there?' and he's like, 'Yes.' So I went to try and find Randy, and I'm like, 'Hey, this guy's outside, this construction guy. I think he's saying that they are going to blow up the building. We'll have to move the bus because it's about to explode.' And he's just like, 'Yeah, yeah, whatever, it's probably bullshit.' He had no interest in investigating or checking it out, or dealing with it in any way. And I was like, 'Okay, at least I've told him.' And sure enough, they started blasting and demolishing all the other buildings around us — not the one they were going to play in, but all the other buildings around it. They all started collapsing. We'd basically pulled into this demolition site!

"That was at the end of several weeks that were just miserable, being in all these weird broken places, dealing with sketchy, corrupt Eastern European mafia-type dudes, like this one concert promoter — we saw him getting into the back of an ambulance with an oxygen mask on and everything. All of a sudden he just jumps into the back of an ambulance with a bag of money and disappears, like it was a fake injury so he could get out with all the money. All these weird crazy things kept happening on that tour. But the kids were amazing. The kids that would come out probably didn't get to see a band like this very often, and it seemed to mean the world to them. They were just going nuts, painting their faces, and jumping off of speaker stacks and stuff, doing this kind of out of control stuff, at least more than I'd seen at shows. Like stage diving from 20-foot PA stacks and stuff like that into the crowd. It seemed always on the verge of someone getting a broken neck or getting killed. Just out of control."

The rest of the tour ended up being cancelled, to the disappointment of the Mr. T Experience. "It was our big chance, the *Insomniac* tour," says Portman. "But typically, our big chance didn't end up going that well because that tour was cancelled. We had two weeks of the stadium experience." Nor did the footage that had been shot get used. "We tried at the time to put it together as some sort of tour documentary, but because they cancelled the rest of the tour, it was a weird time for the band," Bangs explains. "A lot of the shows we thought we'd get a lot more proper concert footage, but that never happened."

An incident that happened when a show in Prague was filmed seemed to summarise the whole unhappy experience of the tour. "They filmed a full-blown concert film shot on 16mm and there was a multi-track recording of the whole show," remembers Bangs. "At the end of the show, they had a section where they would turn on strobe lights, knock over the drums and jump around and stuff like that, smash guitars. And one of the onstage camera operators, who was wearing a steady-cam type rig, was an epileptic. And he didn't know about the strobes. So during the finale the camera guy is just sort of flopping around on stage having a full-blown epileptic fit because of the strobe lights. It was kind of this disaster shoot. So I think they just scrapped all the footage and never really used it for anything. It was kind of like, let's just put all this film away and move on." Some songs recorded during this and earlier tours later appeared on the import releases *Bowling Bowling Bowling Parking Parking*, released in 1996, and *Foot In Mouth*, released in 1997.

By the end, everyone was more than ready to call it quits. "I traveled with them back to the airport, and we all changed our tickets and jumped on flights to go home," says Bangs. "I shot this footage of them on the cab heading back. They were depressed and just ready to be out of there and go home and get away from all this craziness. They'd been working non-stop from the point that *Dookie* had come out. They had just relentlessly worked — toured extensively, gone straight in and done a new record, and then back out on the road to promote that. They'd gone through this incredible life change of suddenly selling all these records. And they'd started instant families, they had all gotten married or had children within that time period as well. Everyone had loved ones at home that they were away from, they had not taken a break or properly rested or recovered, or wrapped their head around what they'd gone through with the explosion of *Dookie*. It was just kind of crazy that they'd worked so hard and not taken time to get adjusted.

"It was really good that they just put it down and walked away for a little bit."

CHAPTER 7

Back From The Brink

"I'll tell you the truth — I had more fun a couple years ago."
— *Mike to* Rolling Stone, *December 28, 1995*

The spring '96 tour had not yet begun when Billie Joe met up with Tom Lantham of *Rip* magazine at a Berkeley diner for an interview. Lantham's story, "The Band You Love To Hate," was printed in the magazine's April issue, and had it come out earlier, the tour's cancellation would probably not have been as surprising. Perhaps reflecting his mood, Billie Joe was dressed entirely in black, and, in between staring "morosely at the floor," gave one of the more revealing interviews of his life.

After beginning by saying, "When I came here today, I said I didn't wanna talk about anything good, because I don't really have anything good to talk about," Billie Joe repeatedly touched on his own unhappiness ("I'm a pretty miserable person right now"; "I'm just not enjoying life right now.") But more important were the underlying reasons for that unhappiness — specifically, the loss of an emotional connection with the music. Billie Joe pointed to the impersonality of playing large rock shows as a factor: "Before we did this last US tour... I was like,

'Yeah! I'm excited! I wanna play these arenas!' And then just every night, it started sucking, it felt like a routine or something... sometimes I feel like we're losing our passion for playing music. And that's the fucked-up thing, when you lose passion for what you love, then it's like, 'Is this marriage headed for divorce or what?'" Still, in spite of such statements as, "I just don't know if I really wanna be involved in the rock world anymore at all... There isn't a day goes by in the past year-and-a-half that I haven't thought about quitting," Billie Joe also made it clear that he hadn't completely given up the fight. "No matter what, I'm gonna be writing songs for the rest of my life," he said. "I definitely want to be respected as a musician," then tellingly added, "Well, more as a songwriter than as a musician."

Billie Joe's comments illustrated the growing pressures the band had been feeling since their explosive success in 1994. They had been able to take some time off at the beginning of 1995, when it was clearly needed ("I'm sure every one of us, in our own way this year [1994], has wanted to blow our fucking head off," Mike told *Rolling Stone*, though he assuringly added, "But I think we're all not that type of personality"), but even then, Billie Joe had needed to start working on songs for *Insomniac*. And on the album's release the band had gone straight back into constant touring. It was clear the band hadn't fully adjusted to their new-found status as rock stars.

Nor had *Insomniac* performed up to expectations. By early 1996, the album had only been certified double-Platinum in the US (sales would eventually reach over four million in the US, eight million worldwide), a far cry from *Dookie's* sales. Billie Joe explained to *Rip* that the lack of much advance promotion, coupled with the 'Geek Stink Breath' video having received little exposure, probably worked against the record's chances of success: "I think we did alienate a lot of people. So that was expected, that it wasn't going to sell a lot of records." But even extensive interviews and a video that constantly aired may not have mattered; the next record released after a blockbuster album rarely achieves the same sales. And Billie Joe was already looking ahead, telling *Rip* on the next record he hoped to "go into different styles, go across my boundaries of the two-and-a-half minute punk song with a three-and-a-half minute jazz song, or maybe get into a little bit of swing or rockabilly." The band's next album would indeed touch on a broader range of musical styles.

And the promotion of *Insomniac* wasn't finished yet. On March 9, the record won Outstanding Hard Music Album at the Bay Area Music Awards, and Tré received another Outstanding Drummer award. The same month saw the release of the album's next single, the double A-side 'Brain Stew'/'Jaded' (on the record 'Brain Stew' segues into 'Jaded'), which reached number three Modern Rock, number eight Mainstream Rock, and number 35 Airplay in the US; in the UK, the single reached number 28.

The song's video was directed by Kevin Kerslake. Kerslake came from a musical family and had been a vocalist and guitarist in the band Rimpest, but had always been more interested in film. He began his work in video after working with Kim Gordon, bass player with Sonic Youth, on a feature film, *Sometimes Through The Wall*. The film was never finished, but had included a sequence of Gordon sitting on top of a moving train, with Sonic Youth's 'Shadow Of A Doubt' as the sound-track. The rest of the band had liked the footage, and, with shots of the band inserted, 'Shadow Of A Doubt' became Kerslake's first video. Kerslake went on to direct Sonic Youth's 'Beauty Lies In The Eye' and 'Candle', and is probably best known for his work with Nirvana, which included the videos 'Come As You Are', 'Lithium', 'In Bloom' (which won Best Alternative Video at the MTV Video Music Awards), and 'Sliver'.

Kerslake was flown out to meet Green Day on their fall '95 tour, "to meet them, to go to a show, to see if we got along," he says. "It was a very familial scene backstage, because they had, like, babies and mothers and nannies and all that stuff. And we got along, so let's do the video! It was totally painless and uneventful in terms of how the job was awarded. And then it was the usual manner in which videos are submitted to directors: 'We have this much money, and come up with your idea.' I prefer it, actually, to be that way. Sometimes you might get something like, 'We need to see performance' or 'The band wants to act,' or 'Show them as little as possible,' but this came over with very little in terms of specs."

Kerslake's idea was fairly straight-forward; "taking some of the icons of their previous videos and dragging them through the dump, and then have all sorts of surreal visuals pop up, whether that's hula girls, or whatever else." The "icon" in this case was the couch that had featured so prominently in 'Longview'. ("It wasn't the same couch, but I wanted to make it have the same feel.") The video's first half accordingly shows the group on the couch being dragged through the dump by a bulldozer, intercut with shots of hula girls, various animals, and an old woman who lip-syncs some of the song's lyrics. "She was good, but she took a lot of work," says Kerslake. "To have an 80-year-old lady sing a punk-rock song was a fight. She wasn't fiery or anything, she was really sweet. But she had these faces that just evoked a fair amount of venom, and I liked all that spiteful energy."

The video's first half concludes with the band hurling Tré's drum set into the dump where it's unceremoniously crushed beneath the bulldozer. Then, as a horse gets to its feet and runs away, the scene shifts to Green Day bashing out 'Jaded' in a cluttered room. Heightening the transition between the songs is that 'Brain Stew' is shot in sepia tone, while 'Jaded' is in almost lurid colour. "Whenever you see Green Day, you want to see them live," Kerslake. "I just figured if we're going to get into some of the bratty punk stuff, to do that really crude and raw, almost like Super-8. I probably even referenced 'Sliver'. I've done a lot of videos with that feel, but that's probably the most well known. And I simply wanted to distinguish between the songs; if I was going to go into the garage phase, with tweaked-out colours, I thought it might be cool to play with a more antiquated look in the first part, giving it a look like found footage, like somebody pissed on the film can and it's been lying in the sun for decades. That was the feeling that I was shooting for." Providing some continuity between the two songs are the hula girls, who appear in both songs, and a close-up shot of wriggling worms ("It was fun to put your hands in there, actually").

The video was shot over two days in Los Angeles: "One day for 'Jaded' and one day for 'Brain Stew'," says Kerslake. "It's a pretty slow video, there's not a lot to do, just some animal wrangling. Set construction was difficult, because we created that junk yard. It was too toxic to shoot in a real one. So we had to create these large wall structures which gave you some sort of mass, and then you just basically piled stuff on that, to give it the irregularity of a trash heap. And then there was making a course for the bulldozer, hitching the couch to it and dragging it through that, and doing various portraits within that scenario."

The band members were quick to give a thumbs-up to the end result. "It's funny, this job was so uneventful, in a sense," Kerslake says. "There was never really much disagreement. Looking back at it now, it's funny to see what you can get away with, because the band's not in it very much, until the very end. So tonally, it has this sort of severity that I miss these days. I think that now everybody wants to see their product on screen a little more.

"I'm still pretty stoked about the video because it was pretty committed to absurdity," he continues. "There's nothing in it that wants to make any sense. It feels like it's giving you the finger, or giving any sort of straight talk the finger. And that's cool, to have that sort of teenage rebellion. Sometimes you do videos, and you want them to be really smart or tell a great story, or just have a great performance, and sometimes you just want to throw paint on the wall and let the splatter stay. Or just go into a certain realm and just want it to feel grim. And I feel like that's in there too, just this bleak hopelessness, that I was happy to keep. It's not necessarily that you have to exaggerate, or go to great lengths to say, 'Oh, woe is us, life is fucked, we can't make sense of anything,' just embody it in the flow of images or the disconnect from one image to the next. So it happens on a more subtle level." And because the split between the two songs was clear in the video, each section was occasionally aired separately on TV.

After returning from the cancelled European tour, the band appeared on *The Late Show* on May 9, which was taping in San Francisco all week. Aaron Elliott tagged along, welcoming the chance to be a "tourist" in "the world of fame and fortune." As he recounted in *Cometbus #41*, "I got to watch all the cameramen and see the behind-the-scenes workings of a TV show... I ran around stealing everything that wasn't tied down," including an effigy of David Letterman's head, made of chocolate. The group also appeared on *Saturday Night Special* on May 18. On both shows they performed their latest single, 'Walking Contradiction', which reached number 21 Modern Rock and number 25 Mainstream Rock. The video, directed by Roman Coppola, was shot in LA, mostly at the intersection of Centre Street and 7th Street, and showed the band members obliviously creating havoc wherever they go; a simple walk down the street results in a runaway van, a flying police car, and the short-circuiting of the area's electricity. Billie Joe later admitted to being especially scared during the filming of one scene which had him walking across the intersection as cars zip by, missing him by inches. ("I thought I was gonna die right there with all the cameras on me.") The clip was nominated for an MTV Video Music Award for Best Special Effects, and it also received a Grammy nomination for Best Music Video Short Form, losing in the latter category to The Beatles' impressive video for their "reunion" single, 'Free As A Bird'.

But after those appearances, the band seemingly dropped out of sight; for the first time in their career, they wouldn't play another concert for nearly a year, a sign of just how badly they needed a break. There were also some changes going on behind the scenes. Despite Billie Joe's telling *Rolling Stone,* "We'll never have a serious corporate manager again," the band decided that after the fiasco of the European tour they needed someone looking after their interests and signed on with Atlas/Third Rail Management, where they were first looked after by Rob Cavallo's father Bob, and then Pat Magnarella. Magnarella had previously worked as a booking agent at Venture Bookings and as a music agent at Triad Artists. He also managed The Goo Goo Dolls and The All American Rejects. And there were further developments on the personal front, with Mike marrying his girlfriend, Anastasia, in August; their daughter, Estelle Desiree, was born in April 1997.

The band also spent plenty of time writing and relaxing, happily without the pressure of any looming deadlines. "We would meet up a bunch," says Lance Bangs. "We went up to Seattle in maybe '96 in October, and just sort of hung out awhile and took a vacation. Just kind of went different places and played pinball and hung out with the kids and stuff. Chris [Bilheimer] was around for some of that too. From there I guess I went down [to California] and started filming them in rehearsals and songwriting sessions. They seemed to write songs and practise a lot; maybe they went through lots of time of not seeing each other, but my sense was that they were still pretty social and involved in each other's lives, spending time working on songs and having fun. They had something that impressed me when they were on tour; they would always have a room set up with some instruments where they could just goof around and play instrumental songs, play accordion and drums, maracas, and make music together. They warmed up that way instead of running on stage, playing the show, and then not seeing each other again. It seemed like a really smart thing, it was a good sign of their camaraderie and their relationship with each other."

Billie Joe also built a home studio in his basement, and was involved in a number of side projects. He'd begun producing other bands: Social Unrest's 1995 album *New Lows*, Dead & Gone's *T.V. Baby* (1996) and *God Loves Everyone But You* (1997), and The Criminals' 1997 album *Never Been Caught*. His own side band, Pinhead Gunpowder, was also releasing records: *Carry The Banner* in 1994, the same year Jason White replaced Mike Kersh on guitar; *Jump Salty* in 1995 (a compilation of the *Trundle & Spring* and *Fahiza* EPs), and *Goodbye Ellston Avenue* in 1997, along with appearances on various compilations. In 1997, Billie Joe also co-founded a label, Adeline Records, named after a street that starts in Berkeley and runs south through Emeryville to the Oakland Inner Harbor Channel. Adeline's other founders were Billie Joe's wife Adrienne, Lynn Theibaud, and Jim Theibaud (an owner of Real Skateboards). "I think of Adeline as a punk-rock label," Billie Joe told *Alternative Press*. "Adeline is a collective — people coming together and doing their own thing when they don't like anything else. It's really putting your money where your mouth is, and that's the beauty of punk rock — you can bitch and complain, but unless you're doing anything about it, then shut up." Pinhead Gunpowder and Mike's side band, The Frustrators, would release records on the label. Adeline would also release the vinyl versions of Green Day's singles and albums.

In the spring of 1997, the band began preparing to head into the studio, playing what was essentially a warm-up show in February, inviting 150 friends to see them at a warehouse in Oakland. The show also celebrated the 10-year anniversary of Cinderblock, a rock merchandise company founded by Jeffrey Bischoff, who was also a member of the Lookout band, Tilt. Huevos Rancheros and One Man Army were also on the bill, and Jello Biafra performed a spoken-word piece. A surprise birthday party was held the same month for Billie Joe at San Francisco club Bottom of the Hill, in honor of his twenty-fifth birthday. "Pansy

Division played," says Jon Ginoli, "and everybody from Pinhead Gunpowder, Billie's side band, was there, and they ended up playing at the end. And there was a drag queen that they knew from New York, that we knew, too. It was just a real nice time, a real nice surprise."

Pansy Division and Green Day were also on a compilation issued around the same time, *Generations 1: A Punk Look at Human Rights* (royalties were donated to the Human Rights Action Center). "We had been asked to be on this compilation," says Ginoli. "And we wanted to give them a particular song that had been on a single, but not on an album, and they said, 'No, we need an exclusive track.' So we had a week to come up with a song. Our new drummer, Luis [Illades], had just joined our band, but he lived in San Diego at that point, he hadn't moved up here. So I forget how he got involved, but we ended up having Tré be our drummer, and we recorded at his house in Oakland. And then we went over a couple days later to Billie Joe's house in Berkeley and mixed it." Pansy Division's song was, 'Can't Make Love'; Green Day's was 'Do Da Da'.

Green Day then decamped to Los Angeles. Initial press reports about their arrival didn't concern the upcoming recording, but rather the juvenile hijinks the group got up to during a stay at the Sunset Marquis [hotel] in March — walking naked around the halls; pestering The Rolling Stones, also staying at the hotel, with late night phone calls; throwing a TV out the window; and Mike ultimately topping that cliché bit of rock-star bad boy behaviour by defecating off the balcony of his room.

The recording sessions for *Nimrod*, which began March 31, were held at Ocean Way Recording, and Billie Joe again had a batch of songs ready: 40, according to some reports, 18 of which made the album (another four appeared on the album as bonus tracks). The band relaxed during the sessions by playing several covers of songs by The Rolling Stones and Elvis Costello (Costello's 'Alison' and the Stones' '19th Nervous Breakdown' were reportedly recorded), among others, none of which have come to light. Ocean Way, formerly United Western Studios, opened in 1952, and had seen the recording of such classics as The Beach Boys' 'Good Vibrations', and The Mamas And Papas' 'California Dreamin'. More recently, artists ranging from Tori Amos to Dr. Dre,

Elton John, and k.d. lang had recorded there. It would now be their home for the next four months, at that time the longest they'd ever taken to work on an album. As Billie Joe told *Billboard*, "We really bled over this record to the point of straight-up delirium."

The songs were a decidedly varied bunch in comparison to the band's earlier recordings. Though tracks like the opening song, 'Nice Guys Finish Last', had Green Day's trademark pop-punk blast, there were also plenty of indications the band was becoming more musically adventurous. "We wanted to stretch as much as possible, but at the same time we never want to abandon the sound that we know how to do best," Billie Joe told writer Jaan Uhelszki. The first single, 'Hitchin' A Ride', about heading out to party after falling off the wagon, is an excellent example. Beginning with a plaintive violin line (courtesy of That Dog's Petra Haden) before the verse, the song then alternates between verses delivered with an old-timey rockabilly swing and choruses of full-on rock. (Billie Joe also cited the inspiration of Big Band performers like Cab Calloway.) The song builds to a frenzied climax that abruptly stops, then concludes with a quiet strum of the guitar. It would become a live favourite, which the band would stretch out endlessly, so Billie Joe could engage in call-and-response antics with the audience.

'King For A Day' was destined to be another live favourite, especially due to the ska influence of the horn section, using players from the band No Doubt for the recording. The song took on the unlikely topic of cross-dressing, though perhaps not so unusual for a band that was known to appear onstage in dresses themselves (though Mike had said in 1994, "Drag's really getting kind of trendy, so we stopped. Basically, now we'll only do it in places that we know are really homophobic"). Billie Joe later expressed his hopes that the frat-boy element in their audience would sing along to the number without realising what the song was about.

Some of the love songs also show a new maturity. Gone is the pain of the unrequited relationships of the early albums, replaced by songs dealing with the pain of working through difficult periods as a couple. 'Redundant's' sense of resignation is bittersweet, but also blissfully tuneful; 'Scattered' and 'Worry Rock' are faster paced, but similarly themed. And the self-explanatory, 'Walking Alone' could easily be a sequel to '86', its mournful sentiments underscored by Billie Joe's bluesy harmonica.

And this time the anger was just as likely to be directed outwards as inwards. There's the sheer, malevolent rage of 'Take Back', or the jabs at the synthetic, soulless "amannequins" in 'Prosthetic Head', certainly a song that reflected the plastic, superficial culture of LA. There were also signs of a political sensibility beginning to raise its head in 'Reject', in which the narrator's happy to be a "reject all-American." The use of the phrase was not coincidental; it was also the title of riot grrrl band Bikini Kill's 1996 album, which Billie Joe had admired. "I really liked the way Bikini Kill's last record came out," he told journalist Craig Rosen. "They challenged themselves more. They have some really rough punk-rock songs and these delicate pretty songs" — essentially the formula Green Day followed on *Nimrod*.

And nowhere was that contrast between rough punk and pretty songs better seen than in aggressive numbers like 'Platypus (I Hate You)' and 'Jinx' (the latter of which neatly segues into 'Haushinka', which had been written during the *Kerplunk* era and was also demoed for *Dookie*), and what would be *Nimrod*'s most acclaimed track, 'Good Riddance (Time of Your Life)'. The song, which Billie said had been written in 10 minutes, was unlike anything Green Day had done before, being an acoustic number with an accompanying string section. "It was an acoustic song from the get-go," Billie Joe told *Guitar World*. "If I'd put drums on it, it would have turned into a power ballad, and God forbid that ever happens!"

The tuneful melody and nostalgic lyric made the song a popular choice for weddings and graduation ceremonies, though ironically it had been inspired by a break-up Billie Joe had when the band was working on *Dookie*; hence the bitter title, 'Good Riddance', which people often overlooked in favour of the song's subtitle, the more positive 'Time of Your Life'. More than anything, it showed the band was willing to step outside of the one-note, bratty persona many had of them. Billie Joe agreed, telling *Guitar World* the song "had really freed us, in a lot of respects, to be able to do different things. To get into more sensitive content without feeling like you're selling yourself out. Or that you're doing something because you need a hit."

146

Basement of the Ashby Avenue house, 1993, where the band's first video,
'Longview', was filmed. *(John Popplewell/Retna)*

Billie Joe at the Shoreline Amphitheatre, Mountain View, California, June 10, 1994, the same month *Dookie* went gold in America. *(Tim Mosenfelder/Contributor/Getty Images)*

Mike at Green Day's landmark appearance at the Woodstock festival, August 14, 1994. The group's set ended in a massive mudfight. *(Neal Preston/Retna)*

Kings of the Road: Tré, Billie Joe, and Mike in 1994, the year Green Day broke through to the mainstream. *(Ken Schles/Contributor/Getty Images)*

Billie Joe behind the drums at New York radio station Z-100's "Acoustic Christmas" concert, Madison Square Garden, December 5, 1994. *(Patti Ouderkirk/Photoweb/WireImage)*

Mike and Billie Joe, Madison Square Garden, December 5, 1994. Billie Joe routinely shed his clothes at shows, though he didn't often perform completely nude. *(Chris Cassidy/Retna)*

Green Day, San Francisco, December, 1995. That night, the group performed at the Oakland Coliseum. *(Jay Blakesberg/Retna)*

Green Day. 1997. The band branched out in a new musical direction that year, with the release of *Nimrod*, which included the huge hit 'Good Riddance (Time Of Your Life)'. *(Stephen Sweet/Rex Features)*

Green Day at the *Kerrang!* awards, August 25, 1998; the group won
the Best Live Performance award. *(LFI)*

Green Day arrives at the September 10
1998, MTV Video Music Awards, Universal
Amphitheater, Los Angeles. After years of being
nominated, the video for 'Good Riddance
(Time of Your Life)' won Best Alternative Video.
"Susan Lucci, eat your heart out!" said Billie Joe.
(Jim Smeal/WireImage)

Yeah, baby! Green Day arrives for the world
premiere of *Austin Powers: Spy Who Shagged Me*
June 8, 1999. The group's instrumental,
'Espionage,' appeared on the film's soundtrack
and was nominated for a Grammy.
(Steve Granitz/WireImage)

Billie Joe and Mike, at the free "Take Back San Francisco" concert, billed as an "anti-gentrification celebration", at Civic Center Plaza, San Francisco, November 5, 2000. The show followed a "Million Band March" that drew only around 500 people; the concert attracted 2,000. *(John Shearer/WireImage)*

Billie Joe and Mike at Wembley Arena, London, December 8, 2000. *(Jon Super/Redferns)*

Green Day, 2000, the year of *Warning*'s release. *(Kevin Estrada/Retna)*

The album was titled *Nimrod*, or, as presented on the album cover, *nimrod.*, and was actually a word that had several meanings. In the Bible, Nimrod is a descendant of Noah, "a mighty hunter before the Lord" (Genesis 10:9), founder of the kingdom of Babel. It's also the name of a town in Minnesota, the name of a villain in Marvel Comics' *X-Men* series, the title of the ninth movement of Edward Elgar's *Enigma Variations*, and — humourously, considering Green Day's penchant for illicit substances — an acronym for an anti-drug organisation in Rochester, New York (Neighborhoods In Motion to Root Out Drugs). But in its slang meaning, it referred to a dimwit, or a dork — it had been Bugs Bunny's nickname for his easily outwitted nemesis, the would-be hunter Elmer Fudd, in Looney Tunes cartoons of the Forties — certainly a definition more in keeping with Green Day's prevailing attitude. For the album's artwork, Green Day decided to draw on the talents of Chris Bilheimer, who had met the group — with Lance Bangs — in the spring of 1995.

Bilheimer was raised in Savannah, Georgia, and was interested in art from an early age — drawing, painting, photography, and graphic design — taking summer classes at the Savannah College of Art and Design, beginning at age 14. He became interested in music through his older sister, who, while attending the University of Georgia in Athens, worked at the college radio station and provided her brother with mix tapes of what was popular on college radio in the mid-'80s. "That's when I first heard R.E.M., U2, and Violent Femmes," he says. "I thought, 'Oh wow, there's this whole other world out there.'"

Bilheimer eventually moved to Athens himself, and unsuccessfully tried his hand as a musician. "I really, really wanted to be a part of the music scene, but I just don't rock. At all," he says. "Art was the only creative way to be involved." So he began designing T-shirts for bands, as well as handling stage lighting at clubs and designing sets for bands, "just trying to do as many creative things for the bands and performances as I could." He then moved on to designing posters and record sleeves for local bands. "There weren't that many people doing it," he says. "I barely knew how to do it! I kind of got into graphic design as an afterthought. I'm pretty much completely self-taught. I was laying out flyers by using letraset type, really crude methods.

Someone said, 'You know, you can stretch type on this computer called a Macintosh.' I'm like, 'Wow, that sounds interesting.' The University had a graphic design lab and it was open to non-design students on weekends, so I would just spend the weekend in there teaching myself how to use Macs. I just sort of fell into it."

Bilheimer met Michael Stipe through a mutual friend in 1989 and began working for R.E.M. at the end of 1993; the first album he designed for the group was *Monster*, released the following year. At the time of meeting Green Day, Bilheimer, unlike Bangs, was unfamiliar with the group. "I had never heard of them before *Dookie*," he admits. "I really didn't pay a huge amount of attention to bands outside of Athens. I've never been the most musically literate person. That was one of the joys about being around Lance all the time, that he's one of the most voracious consumers of music. Just by proxy I would find out about stuff." For the next few years, Bilheimer was simply a friend, seeing Billie Joe "a couple times a year. I went out for his twenty-fifth birthday party. I had fucked up and didn't get a hotel reservation, so I ended up having to sleep on his couch, and I watched *Teletubbies* with Joey the next morning. A couple of times I was in Seattle [where R.E.M.'s Peter Buck had relocated] and he'd come up to visit friends up there. We'd go out and play air-hockey and goof around in Seattle." But the offer to work on *Nimrod* came totally out the blue.

"They went through three art directors, some of them at Warner Bros. and some freelance people," Bilheimer says. "They were just hating everything, apparently. They called me, Pat [Magnarella] called me, said, 'We are desperate and way behind schedule, and we've gone through three people. Can you come out here and talk to the guys?' I went out there, and the first thing Billie Joe did was tell me, 'We try not to work with friends because it can really fuck up friendships. That's why we've never asked you to do anything before, but we're pretty desperate at this point.'"

By then, Bilheimer was familiar with the group's output, both musically and visually. "I loved the art for *Insomniac*, the Winston Smith collage," he says. "Their previous cover stuff was pretty cartoony, so it was nice to see something a little bit darker, a little bit edgier, a little bit angrier. By *Nimrod* they had definitely matured as songwriters, with their subject matter and everything. I felt like it was really important to do that with the artwork, to step it up to be a little more mature and have a darker kind of look. *Insomniac* showed me a little bit of the progression that I thought should be taken further."

Just working with the record's title, Bilheimer had come up with a few different ideas "and one of them was almost identical to what ended up being on the cover. I had seen a photograph, it was a poster for a politician. It said, 'Elect Blah Blah,' and the poster had been re-pasted to a wall and someone had ripped the face off the person. It was this portrait of this typical white, middle-aged male, corporate politician American kind of guy, and someone had completely taken his identity away through vandalism. It was just really striking, and thematically it just seemed to really fit them. I had taken this photograph I had seen, and they thought it was a really cool idea. I went from there to doing basically the same thing, which is taking people and labeling them, actually making little labels that said 'nimrod,' and using that to take away the people's identity."

The cover featured a picture of two men in suits and ties, taken from an encyclopedia, with yellow circles (on US copies; overseas copies had orange circles) reading "nimrod" over their faces, and a similar tactic was employed on the back cover and the CD's booklet, using photos from a yearbook Bilheimer had bought in a used bookstore in Los Angeles. "I tried to find one from the era of the *Leave It To Beaver* idyllic '50's America," he explains. "I tried to, once again, break down that image of people's perceptions of a happy polite idyllic society." The circles convey an air of something being hidden — or censored, something especially seen in the way the lyrics are presented in the booklet, with lines heavily blacked out as if you're looking at an FBI file, something Bilheimer wishes he'd taken "a little further, that whole idea of blacking out of the lyrics so they seemed like they were part of something else and you're only seeing a part of it."

The picture on the final page of the booklet has the band wrapped up in duct tape, screaming (save for Mike, who has tape over his mouth). "That was a joke," Bilheimer says. "We were talking about band photos and I was like, 'You always see these photos of the band and they're all standing unnaturally close to each other,' and just how awkward and forced it looks, 'So why don't we actually give you a reason to be that crammed up and why don't I just duct tape you guys to each other?' That was purely just kind of a smart-ass response to taking publicity photos. It was not intended to go in the package necessarily. It just turned out that way because the photos were pretty fucking funny."

Bilheimer's design work was not just limited to the record, but all the images associated with the release, from promotional postcards and posters to ads and backstage passes and the covers for the different singles. "When you sign onto a project, like for Green Day, you end up doing everything," he says. "Every single advertisement in every magazine. Every poster. Everything you see of theirs." In the course of working on *Nimrod*, Bilheimer had also come up with another idea that played off the circle. "I had this concept of taking other Warner Bros. or Reprise artists' promotional items, like, say, the life-size Madonna cardboard cut-out that goes in the store, and covering them with 'nimrod' stickers," he says. "I thought this was a genius idea because you don't actually have to spend any money on making new stuff. And it was sort of cross-promoting the other artists. You're also getting rid of stuff that's just going to end up in a landfill. There was also supposedly going to be a campaign hiring some vandals to actually vandalize some billboards, for movies and that sort of thing. Supposedly that happened, but I never actually saw any."

A subsequent story in *Billboard* quoted Linnea Nan, director of artist development and creative marketing for Reprise, as saying, "We're not telling [retail outlets] to sticker POP [point of purchase] for hot new releases, but we're leaving it at the store's discretion and hoping that they'll have some fun with it," with the writer adding, "Nan is optimistic that the sticker campaign will spark curiosity and intrigue with consumers, before it is revealed later in the campaign that 'Nimrod' is the title of the new Green Day album."

In building up to the album's release, the group — billing themselves as The Nimrods — did a surprise show on July 19 at trendy LA club, The Viper Room (co-owned by actor Johnny Depp, and more notorious as the place outside of which actor River Phoenix collapsed and died on October 31, 1993). They then traveled to Japan, where they were schedule to play the Mount Fuji Rock Festival on July 26 to 27. But the event was cancelled on the first day when Typhoon Rosie hit the region, and the bands ended up spending their time at a nearby amusement park, where a fight almost broke out after Tré shot Foo Fighter Taylor Hawkins with a BB gun. A brief European tour started in September, taking in six cities (Milan, Vienna, Hamburg, Cologne, Paris, and London). The album's first single, 'Hitchin' A Ride', was sent to radio in late August, in advance of a proposed September release date in an attempt to thwart leaks of the song.

Nimrod was released October 14 in the US, where it sold 82,000 copies in the first week. It was released on October 11 in the UK, and reached number 10 in both countries. The day of *Nimrod*'s US release, the band also appeared on *The Late Show*, performing 'Hitchin' A Ride'. Paul Shaffer, the leader of the show's house band, played the song's violin part on his keyboard. Yellow "Nimrod" circles decorated Tré's drum riser, and he somersaulted over his kit at the song's conclusion, then dashed off-stage, to host David Letterman's amusement. Afterwards, the band threw a party at the club Don Hill's. During the first part of the evening, the house band performed songs from the new album, with vocals provided by an assortment of drag queens. Green Day finally took to the stage themselves for an hour-long set, throwing in plenty of covers (such as the perennial favourite, Survivor's 'Eye Of The Tiger'), including one from their Sweet Children days, The Who's 'My Generation' (during which an over-excited fan cut his hand open on broken glass). The set ended at 2:30 am, when Billie Joe overturned Tré's drum kit.

'Hitchin' A Ride' reached number 5 Modern Rock, number nine Mainstream Rock, and number 25 in the U.K; the video had its world premiere on MTV on September 16. "That one was really hard to do," says Mark Kohr, who again directed. "At the time, I was keeping all these people working for me, and I was just rolling from one video to the next. It was hard, and we had done that for two years at that point, or maybe even longer, I can't remember. And we were just shot. We were like, 'We're going to take a break, almost done...' And then 'Hitchin' A Ride' came along, and I was like 'Oh God, OK, well, I guess not.'"

Billie Joe's only direction had been that "he wanted to have some dancing girls in it, some pretty girls, but he didn't want it to be overt, didn't want it to be too much. And in hindsight, I think I even pulled it back too far. I wish that I had just made that video be that sort of weird, sort of cool Twenties theatrical thing that it is, but done essentially as a dance piece."

The video has a vintage feel, opening with the group on stage of what appears to be a vaudeville theatre; the action later cuts back and forth between the stage and a bar, both populated with an odd assortment of characters and artifacts. "I grew up loving musicals, Fred Astaire and Gene Kelly and all that stuff," says Kohr. "And you know in *Singin' In The Rain*, there's that whole sequence with these long conveyor belts [the 'Gotta Dance' number toward the end of the film] and I always wanted to do a thing with conveyor belts. And in that video, of course, it opens up with them walking on a street that's staying still, with other people walking around them, but they're walking in the same place.

"And then it just sort of grew," Kohr continues. "In the song it talks about a fountain of youth, so I thought why don't we make the fountain of youth like this bar? And the people in it are just exhausted, and they're kind of like zombies almost; their teeth look bad and they have dust on them, and their faces are kind of white. And the band are at the back of this bar, but they're under the roots of this tree. And I can't remember why I made those symbols, but in the song it talks about a pot of gold, and so I had a pot of gold at the base of the tree. And it's actually empty, and then there's a mosquito that comes out, so it's kind of like, money comes and bites you.

"I was working almost with those Betty Boop and early cartoons, where you would have these weird things happen and trippy stuff. I was thinking about how in those Max Fleischer cartoons everything moved to the beat, the bottles moved to the beat, everything moved, everyone's in motion. And then I had that one bartender that's actually a giant, he's like 8´ or 7´9″, he was the tallest guy in LA at the time. And then I had one guy who's really short but who's not a midget. So I had the tall and the short guy, and when Billie goes to fight the giant guy in the end, he's really small by comparison, and it looked hilarious at the time. I was just trying to make it like a trippy adventure, vaudeville thing."

Considering the intricacies of the video, it's surprising that Kohr was able to shoot it in one day. "I wish that photographically it read better, but if I had more time, maybe I could have pulled that off," he says. "There were a lot of things I wish I could change with that one, and make it even better, because I always wanted to do a piece like that. It always kind of bummed me out, because I wanted to make that so good and I wanted to make a video like that so cool, and I had to shoot it in a day and I was exhausted, and my whole crew was exhausted. It was just really tough, but the band was really great, everyone was really great."

The band began their next tour to support *Nimrod* on October 30 in Dallas, which essentially lasted until the end of 1998; they played dates during 14 out of the next 15 months. There was the usual revelry on the road. On November 11, the band made an appearance on the show *Late Night With Conan O'Brien*, then played an in-store at Tower Records on 4th and Broadway in New York, with predictably chaotic results. "You can start a riot," Billie Joe told the crowd, "You can do anything you want, 'cause you're not at Tower Records, you're at a Green Day concert!" The audience didn't riot but did cause some damage to the premises, with Billie Joe further adding to mayhem by dousing the audience with beer and water, spray painting "Nimrod" on the walls and "Fuck you" on a window, and once again dropping his pants to moon the crowd. He was restrained from throwing a monitor from the landing where the band was playing by a Tower staffer who wasn't able to keep Tré from throwing his bass drum. But a *RollingStone.com* story noted, "Reports that damages totaled $50,000 are excessive. A Tower spokesman says there was only $100 at the most." "It was just good fun," Billie Joe told *MTV online*. "[In-stores] give you the perfect opportunity to make a complete fool of yourself."

Undeterred, the band played another free concert in the alley behind the downtown HMV record store in Toronto, Ontario, on November 19; their concert that night at the Phoenix Concert Theatre had sold out in six minutes, so the free show was added. No mishaps were reported. The same month the group also appeared in animated form on the cartoon series *King Of The Hill*, cast as the garage band Cane And The Stubborn Stains. And teacher/fan John Goar caught the group again in Seattle when they played club DV8 on December 2. "The venue was small and intimate," he says (Green Day had previously played the club in 1994 when it was known as Oz.) "I could imagine that Billie Joe was looking right at me. When the band was coming on the stage, I tried to yell at Billie Joe to get his attention, but no dice." Goar later wrote about the show for *greenday.net*.

The group also irked KROQ with their antics at the station's Almost Acoustic Christmas show in LA in December. First they threw a Christmas tree into the audience; "Well, someone had to do it!" Billie Joe told writer Jane Ganahl by way of explanation. "It was sitting there two days and nobody had thrown it in!" The group provoked further outrage by spray painting the set, trying to stop the show's rotating stage in the middle of another band's set, throwing a bottle through a window, and Billie Joe again mooning the audience. ("I do that sometimes when things aren't going well.") The police were called, and another indecent exposure arrest loomed. But ultimately, charges weren't pressed as the band had "played a really awesome set," in the words of a KROQ representative.

The US leg concluded with three nights at San Francisco's venerated Fillmore Theater. The reviews were mixed. Craig Marine of the *San Francisco Examiner*, sounding like a disgruntled East Bay punk, wrote, "For all of the band's high-energy machinations, they are so eager to please the crowd that they come across as some sort of schmaltzy lounge act, what with lead vocalist Billie Joe Armstrong's constant butt-kissing chatter... he has also become the thing most true punks would probably hate to be the most — a frat boy poster child." Conversely, James Sullivan, in the *San Francisco Chronicle*, said, "The first rule of punk is tenacity — the determination to do whatever you're told you can't... Green Day made it clear that it has tenacity in spades, punching through 20 glorious songs that assured its fans that the band has no intention of fading into the early retirement of so many fast-rising pop phenoms," adding that the band's songs "sounded as fresh as they did when *Dookie* was released."

They certainly remained a hit with the audience. All three concerts were sold out and the crowd was becoming more mixed in age, with teenagers moshing and crowd-surfing down front, while adults bopped away at the back. And instead of stripping, during the first show Billie Joe put *on* clothing, piling on the T-shirts and a bra that had been hurled on stage. But the show's end involved the usual destruction, Tré stabbing his drum kit during the encore, leaving Billie Joe to perform 'Good Riddance' solo.

After a break for the holidays, the European tour began on January 20, 1998 in Belfast. January also saw the release of 'Good Riddance' as a single. The group — or, rather, Billie Joe, who sang solo in the spotlight, somberly dressed in black — performed the song on *The Late Show* prior to the European tour (host David Letterman even introduced Billie Joe by name, as Mike and Tré, though in attendance, did not perform on the show. "These guys are looking for day labour, so if have anything you need done around the house. . ." said Letterman). While in the UK, Billie Joe also performed the song on the long-running music show, *Top Of The Pops*.

The song was quickly becoming, in DJ Dean Carlson's words, "a multi-format smash. Prior to that, they really were more branded as an alternative band, whether it was as part of the punk revival or as the new Buzzcocks for another generation. But this was a record that was such an across-the-board smash that everyone played it. There was a time in radio when you would just play a record that, on paper, didn't make sense for that station, but when you listened to it, it totally made sense, because it just transcended the image of the band. You just played the song because it sounded so good. And you didn't care about what the band looked like or the average age of their audience, it's just the song itself appealed to such a wide audience. And that doesn't happen very often, but that was one of those songs. I think there was a sentiment in that song that just made it universal. That's what made that song go beyond just being a Green Day song and become a classic pop song. And those records are just hard to deny. There are always records like that; just because a record is accessible doesn't mean it's diluted or softened. It just means that the strength of the song completely transcends the image of the band. And I'm a sucker for a really great pop record."

In the US, the single reached number 11 on the Airplay chart (their highest placing on that chart since 'When I Come Around' in 1995), number two Modern Rock, and number seven Mainstream Rock. In the UK, the single reached number 11 (the highest placing in the UK chart since 'Basket Case'). The song gained further exposure when it appeared at the end of the *Sienfeld* clip show that aired before the final episode of the comedy series on May 14, after which the album jumped 20 places on the *Billboard* chart. It was also featured in two episodes of the medical drama, *ER* (though skeptics couldn't help noting that Warner Bros., coincidentally, owned both Green Day's label and the companies that produced the TV shows). It was also chosen as the official theme song for that year's PGA Golf Tour. Mike wondered how many of the people that heard the song even realised it was Green Day. "They just go, 'I heard this really good song a couple of years ago and I don't know who sang it,'" he told the *Las Vegas Sun* in 2001. He added he'd seen the song turn up in all sorts of unexpected places, such as on an enrollment cassette for the College Of The Redwoods up north in California.

The video for 'Good Riddance' also made an impact. "That one was a gift from the gods," says Mark Kohr. "They put it out to me and to other directors, and I wrote up a concept. I didn't talk with Billie, I just thought, I'm just going to give it a go, see what I come up with."

Kohr's original idea was not too dissimilar to the underlying scenario of 'When I Come Around'; a series of people caught up in their own lives, yet somehow linked together. "It was really kind of cool," he explains. "It was like this black-and-white thing where there were people in an urban setting, and people waiting in line at a supermarket, and you could see that they were just in their own thoughts. And then there was a couple and they were driving a car along an urban park, in a cool old car, and then there was a mortician doing the makeup on a dead person. And you would see each one of these scenarios, you would see these little stories, these ordinary stories, and then fireworks were going to come out of the park. I've experienced this from time to time in my life, where I'm just going along, and all of sudden there are fireworks going off, and it's not the Fourth of July. And I go, 'That's kind of wild. Fireworks — how cool!' and I see them in the distance, and I watch them, and then they're done. And that's what I wanted to have happen — I wanted to have these fireworks go off, and I wanted to have all these people look up, like the mortician guy doing the makeup on the dead person somehow turns and sees the fireworks, and the people waiting in line at the store, they look out the window and they see the fireworks. And this couple that are driving along see the fireworks through the trees and they stop their car and they sit on the hood. And I just wanted to have this scene that like, bound everybody together."

But Kohr's idea was rejected. "I got this word back, 'Well, Billie doesn't like any of the ideas from any of the directors, because there's a dead person in all of them,'" he says. So he was surprised to be contacted by the group again in November '97. "They called and asked me, 'Mark, could you come with us and spend a few days with us in New York, and we'll come up with an idea.' And I said, 'Well, sure.' They flew me to New York, and I hung out with them for a few days, and it was a great time; you know, hanging out, go on MTV, they did a show at Roseland, and all this stuff happened. And we didn't talk about the video at all, for a day and half. Maybe it was even three days. And then they went to be on Conan, and Billie was like, 'Why don't we talk about the video?' And I was like, 'Sure.' Because, again, I wanted to let this emerge, I didn't want to force it. But of course, secretly, I had a little anxiety, because at some point, we're going to have to talk about this thing."

Once the entourage arrived at the TV studios, "Billie sweeps everyone else out of the green room, and it's just me and Mike and Billie and Tré," says Kohr. "And Billie says, 'You know, I'd kind of like to do this like a Pogues video, where they're working class, and we have shots of working-class people, kind of like they're like drunk or something. And they're in real ordinary places.' And I was like, 'Okay, anything else?' And he was like, 'No. Well, no, I know. . . and I'm playing a guitar, and I'm like sitting on a bed that's on the floor, and there are flyers on the wall.' And I was like, 'Okay, that sounds good. Great.' And again, it's that I have the faith. I know that Billie's given me it all, he's told me everything that he wants. All I need to do is ask myself, 'What does he mean by that? What do I work with there?'"

Kohr ended up combining Billie's suggestions with his original idea for the video. "So I took his idea, and I was like, I want to do these ordinary people," he explains. "But I changed it a little bit in that I was like, I want them all to be caught in a moment of clarity, where their brain turns off and they stop thinking about all the things in their life. And their physical reality surrounding them is very clear, just for a moment. And that's how I directed all the people. And I also wanted to do these different camera tricks, where I shot them once with a hand-held camera that has a slow frame, and then I shot them with a camera on a dolly with a real fast frame, same angle, same camera track, and combined those two so that it appears I'm going from this really fast motion shot to this super slow-motion shot. Because I wanted it to feel like this moment is happening simultaneously to everybody. And that it's a common thing that happens to people. Essentially, it's sort of like that eventually, everyone has that moment of clarity, or awakening, or Buddha-ness, or whatever you want to call it. It's existential, it's sort of internal, I don't know how to say this. I'm probably going to come off like an idiot, but it comes out of that feeling that people have only as individuals, when they're alone, when they reflect on themselves. It's that whole kind of 'I am' thing, but it's a very internalised feeling. It's not loneliness, it's more like the sensitivity of being alive."

The combination of Billie Joe's ideas and Kohr's presentation resulted in a compelling video. Billie Joe serves as the narrator of the piece, with frequent cuts to him performing the song in a somewhat disheveled apartment. The other shots are of people going about their daily, ordinary activities — waiting for a bus, shopping at a hardware store, working at a dry cleaners — the camera zooming in as they have their "moment of clarity." The people featured were "a combination of people we knew or had access to and actors," says Kohr. "If you'll notice, the woman who's at the beginning and the end of the video — she's the only one we photographed twice, by the way — she is also in the 'Hitchin' A Ride' video. She is the one with the Betty Boop head on that the ape knocks off her head." Making sure they were included, Mike appears filling up his car at a gas station; Tré is seen recovering from an accident.

Kohr describes the shoot as "a joy, because we had three days to shoot, and we had all the money we needed. Even though I was doing this unusual thing, where I was shooting all these people only once. You know, when you do a film shoot, you do a lot of coverage? Well, in this shoot, I was shooting each person *once*; then we'd move to a whole new location and just do one shot, and then we'd move to another location and just do one shot. And luckily, the record company had faith in me, because I had a track record and all that jazz. And then, after I put it together, and Billie was like, 'Man, that thing you did with the fast and slow motion, I didn't understand what you meant before, but that turned out great.' And Adrienne really liked it, too. And we put it out there, and it just did so well; audiences loved it, people would watch that video and they would cry. And I saw that the effects reverberated through the visual community; I saw versions of the techniques in television commercials, in movies, and on TV shows. And I was like, 'That's great.' I know it sounds funny, but sometimes when you do something, and you put it out there, and it's echoed, some people would say that's plagiarism, but with me, I just go, 'Oh, I created something that had that kind of impact.'"

On March 8, *Nimrod* won Best Rock/Pop album at the renamed California Music Awards (*BAM* magazine having folded). Later that month, the group headed to Japan, and then Australia. While in Melbourne, they appeared on the show *Recovery TV*, but were only scheduled as an interview. They ended up commandeering the instruments of the house band and launching into an unscheduled performance of 'The Grouch', a song whose chorus was replete with the phrase "fuck you." Though no one was seen getting unduly upset by the performance, the group was nonetheless escorted out of the building immediately afterwards by studio security.

By April, *Nimrod* was certified Platinum; it would eventually sell over two million. The same month, the band taped a show for MTV in front of a live audience at Bottom of the Hill in San Francisco on April 17. "Okay, when the video cameras come on, act really punk!" Billie Joe told the packed house, who duly went into what was described as "a frenzied nonstop mosh." The performance was wonderfully energetic, the intimacy of the small club setting greatly enhancing the atmosphere. Billie Joe enjoyed playing with the crowd; during the instrumental break in 'Hitchin' A Ride' he donned a black jacket, shook two plastic skulls at the audience, and intoned, "Ladies and gentlemen, you're all a bunch of sinners! You're all going to hell!" to delighted cheers. When using the occasional swear word in talking to the audience, he then seemingly caught himself, disingenuously proclaiming, "Oh, wait a minute! Television, you can't cuss!" then proceeded to give the censors lots of work blanking out the swear words in songs like 'The Grouch' (the censors didn't always blank out times when the audience itself would swear, while singing along). During an especially frantic 'She', Mike hit himself in the face with his own bass; Billie Joe didn't even notice until someone in the audience pointed it out. "What's that? Holy shit! What just happened?" he said. "I'm sorry, I think I just broke my nose!" said Mike, who exited the stage holding a towel to his bleeding face. Billie Joe then said he'd play the next number, 'Redundant', acoustically, "But you have to slam dance extra hard" (it was actually just a solo performance as he used his electric guitar). The broadcast ended with 'Good Riddance', but the final song was 'One Of My Lies'. "Green Day was at their finest," concluded the *San Francisco Examiner*. "Yeah, they're punk, but they're also very fine — and occasionally brilliant — musicians."

Another US tour began April 30 in Houston, and the group also had a new song to promote, 'Redundant', which in the US reached number 16 on the Modern Rock chart, and number 27 in the UK. The video, again directed by Mark Kohr, has the band playing just outside a living room, where one person after another walks through, performing the same activity each time. "I was looking for a gag that dealt with the idea of how in life, we end up doing the same things over and over again," he explains. "Because the song has the line about being stuck in repetition over and over, I was looking for a gag that would be this circle which would be broken at the end." This was conveyed through the action of the first person, a woman who walks into the room, picks up the newspaper on the floor, and walks out. A new newspaper is tossed on the floor and she walks through again — until the end, when Billie Joe picks it up first. "When you break the circle, it's scary," says Kohr. "Like when the newspaper falls, and falls, and falls, and falls, and then Billie goes to pick it up, and she goes to pick it up in the same place, and it's like, 'Ahh! Where did it go?'" Seeing no newspaper, the video's last shot is of the woman screaming.

On May 16 the group played the HFStival in Washington, D.C., named after the sponsoring radio station WHFS; other acts on the bill included the Foo Fighters, Everclear, Bad Religion, and The B-52s. During the course of their set, Tré lit his drum kit on fire, which was seen as a way of heightening the excitement beyond merely battering one's instrument into pieces. "We never plan to do shit," Tré told *RollingStone.com*. "But we always keep the implements of our destruction on hand in case need be. I had an axe and other things." Standing amidst the destruction, Billie Joe performed 'Good Riddance', a song that was fast becoming an obvious set closer.

The atmosphere was more highly charged the following month at the sixth annual KROQ Weenie Roast & Fiesta on June 20 at Irvine Meadows Amphitheatre in Irvine, California (now the Verizon Wireless Amphitheater). The *Los Angeles Times* reviewer was unimpressed with the lineup (which included The Prodigy, Cherry Poppin' Daddies, Creed, and Blink-182, among others), which he called "Unspectacular. . . way overcrowded with inconsequential newcomers." But Green Day came in for praise: "The puerile but feisty Bay Area trio played with the fire and authority that everybody else lacked, packed plenty of action into its set, and let a catchy array of tunes do the rest. . . on stage, Armstrong was his usual antic self, mugging and scampering cartoonishly, cussing to be cutely naughty, stripping to his undies and serving as ringleader for assorted pranks."

What wasn't mentioned was the unexpected appearance during the band's set of Arion Salazar, bassist with Third Eye Blind, who ran on stage and hugged Mike. Mike was annoyed at having the band's act interrupted, and a brief skirmish broke out. Backstage, the fight began again, ending with Mike getting hit in the head with a beer bottle, resulting in a fractured skull and twenty stitches. It was not clear who had hit Mike, but Salazar nonetheless issued a public apology, that read in part, "I am sorry that my attempt at doing something I thought would be funny escalated into Mike getting hurt. . . My heart goes out to him and I hope he recovers quickly. We have many friends in common and I just hope that he can accept my sincerest apology. I am sorry, Mike."

The band then returned to Europe, and Lance Bangs accompanied them on what was a much happier tour. "I was in Los Angeles working on *Being John Malcovich*, documenting the production of that film," he says. "They would fly me out to go tour with them and shoot footage. Billie Joe was definitely a music fan, wanting to see early footage of The Clash and tracking down information or books about Dylan. He seemed to have that sensibility, knowing that he needed to have things documented and put away for awhile so they would exist at least. Which was a pretty bright thing to be aware of. It was never like it was coming from management or anything, it was mostly Billie Joe being interested about having someone go and shoot some footage.

"And again, it was amazing how many kids were just going nuts and painting their faces and making shirts and jumping in the crowd and going crazy at their shows," Bangs continues. "That definitely won me over. Pretty early on when I had been touring with them, I had come from a more indie rock sad music background. But I was won over by their live shows. What they were doing was really great live." Bangs' footage would end up in numerous short documentary shows about the band that appeared on music stations like MTV and VH1: *Behind the Music*, *VH1 Ultimate Albums*, *Driven*, and other similar programs.

The band's incessant touring paid off when they won the Best Live Performance award at that year's *Kerrang!* awards ceremony. More awards followed on September 10, when the group attended the MTV Video Music Awards, held at the Universal Amphitheater in LA, and, after being nominees since the release of *Dookie*, finally won a Best Alternative Video award for 'Good Riddance'. "No way!" said Tré when the group reached the podium. "Susan Lucci, eat your heart out!" Billie Joe said when it was his turn to speak, in reference to the *All My Children* soap opera star who at that time had been repeatedly nominated for an Emmy award and had yet to win. He then thanked Rob Cavallo, Pat Magnarella, and, scratching his head to remember who else he might have left out, finally blurted, "And Mark Kohr! I don't know if Mark Kohr is here but he's the one who introduced us to making videos. And he made this one, he's made almost every single one that we have done, so I just want to say thanks to him." He also said hello to his wife, who would soon give birth to the couple's second son, Jakob Danger Armstrong (giving Billie Joe a reason to get another tattoo).

After a trip to South America, touring finally ended in December, with more appearances at radio station-sponsored holiday shows. The last single from *Nimrod* was also released, though the song was actually promoted as being from the soundtrack of *Varsity Blues* — 'Nice Guys Finish Last', which reached number 31 Modern Rock. The video marked the first time the group worked with director Evan Bernard, and recast a Green Day show as an American football match, complete with cheerleaders, a pep-talking coach, and bizarrely dressed fans. The band is seen trashing their locker room after their "victory", as the announcer solemnly intones, "Nice guys finish last, but on this fateful December afternoon, Green Day finished first!" The video was shot in Los Angeles November 22 to 23. The number later received a nomination for an MTV Movie Award for Best Song.

Over the course of promoting *Nimrod*, the newly recharged Green Day had played close to 200 shows. But they were learning to pace themselves, and they would not tour again so extensively for another year and a half. There would also be another long break before they recorded their next album, which would again see them exploring new musical directions. Green Day was growing up, but they certainly weren't about to start growing old.

CHAPTER 8

Going Down To Jingle Town

"You can't keep writing the same song over and over again. Lyrically, I think there's a lot more said on this album then there has been in the past."
— *Billie Joe to* Teen People, *November 2000*

At the beginning of 1999, it was announced that Green Day would open for The Rolling Stones on five dates in February. But the band pulled out almost as soon as the announcement was made. The official reason given was that they wanted to get to work on their new album, but in fact they wouldn't start recording until the following year. As when the European *Insomniac* tour was cancelled in 1996, the band needed a break after the relentless touring of the previous year. Tré also later spoke of the turbulence in their personal lives; both he and Mike divorced their wives during this period (Tré remarried in March 2000). Mike also had some health issues to sort out; what he feared was a heart condition turned out to be simply a digestive disorder. For his part, Billie Joe admitted his own marriage had been "pretty rocky," but he and Adrienne managed to keep their relationship together.

The band also managed to keep the relationship between themselves together, taking a month and a half off after the *Nimrod* touring had ended, then going back into their usual routine of rehearsal. "Band practise isn't an event for us," Mike told *Guitar World*. "It's what we do. We enjoy it, but we take it very seriously. We always have." Songs began to materialise during rehearsals, but instead of deliberately trying to build up a backlog, as Billie Joe had for *Nimrod*, the band opted to let the songs emerge naturally. "We wanted to make this record in our practise space," Billie Joe told *Guitar World*. "No writing in the studio. Sometimes I think being in the studio can have disadvantages creatively. You can feel stifled a little bit."

"The last record was just us going in and pounding out songs," Mike told the *Denver Rocky Mountain News*. "We were saying, 'Let's just keep writing tons of songs and find the record within that.' This time, Billie wasn't forcing himself to write songs. We were letting the songs happen and letting the inspirational moments show up when they do."

But what was more unusual was that the band played only two shows over the next 17 months, the fewest they'd ever played in their entire career. Even more unusually, the two they did play were concerts more associated with an acoustic performing style. The shows were two of Neil Young's annual Bridge School Benefit concerts, the Bridge School being an organisation that works with children who have physical and speech impairments. Young had long been a supporter of the school, as his wife Pegi was a co-founder; the Youngs' son also attended the school.

The 1999 Bridge School Benefit shows were held October 30 and 31 at Shoreline Amphitheater in Mountain View, California. Young, Pearl Jam, a reunited Who, Tom Waits, Brian Wilson, and Lucinda Williams were among the others on the bill. Improbably enough, Green Day's set began with 'Geek Stink Breath', and though they toned their antics down somewhat — nothing was set on fire — Tré nonetheless managed to break several drumsticks, later tossing one to the Bridge School students sitting on a riser at the back of the stage, and Billie Joe added a tuneful kazoo part to 'When I Come Around', which finally brought the audience to its feet. "Green Day proved that punk rock can translate to acoustic instruments — it's called rockabilly," wrote *Metro*. "These multi-Platinum East Bay punks certainly surprised some people in the crowd with their deep musicality." The group also debuted the song that would become the title track of their next album, 'Warning', and debuted a new live member as well, Billie Joe's band mate in Pinhead Gunpowder, Jason White.

Lance Bangs shot the group in rehearsal and was present for the shows. "It was great because it was really the first time I'd seen them play with Jason," he says. "He's a really great guy. And it was just good to see, when they stripped things down, what the songs were like. Their songs worked in that format; they're classic, well-written songs. They won over a lot of the audience, they were really impressed with how the songs held up. It was just a really fun weekend. They felt like they were slightly out of their element, because it was mostly older, more established song-writer-type people. But they definitely came over really well, the crowd was totally into them. It was a blast." Having a second guitarist not only added to the sound, it also freed up Billie Joe as a performer, allowing him to move around the stage without worrying about always having to play his instrument.

Bangs had also put together a video for another song on *Nimrod*, 'Last Ride In', which was put out around this time, though the song itself was not released as a single. "They just liked that song," says Bangs. "It was a nice little instrumental thing. Different than what they are known for; it has more of a surf rock type feel. And they just wanted to make a film to go with that song." The video offers a distillation of the kind of footage Bangs had been filming, with shots of the band rehearsing, and on stage.

"They wanted to make use of all that footage that had been shot," Bangs explains. "Billie Joe had also gotten a Super-8 camera and shot some footage of his family vacation and water skiing and things like that. I got that transferred for him and started going through all the footage through the years, and pulled various moments together in that song. And the video definitely aired on MTV. I don't think you could buy a CD single of that song, necessarily, but it was definitely put out and pro-moted on MTV."

The similarly flavoured instrumental, 'Espionage' — featured in the film *Austin Powers: The Spy Who Shagged Me* — was also released that year. The song was nominated for a Grammy for Best Rock Instrumental Performance, but lost to 'The Calling' by Santana, featuring Eric Clapton.

The members also continued their own involvement with various side projects. Billie Joe duetted with former Avengers lead singer Penelope Houston, now a singer-songwriter solo act, on the song 'The Angel And The Jerk'; it appeared on the 1999 compilation *Friends Again,* as well Houston's own 1999 album *Tongue.* He also produced One Man Army's 2000 album *Last Word Spoken* on Adeline. And there were further releases from Pinhead Gunpowder: *Shoot The Moon,* released in 1999 on Adeline, and three EPs released in 2000, a split EP with Dillinger Four on Adeline, a self-titled EP on THD Records, and *8 Chords, 328 Words* on Lookout (all three EPs, and an additional unreleased track, would be compiled by Lookout on 2003's *Compulsive Disclosure*).

Meanwhile, Mike had his own side projects. He appeared on Screeching Weasel's *Thank You Very Little,* released in 2000 on Panic Button. He also formed a side band, The Frustrators. Mike had been jamming regularly with guitarist Terry Linehan and drummer Art Tedeschi (who had played together in the band Waterdog), and the three decided to add a lead singer. Tedeschi brought in singer/guitarist Jason Chandler, with whom he'd played in the band Violent Anal Death (Chandler, Linehan, and Tedeschi were all originally from the East Coast). In 2000, the band's song 'Trout' appeared on the Adeline compilation *Might As Well — Can't Dance,* and they also released an EP on the label the same year, *Bored In The USA,* with a cover, designed by Chandler, parodying Bruce Springsteen's *Born In The USA* album. ("Eight catchy tunes about cars, rotting food, midgets used for sport, and sex!" boasted the label's website.) There was a minor controversy when the band's song, 'The Great Australian Midget Toss', was played during a Lakers' basketball game in Los Angeles, resulting in complaints from an organisation called The Little People of America. "This sends out the wrong message to short-statured individuals and their families," LPA representative Casey Hubelbank told the Associated Press. "[The] fact that the song was used as a taunt at a major sporting event only makes it worse... We don't like to throw the word 'boycott' around, but in this case can you blame us?" The band's response appeared on their website, in which they stressed that, "The song is meant as a farce. If anyone in this world listens to our song and finds in it some call toward violence, then that person should seek counseling," and concluding, "If anyone has taken offense at our jokes, we do apologise for the misunderstanding." No boycott ever materialised.

Expectant fans who wanted new Green Day material in 1999 had to content themselves with the group's contribution to the compilation album *Short Music For Short People*, released on Fat Wreck Chords (run by "Fat" Mike Burkett, singer/bassist in NOFX). The album's title referred to the fact that all of the "songs" were 30 seconds in length, enabling a total of 101 acts to appear on the record. The Green Day track was 'The Ballad of Wilhelm Fink'.

Finally, three years after the recording of *Nimrod*, the band began making preparations to record their next album. They also decided to make a few changes. The band had previously co-produced their albums, and had shared that duty with the same two people: Andy Ernst, who co-produced the albums on Lookout, and Rob Cavallo who had taken over when the group signed to Reprise. This time, they decided to go outside their circle and picked Scott Litt, who'd previously worked with The Replacements, R.E.M., and Nirvana, among others, to produce. And in addition to a new producer, the band was also going to be working at a new studio: Oakland's Studio 880.

Studio 880 is located on a dead-end street, virtually next to an over-pass of Interstate 880. "It took so much effort to shut out the noise from the freeway, we have a mutual respect for each other," says John Lucasey, the studio's owner. High gates topped with barbed wire surround the location, and you need to press an outside buzzer for admittance. There's no address on the outside indicating that you're at Studio 880; you just have to know that it's there.

When the gate slides back, the first thing you see is a huge parking lot. Immediately to the right is a fence with a high gate that leads to a covered patio, and what's called the '880 Entertainment Complex,' a building with four studios, pre-production rooms, and offices. The décor in the lobby is Tiki-room ambience, with wood-carved columns holding up the balconies, bamboo torches jutting out from their sides, and a large Tiki god (from the set of the first *Scooby Doo* movie) surveying all from the top of the stairs with eerie, glowing red eyes. Tropical foliage appears to spill from the ceiling, and from somewhere in the distance you can hear the gentle sound of trickling water. "Some people call it the Rain

Forest Café," Lucasey jokes. At the far end of the parking lot is the door to the main studio complex.

Lucasey's family previously owned a factory on the spot he now calls "the house that Green Day built." "I grew up in this building," he says. "The control room, where we mix all the hits now, used to be where the machine shop was. I worked there during the summer when I was in high school, as a tool and dye apprentice. And I used to drive a fork-lift through where all the studios are now. So it all means a lot to me." The immediate neighbourhood around the studio is called "Jingle Town," a reference to the young hipsters that used to frequent the area back in the Thirties, "hip dudes in these long, pinstriped zoot suits with deep pockets," Lucasey explains. "And they'd hang out on the corners, and they'd always have change in their pockets and jingle it. That was kind of their trade mark, so they called it Jingle Town 'cause of that."

Lucasey had been interested in music since he was a teenager. "I wanted to become a musician, but I couldn't afford lessons," he says. "Then, after I'd finally learned, all my friends had become better musicians than I did." Still wanting to be involved in music somehow, Lucasey designed stages for his musician friends, tried his hand at songwriting, and became increasingly interested in the workings of recording studios. "But I also had a wild side," he says, which resulted in his moving to Los Angeles in 1984 where he worked as a stunt man for some years.

When he decided to get back into music again, he didn't want to work in LA. "I didn't like the music scene there," he explains. "And I knew something special was going to happen in the Bay Area because there are so many characters here, so much original talent. Los Angeles is a neat place, but everybody puts on their showcase face there. People who play shows here, they're playing shows because they love to be in a band, it's not about, 'How do we become rock stars?'"

So Lucasey returned to the Bay Area in 1991, initially opening a small studio in Oakland. He then relocated to Walnut Creek, opening Lucasey Video and Audio Productions on North Main Street. "My dream was to own a big recording studio, but this was a little tiny place," he says. "And it was off in Walnut Creek where there were no bands. But there was this used music store, Black Market Music, down the street, and I used to always visit and hang out at there. And one of the guys who worked there was a guy named Bill Schneider. He also had a band and he had no money, and I always took in the little refugee bands and said, 'Here's some free recording time... if you make some money then you pay me, alright?' So I gave them free recording time."

Lucasey's generosity would bring him an unexpected payoff when Schneider began working for Green Day as their roadie and, later, guitar tech (not to mention playing with Billie Joe in Pinhead Gunpowder). Lucasey eventually moved to Oakland and opened Studio 880 in 1998. "And one day I heard on the radio that Green Day was looking to do an album again," he recalls. "They were saying, 'Yeah, they're going to Los Angeles and meeting with studios.' So I was like, "I wonder if my friend Bill Schneider still works with Green Day?' So I just called him up and he's all, 'Hey John, long time no talk!' He told me he was still working for Green Day and I go, 'Well, I opened this new studio in Oakland. It's a lot bigger than the last one. I heard Green Day's looking for a new place to record... would you mind telling them about my studio? Could you have 'em come in and check out my place?' Then all of a sudden he's, 'Ahhhhh, you know, John, to be honest with you, they're kind of a big band, they're not like a little demo band. These guys are big time.' So I said, 'You know what Bill, you're right. I don't know how to describe my place, so all I'm going to say is one thing, and if you can't, you can't. But remember that time I gave you that free recording time with your band?' And he goes, 'Yeah...' And I said, 'All I'm asking you is just to mention it to them, and just tell them that I'm inviting them down. And if they say, 'No, F-off,' at least you tried. This is the only favour I'm asking.'

"So, about two hours later, Bill called me," he continues. "And he had this little trembling voice, and he's like, 'Uh, John? Dude, they're gonna come down!' And I was like, 'What? They're really?' And he says, 'Yeah! I'm just as shocked as you! They wanna come down tomorrow.' I was like, 'Oh my God. This is really cool.' So they came in the next day. And it was funny, because I saw them out in the parking lot, and at the time the place was one-sixth of what it is now, and from the parking lot it just looked like a warehouse. And they were like, 'Hey, what's up dude?' Then they walked in and their jaws just went to the floor. It was just amazing, it was just — I saw it right in their eyes, they're like, 'This is in our back-yard, and we're like ten minutes away from here. This is amazing.'"

Michael Rosen, who was Studio 880's studio manager at the time, remembers the Green Day connection coming about somewhat differ-ently. He says he contacted the band after learning they wanted to record in Oakland. "I had gone to Los Angeles, and a friend of mine who managed Cello Studios, we had lunch, and she told me that Green Day was looking for a studio up in the Bay Area," he says. "They wanted to be in Oakland. They specifically didn't want to be in the Bay Area, they wanted to be in Oakland, because they wanted to come back to their roots. They wanted to be near their homes; they had done enough trav-eling, and they wanted to do something that was in their backyard. I actually worked at Fantasy when they did *Dookie*, and I think they liked that studio, but they wanted this to be a little grittier. There's a little more cachet, a little more street-cred, perhaps, in Oakland."

But both agree that once Green Day had given the thumbs-up, Rob Cavallo, Scott Litt, and Alan Sides, a studio designer and owner of Ocean Way (where the record would be mixed) inspected the facilities and requested certain modifications, which Lucasey was happy to do. "No problem!" Lucasey says. "I redid the hardwood floors and we made the room just sound amazing. I was willing to accommodate them. It's a world-class setting that they could tailor to make a certain sound, which became a very successful sound — we definitely have a very distinctive sound coming from the studio. It just had the vibe, you know; the studio's here in Jingle Town, it's kind of the barrio, and it's a world-class place."

"The neighbourhood was really something," Mike later told *Guitar World*. "There were people out there selling drugs and shit. But on the other hand, there's a lot of 'community' in the Latino community."

"Every time a truck went by [on the freeway], you could feel it, and you can hear it in the frequencies the microphones pick up," said Billie Joe in the same article. "We said, 'This is a great place! It's 10 minutes from where we live. We can still have our lives at home, but still not be distracted when we're working in the studio."

Pre-production started in February, but within a few days Litt had bowed out of the project. "Scott had come by the studio," says Rosen.

"Every producer and engineer, especially when you work with a big band, you want to see where you'll be working, that the studio has everything that you need. So Scott had come by and talked about a couple of things that he might want to do in the studio, and then we never saw him again. I heard through the grapevine that the band wasn't sharing his vision for what they were doing, that they didn't like his vibe, or something like that. But that was it. We never saw hide nor hair of him again."

Instead of bringing in another producer, Green Day decided to produce themselves for the first time, working mainly with their engineer, Ken Allardyce, and with Rosen "making sure everything ran smoothly as far as their session, getting anything they needed — runners, coffee, equipment. Everything from soup to nuts." The sessions finally began April 1.

As the band had been working on material for some time, "when Billie Joe came in he had a pretty clear picture of what he wanted to do on the record and went right at it," says Rosen. "Billie Joe's a pretty smart guy. He has a very strong sense of what he wants and how to go about getting it. The only confusion was that Rob Cavallo sort of produced that record as well, but he didn't spend a lot of time up there. He was the executive producer and he would come and go from Los Angeles every couple of weeks. He would come in and go, 'These monitors sounds like crap, why don't you get new monitors?' And I'd have to run around and find someone to rent some monitors for a day or two and change everything. Then he'd leave and they'd go back to what they were doing before, and they'd be like, 'We were fine, what is this guy going on about?' See, they were trying to do things for the first time without him, so it was kind of a strange dynamic. It's kind of like how it is with your parents, when you go away to college or something like that. They wanted to do things on their own, yet they counted on his input. They definitely respected him and counted on him."

"Rob looks like Joe Business when he comes in," is Lucasey's assessment. "He's always on the phone with Jewel or whoever, talking talking talking, going fast at it. And then he sits down, and he picks up a guitar and you're like, 'Oh shit, this guy can actually play.' And then he'll challenge you. He'll say, 'Name a song.' And I'll try and name like the most off-the-wall Beatles songs, or the strangest songs from the Sixties and Seventies, and he can play every single one of those songs. 'Cause he really believes in music. He really knows music. He also knows what will sell, too. He's definitely earned the respect of Billie Joe, and that is one hard fucking thing to do. They definitely work together well."

If on *Nimrod* the group had dabbled their toes in musical experimentation, on *Warning* they took the full plunge, bringing in ever more diverse instruments, creating an album that's the most different, musically, of any of Green Day's records. After three opening drumbeats, the first sound you hear on *Warning* is the vigorous strumming of a brace of acoustic guitars — certainly an unexpected opening on a Green Day album. The song itself cleverly takes the same cautionary phrases that everyone sees when they buy a new appliance and turns them into lyrics — and, more subversively, subtle statements of dissent. In considering the warning about not crossing police lines, for example, the question is raised, who is more dangerous — the cop or the private citizen? And was it better — or safer — to knuckle under or "question everything"?

In the case of 'Minority', the answer was definitely the latter. Musically, the song has an engaging swing, with the feel of a Pogues' song, but with a proud statement of defiance in place of drunken revelry. It's preferable to stand against authority, goes the song's message, even if it means being in the minority. There were also swipes at consumerism in both 'Fashion Victim' and the album's closing song, 'Macy's Day Parade', though the sadness in the latter number is somewhat mitigated by the singer's determination to hold onto one "brand new hope."

Instead of the celebratory apathy of the loser that had been the subtext of songs like 'Longview', Green Day's songs were now giving more serious consideration to the world around them. And appearances to the contrary, these were actually issues that had always concerned the band. In 1995, Billie Joe had told *Oor*, "I refuse to be some sort of politician," but in the same year he'd also told an interviewer for the *San Francisco Chronicle*, in answer to a question if it was difficult to write about dissatisfaction in light of his success, "There's still things that anger me. Your basic racism, police brutality, and shit like that I've been against for a long time, and will always be against... there's things that piss me off every single day." The difference was, now he was beginning to sing about them.

But though the album also featured songs like 'Waiting', which, with its exultant call to "Wake up!" was not as straight-forward as it might first appear (the same could also be said of 'Hold On'), not every song made a "statement". 'Church On Sunday' looked at another troubled relationship, again saved through compromise (or resignation). 'Blood, Sex, And Booze' revisited the terrain of 'Dominated Love Slave', though lacking the tongue-in-cheek delivery of the latter number. For a bit of authenticity, the group hired a dominatrix (credited as "Mistress Simone" on the cover) to whip and humiliate the luckless second engineer, Tone. "The dominatrix was real, it was not a joke," says Rosen. "She was not some little girl pretending to do this, she beat the crap out of the assistant engineer. He was petrified. That poor kid had no idea what was going on. He was being all tough and thinking that he could handle anything. But she beat him; he thought she was playing around, and she was not playing around." Perhaps appropriately, the song also ended up on the soundtrack of the 2001 film, *Freddy Got Fingered*.

And 'Misery' (with lyrics credited to the entire band) has the most unusual musical mix of all, bringing together a farfisa organ playing a motif reminiscent of the silent movie era, an accordion, a mandolin, and string and horn sections, blended into a waltz-tempo number. The music was then paired with lyrics spinning a tale straight out of an independent movie, replete with drugs, a murder, and, of course, a trip to Las Vegas (Billie Joe also cited the Tom Waits' song, 'Rain Dogs', as an influence). This was another unusual aspect of the track; most Green Day songs were in first person and didn't have characters acting out a storyline. It was an element that would be vastly expanded on in the next album.

"*Warning* was them trying to do a different style, trying to reinvent themselves," says Rosen. "You can hear the beginnings of *American Idiot* in that record. *Warning* was what they needed to do to do *American Idiot*, in that they tried to flip things up a little bit. Go for a different style."

"I think a lot of bands, they get a certain fan base and they find safety in that and they're afraid to think outside of their own box," Mike said, looking back at *Warning* in 2001. "We've got to keep it interesting for ourselves, too. If you get bored... or if you stop growing, you die."

And though Rosen emphasises, "When they worked, they worked," the band still managed to make time for visitors and some relaxation. "There were people coming by," says Rosen. "It wasn't an amazing amount, and it wasn't out of control, but they had people coming in and out. They had their friends there. Every Friday night we had a little barbecue; my gofer at the time worked at a really good meat store and he would go and get steaks and all kinds of beef. So they would barbecue and have some people in. It was definitely not all work. Billie Joe's wife would come by with the kids, Tré's wife at the time would come down. They liked to party. Billie Joe was friends with Matthew Fox, that guy who stars in the TV show *Lost* now, and he would show up every couple of weeks and hang out."

Chris Bilheimer and Lance Bangs were also at the sessions, shooting footage that would be used for the album's EPK (electronic press kit), and, later, some mock PSAs. The EPK, hosted by "Cash MaHoy" (comedian David Cross) presented a tongue-in-cheek history of the band and a behind-the-scenes look at the making of *Warning*. "But what now? After all these years, is it still possible for Green Day to make a great record?" asks MaHoy, who smoothly provides the answer, "Of course it is. Don't be an asshole."

"Being in a studio is boring as hell," Bilheimer says. "The best way to describe being in a studio, is that it's long periods of waiting broken up by shorter periods of waiting. It's incredibly boring. So having a really serious look at people in the studio is a snore. I was trying to make something that was entertaining to watch." Bilheimer knew Cross through having done some design work for Cross' TV program *Mr. Show*. "I had been doing some work for them and they sent me the entire four seasons on tape," he explains. "I used to sit with the band and we'd watch all the old episodes at 880. So when I was thinking who would be a good host, David happened to be in town and so I got him to do it. The band was just so excited because they were like, 'He's the funniest guy in the world!' He was incredibly hung-over and had slept for like an hour; he did the whole shoot and then went back to sleep. He said he woke up that evening and he was like, 'Did I do something this morning?' Apparently he has almost no recollection of doing this."

In addition to shots of the band working and goofing around in the studio, Billie Joe and Tré are shown explaining the basics of punk rock to a group of school children, and "Mistress Simone" is seen abusing poor Tone. ("He can't sue us, can he?" asks Billie Joe.) There's also a sequence of Bill Schneider going to the hospital to have a piece of guitar string removed from his eyeball, which not only references another operation seen in a Green Day video (the background music is 'Geek Stink Breath') but also brings to mind Luis Buñuel's 1929 surrealist short *Un Chien Andalou* (co-written with Salvador Dalí), with its infamous sequence of a woman's eye being sliced open. A performance video of 'Warning' was also put together from scenes shot in the studio.

"We would hang out with them and go see other bands play at night in town," says Bangs. "I'd do interviews while we were driving around in Billie Joe's car. He collected these old beat-up cars, I don't know what they were — I don't know anything about cars. They were these really cool old things, in my mind they seemed like Forties or Fifties-era cars. We would just drive around and shoot interview footage, and then just hang out. He had a firepit in the backyard, we would do BBQs at night and stuff and have family members over."

The two also heard the album's songs coming together in the studio. "It wasn't like were going, 'Oh, let's see what Lance and Chris think of this crazy song we are trying,'" says Bangs. "It was more like they would be working on it and we would be there in the room with them and hear it incidentally. They weren't like, 'What's your opinion of this, should we do this or not?' They had fun. Billie Joe is really smart and he seemed like he enjoyed the process and talking a lot to Rob, or whoever was engineering, and making sure the band was taking time to try out different guitar sounds and have ideas and get things right. Obviously keeping things simple enough to not get bogged down, and doing overly meticulous studio things that they couldn't play live, but definitely thinking about what the guitar sounds were, what they could do that was cool. Working on interesting arrangements. We were definitely aware that they were writing on acoustics and trying different things at that point. I first saw that when they would set up those rehearsal rooms while on tour, and do these instrumentals, play the accordion and do surf instrumentals, things like that, rather than just straight pop/punk stuff over and over."

As important as the new developments in their sound, the fact was that Studio 880 was gradually becoming like a second home to the band. Ultimately it would come to be something like Green Day's clubhouse, where they worked, played, and stored equipment. It proved to be an environment well suited to their own often-quirky tastes. American flags adorn several rooms and pictures of Jimi Hendrix are everywhere. "I have a little on-going thing," says Lucasey. "If anybody can tell me how many Jimi Hendrix's are hidden in this building I'll give 'em a free day of recording. And nobody's ever come close!" Studio A also has a disco ball hanging from the ceiling. "When the Green Day guys first saw that, they were like, 'It's coming down,'" Lucasey recalls. "And I said, 'No, you'll get used to it.' And they did."

The group was soon adding their own touches to the place. You'll find "Tré Cool is fine," scrawled in unexpected, out-of-the-way places, such as behind a curtain. A sign on the entry gate by the buzzer reads, "Moving gate can cause serious injury or death" (an observation that could've easily appeared in the lyrics of 'Warning') and features an illustration of an unfortunate person getting crushed by said gate; the sign had been amended by Tré to have the person saying, "Help me, I'm famous!" A coin has been glued to the floor in one place, tempting the unwary to try and pick it up. "And I came in one evening after a session to check around and clean up, and there was this coffee cup sitting there, with coffee and cream in it, right on my credenza," says Lucasey. "And I go to pick it up and it's stuck. Tré had taken some crazy glue and glued Rob Cavallo's cup of coffee to the counter. And I have multiple keys to every door in here because of them. One time I came in and they had changed every lock on my doors, so it took 20 minutes to get through this place."

A lot of the pranks are down to Tré. "Tré's off the wall," Lucasey says. "He's like a little kid, he's the one who starts all the shit, that's for sure. If I find broken TVs, or things like that, the first person I'm going to point my finger at is Tré [in the EPK for *Warning*, Tré can indeed be seen hurling a TV off the roof of Studio 880's main studio complex]. And he's pulled some nasty pranks, but I've always got him back, too, so that kind of evens things out to where he'd probably think twice about doing certain things, 'cause there'd always be retaliation. Which I don't think they were ever used to." Perhaps as a gesture of reconciliation, Tré also brings decorative fish as gifts; a puffer fish hangs from a ceiling in the lounge, and another wall displays a large swordfish.

But their most inventive prank came when the sessions were completed. "It was in the middle of the summer, and it was really hot," Lucasey says. "Green Day had finished up, and every day when I walked into the studio something stank more and more. And we couldn't figure it out. Until it was just like, 'There's 20 dead rats in this building, what the hell is going on?' So, we're tearing apart everything, and looking under everything for this stench, thinking that it's just dead animals; I mean, it went from thinking there's a dead mouse, to a dead rat, to a dead cow, to a dead elephant!

"So what happened was, we'd been getting ready to do some construction," he continues. "And there was a little hole in this wall, in the sheetrock; it was about five feet up the wall. A friend of mine says, 'Maybe the dead rat's behind that,' so he looked down there, and he goes, 'John, I found out what your problem is.' And it was a bunch of lunch meat, delicatessen cold cut slices just dropped behind that. So we had to rip out the wall and take out all these rotten deli slices. But it still stunk. And it took another couple of days before we said, 'You know, these couches really smell bad.' And when we moved them, there were stains on the carpet underneath, so we took out the pillows and there's these precision surgical slits in the couches that they put potato salad and meat in, raw meat, it was horrible. The couches were toast, the carpet was toast, everything was toast.

"Then one of the engineers called from Los Angeles where they were mixing the album to ask about something. And I go, 'Hey, is Tré there? Can I talk to him real quick?' And Tré gets on the phone, and I go, 'I found those gifts you left for me.' And he goes, 'Oh, what gifts are those?' 'Oh, you know, the ones in the couch and behind the wall. And you know what, I've got some gifts for you! But don't worry, I know you're going on tour, I'll just leave them in your mailbox, it'll be there for you when you get back.' And all of a sudden, his voice started getting shaky, and he's all, 'You know, that's not meant for you, John. And it was no disrespect for you, it's meant for your new clients.' (A band that had been scheduled to use the studio after Green Day, but who had ended up canceling.) And then they bought me new couches and new carpet and stuff."

Despite the hijinks, or perhaps because of them, Lucasey and Green Day ended up forming a strong bond. "Instantly, we all became friends," says Lucasey, and it was the kind of friendship that would see the band returning to the studio even when they weren't working there. At the end of the sessions, Billie Joe left behind some more benign graffiti, spray-painting "B + A" on a wall.

The group was pleased with their work. "I think *Warning* is the best record we've ever made," Billie Joe told writer Jaan Uhelszki, though admitting, "but I'm a little biased." In answer to a comment about the album being their "most serious," he replied, "I feel everything we've done has been serious. I think our antics sort of get in the way of what people think." Uhelszki also asked if the album had another 'Good Riddance'. "Twelve of them." Tré was quick to respond, but Billie Joe was more circumspect, noting, "No, we didn't want to repeat that. We didn't want to write another 'Basket Case' after we did that." "It's got depth. It's got different layers," Tré said to another reporter. "It's like each song has its own life, each song has its own feel, its own vibe… Each song could be its own album." He also stressed that though there were acoustic guitars on the record, the sound was not "sappy acoustic" but "more aggressive, percussive acoustic."

Meanwhile, Bilheimer had been working on cover ideas. "I spent two months in the studio with them shooting the EPK and supposedly working on the album cover," he says. "Which was funny, because I was there for an entire month before I ever did a photo shoot. I was supposed to be working on a cover with their photo on it, and I didn't have any photos! Before they started recording, Billie said, 'I want a band photo on the front.' I was trying to think of what way to put them on the cover that doesn't look like every rock band album cover with the band on it. It's hard to do something unique with it. I was trying to think of something a little more classic. I think one of the most classic records of all time is *London Calling* [The Clash]. I wanted to get that feeling of the timeless classic black-and-white shot, a little bit of blurry motion, so it's not necessarily about them and their faces. It's more about setting an environment and a mood. It's a little bit out of focus, it's a little bit taking the focus off of them, not making it a pretty-boy shot of them on the cover."

Bilheimer ended up shooting the group in Chinatown in San Francisco. The photo chosen for the cover (their first album to feature a picture of the group on the cover) has the band walking down the street, slightly out of focus, Billie Joe adding an air of despondency to the shot with his head hanging down. ("I'm sure you can read all sorts of things into that which were all probably happy accidents," says Bilheimer.) An interesting graphic touch was the use of various industrial-looking icons throughout the booklet, such as the man in the circle getting zapped by a bolt of electricity.

"That to me is just an obvious off-shoot of the word 'Warning'," Bilheimer explains. "Those all came out of an industrial safety catalogue. Those were all images of warnings. I just love this idea that there is what I'm assuming is a billion-dollar industry of people whose entire job it is to make sure that people don't hurt themselves doing anything stupid. Like, I'm the designer that has to make sure you don't stick your hand into the giant buzz-saw, so I have to draw a picture of this person putting his hand into the buzz-saw with a line through it. Or the people who design phones that don't have sharp edges so you don't stick them in your eyeball. I was immediately drawn to those sort of icons, because they are also everyday things that you see. Incorporating everyday things into your design makes it accessible, people can relate to it. I try and do that with a lot of my design. The album also marked the first time since *Sweet Children* that a record had taken its name from one of the songs on the album.

The band finally hit the road again with the Warped tour during the summer, "basically to jump-start ourselves into touring mode," Mike explained. "We're like one of those Evel Knievel dolls that has been winding up for quite some time. We're ready to just spring out of the box." The Warped Tour is another of the themed traveling festival shows that emerged in America in the Nineties, along with Lollapalooza, Lilith Fair, and Ozzfest. The Warped Tour's focus was ska/punk rock and "extreme sports" (essentially, sports involving spectacular stunts); the tour's founder, Kevin Lyman, was previously involved with skateboarding shows. The first Warped Tour, held in 1995, featured such acts L7,

Seaweed, Tilt, and Sick Of It All. Once Green Day was added to the bill (which also included such acts as NOFX, the Long Beach Dub Allstars, The Donnas — yet another band that got its start on Lookout — Suicide Machines, Papa Roach, and The Mighty Mighty Bosstones), the tour, which began June 24 in Fresno, California, was quickly extended. Ticket prices were kept under $30. "I'll get to skateboard every day, which will be fun," Billie Joe told Jaan Uhelszki. "But you're not going to get me on the vert ramp."

With so many groups on a variety of stages, each band's set was limited to half an hour. And, reasoning that their new album wasn't due out for a few months, Green Day elected not to preview any songs from *Warning* during their set and stuck to their back catalogue. The set was neatly bracketed by 'Welcome To Paradise' and 'Good Riddance', and included such classics as 'Longview' and 'Basket Case', live favourites like 'Hitchin' A Ride', oldies like 'Going To Pasalacqua', and the occasional cover, such as Generation X's 'Kiss Me Deadly'.

"Green Day nailed the mood at Saturday's annual Vans Warped Tour by opening its set with the punk anthem 'Welcome to Paradise'," wrote the *San Francisco Chronicle* of the group's July 1 show in that city. "For one day, Piers 30-32 in San Francisco were paradise for punks and alterna-teens looking for the spirit of '93, or '84, or '77 — anything but the corporate-rock doldrums of 2000." "You make me proud to be from the Bay Area," Billie Joe exclaimed after the first song, later announcing that the next day was his wedding anniversary. "My wife thinks I'm a pain in the ass," he beamed. "She's right! And," he added, pointing to Mike and Tré, "these are my two other wives!" The set once again ended with Tré setting his drum kit on fire.

"Green Day proved that it's lost none of its goofy, ebullient charm, sounding as fresh and irresistibly pugnacious as it did when the band became the tiny Gilman Street club's first major-label breakthrough back in the early Nineties," said the *Chronicle*. Elsewhere, the band's July 18 date in Pittsburgh was marred by Tré's head being cut open after a cymbal he'd hurled in the air fell back on him.

In August, they played a few shows in Japan, and at the end of the month taped an appearance for the TV show *Farmclub* at Universal Studios, which aired in October; 'Minority' and 'Nice Guys Finish Last' were broadcast, while the studio audience also enjoyed performances of 'Blood, Sex, and Booze', 'Christie Road', and 'Warning'. In September, the group headed to Europe for more promotional appearances. Their time in the UK was especially busy, beginning on September 14, when they taped an appearance on *Top Of The Pops*, performing 'Minority'. The next day, they taped an appearance with Radio 1's Steve Lamacq, and performed that night at King's College in London. The set was a mix of songs from *Warning*, older songs like 'Longview', and more off-the-cuff numbers — as when, after asking the audience, "What cover song do you wanna hear?" Billie Joe answered his own question, playing Generation X's 'Dancing With Myself', confessing afterwards, "We only do this when we've been drinking a lot." For their part, the audience drank to the point where beer began to be hurled at the group; Billie Joe merely closed his eyes when he was soaked and kept on singing. Their last song of the night was The Sex Pistols' 'Holidays In The Sun'. Billie Joe later told writer Ben Myers the gig was, "The best show we've ever played in the UK," and the reviewers agreed. *Rock Sound* wrote, "Green Day may be a bunch of goofy bastards but they're tight as hell too. . . the true heirs to The Ramones spirit."

On September 16 they taped an appearance for *T4 On Sunday*, again performing 'Minority', followed by a late night in-store appearance at the Virgin Megastore on Oxford Street, a free event some fans had waited 12 hours to get tickets for. When someone threw a clown mask onstage during the show, Billie Joe immediately threw back a withering response in reference to the band Slipknot, who wore such masks onstage: "So you've got masks, assholes. Why don't you try writing a good fucking song for a change?" They also spray painted their name on the store's walls.

'Minority' was the group's first single from *Warning*. It topped the Modern Rock chart for six weeks, and reached number 15 Mainstream Rock. In the UK, it reached number 18. The video, directed by Evan Bernard, had the group playing on a parade float, adorned with oversize scowling heads and fists making the heavy metal "devil sign" [first finger and pinky extended, middle two fingers curled under the thumb] — seemingly an idea better suited to the song 'Macy's Day Parade' (indeed, Bernard had told his art director the look he wanted was that of "a punk version of a Macy's Day float"). Other trappings of grand parades are also present: baton-twirlers and marchers holding on to the large balloon effigies (actually computer generated) of the group members.

The video was shot over the weekend of August 19 to 20 in San Diego on near-deserted streets, underscoring what Bernard called the song's mood; "a celebration of being an outsider." Yet it also struck a note of futility and powerlessness — there's virtually no one around to listen to, much less cheer on, the band's anti-authority message. (Billie Joe's acoustic guitar even has a sticker reading "Against All Authority.") One could also read a sense of a defeat into the video's ending, with the group sitting on their now-destroyed float. In reality, the idea to wreck the float didn't come up until the last day of shooting, and, of course, accurately depicted what the end of a Green Day show often looked like. One of the styrofoam fists was later auctioned off.

The group was also starting to become increasingly candid in their political views. This was timely, considering that a US presidential election was held a month after *Warning*'s release. Tré went so far as to tell *Launch.com,* "If you're 18, for Christ's sake, register and keep George W. bullshit out of office because he's the devil, he's totally evil, and he needs to be stopped." The band adopted a more satiric approach with the mock commercials put together on Billie Joe's own purported candidacy for president, "Paid for by The Friends of Billie Joe to Elect Billie Joe. And Tré and Mike." The pro-Billie Joe ad had a voiceover proclaiming, "You need a leader. You need a leader with a flair for leadership and the ability to lead. You need — Billie Joe Armstrong," over shots of Billie Joe strategising with his aides, meeting school children, and jogging with the Secret Service. "A man with a home. A man with a dog. And a wife!" continued the voiceover, show-ing Billie Joe sharing a bench with his "spouse", Tré, fetchingly done up in drag. His slogan was, "Burning a bridge to the 21st century," a play on President Clinton's slogan about building a bridge to the new century. In the spirit of equal time, an anti-Billie Joe ad was also pro-duced, with more cautionary commentary: "You've heard a lot about Billie Joe Armstrong. But what do you really know? Did you know that he's a dick? Did you know that his wife is very ugly?"

Warning was released October 3. In its first week, it debuted at number four in *Billboard*, and sold 156,000 copies. In the UK, it reached the same chart position. (Adeline also released a version on green vinyl.) In December, an enhanced version of the CD was released that featured the EPK, the "Billie Joe for President" ads, and the 'Minority' video. A 64-page booklet was also included, with photos and song lyrics. "The booklet came about because I had a ton of video and photos from the recording sessions, and tons of footage from Lance," Bilheimer explains. "I wanted to have a booklet that had a lot to look at, so you felt that you were getting a lot for your money." The cover photo of the booklet is of a sign posted in a tram at the Atlanta airport that reads, "PLEASE HOLD ON." "I liked the idea of a safety/warning sign whose message actually works as advice for people when they are having troubled times," Bilheimer explains. The CD was also packaged in a green bag, "based on the idea of a hazard materials bag," says Bilheimer. "It just kinda made sense to package something called 'warning' in a hazardous materials bag."

For the most part, the album received favourable reviews. "Green Day has not tried to repeat the formula of its commercial peak," wrote Jon Pareles in the *New York Times*. "While the melodies on later albums have stayed strong, Mr. Armstrong's lyrics have outgrown bratty self-absorption, and the music has sometimes quieted down, with unpunk instruments like acoustic guitar... *Warning* is closer to British Invasion pop from the Sixties than it is to punk from the Seventies." When first reviewed in *Rolling Stone*, the magazine was more critical, with Greg Kot writing the album "invites the question: Who wants to listen to songs of faith, hope, and social commentary from what used to be snot-core's biggest-selling band?" But in the magazine's year-end issue, critic Barry Walters was kinder, saying, "*Warning* is an incredibly enthusiastic record. Even when tempos drop and arrangements embrace artful pop, these tender hooligans still sound like they're pogoing." *Magnet*'s review had a certain degree of prescience, saying that the album showed the band "working with a sense of maturity they have only begun to express."

And though the sales continued the decline from *Dookie* (stalling at one million in the US), the record nonetheless won admiration from some of their old associates from the East Bay. "I thought *Warning*, which I gather has been their lowest-selling record, was a brave attempt to shift gears and try something new," says Lawrence Livermore. "You don't always see that in a band that's been around as long as they had by that time."

"I admired the chances they took with *Warning*," says Frank Portman. "And that's probably actually my favourite one, I have to say. That's 'cause I'm a contrarian, 'cause I think a lot of people think that was where they stopped being punk or whatever. And I don't. I know the feeling of people accusing you of stopping being punk, so I paid more attention to that album."

The group did a few quick performances around the country in September and October, mostly radio and TV appearances. In early October they arrived for a few hectic days in New York. On October 3, they appeared on *The Howard Stern Show*, then appeared on *The Late Show*, performing 'Minority'. On October 4, they appeared on MTV's *Total Request Live* and another radio show, then played a free evening concert at Roseland. After a few songs from *Warning*, the band again threw open the show to requests, saying, "We're going to play anything you fucking want, basically," resulting in a set laden with older songs like 'Christie Road', 'Only Of You', and 'Disappearing Boy', which *RollingStone.com* noted were delivered with "pure glee," in contrast to the songs from *Warning*, which "seemed perfunctory afterthoughts, quickly rendered to make room for everything else the band wanted to squeeze into the show." Tré was called up front to sing 'All By Myself' and 'Dominated Love Slave', swapping instrument roles with Billie Joe; a cover of Billy Idol's 'Dancing By Myself' also turned up. For 'Blitzkrieg Bop', members of the audience were invited onstage to take up the instruments. The set ended with the usual bout of instrument destruction.

The next day in Boston, the tour was momentarily in danger of being delayed when Tré became injured after a cymbal sliced through the webbing between his fingers. Thankfully, the drummer's hand wasn't seriously damaged and after receiving stitches at a local hospital, Tré was back signing Green Day memorabilia at a post-gig signing. The rest of the US tour proceeded smoothly, with one of the more unusual being the Valley 6 Drive-In movie theatre in Auburn, Washington (near Seattle) where the group played on October 10.

Seattle radio station KNDD gave away tickets, and teacher/fan John Goar managed to get one through one his students (the band also made a live appearance on the station that day). The band made their entrance to Frank Sinatra's version of 'My Way'. The persistant drizzle didn't dampen the crowd's enthusiasm, though after a while it did cause the packed audience to look like they were steaming, causing Billie Joe to shout, "Oh, I think we reached the apocalypse now, boy! Well, if I'm going to hell, I'm bringing you right down with me!" A portion of the concert was later broadcast on MTV.

In less than a week, the band was back on the road again, with a short Australian tour in October, followed by more European dates in November and December. In between, the band returned to San Francisco to headline a free event on November 5 called "Take Back San Francisco," billed as an "anti-gentrification celebration." The event was a protest against the real-estate development that was displacing artist spaces, such as Downtown Rehearsal, a venue utilised by hundreds of musicians (Faith No More and Chris Isaak among them), that had been closed the previous August to make way for a new office block. "If the city's willing to build a giant baseball stadium and kick homeless people out of town, do you think anyone's going to care about musicians?" Mike told the *San Francisco Chronicle*. "There are games and there are lives. I think it's a lot easier to win the World Series than it is to stay alive for an entire year in San Francisco." (Ironically, Green Day would play that new baseball stadium in San Francisco in five years.)

The event began with a "Million Band March" from San Francisco's Mission District to Civic Center Plaza, where the concert was being held. The turnout for both was disappointing; a mere 500 musicians participated in the march (with the Gun And Doll Show leading the pack, driving a van that dragged a symbolic "dead musician" behind them), while the show itself drew 2000. But the setting was impressive; Civic Center Plaza is in front of the city's majestic City Hall, which looks more like a state capitol than a municipal building, topped with a golden dome that's 302 feet high.

The lineup included Victoria Williams, Mark Eitzel, Creeper Lagoon, Blind Boys of Alabama, and Zen Guerrilla, among others; Metallica's Kirk Hammett also delivered a speech of support. "We all know why we're here, don't we?" said Billie Joe when Green Day took the stage. "Because I don't think any band has ever played in an office space." When someone in the crowd yelled out the inevitable request for 'Freebird!' the band broke into another Lynyrd Skynyrd song, 'Sweet Home Alabama', substituting "San Francisco" for "Alabama."

The show marked the last time Eric Yee saw Green Day perform live. "Me and my friend Kevin took BART there," he says. "That was the first time I ever saw them play with Jason White, the first time I had seen them as a four piece. I remember they played forever, they played all old songs. That was pretty cool. It was pretty fun. Musically they were always tight. I've never seen them play bad. I don't think there's any difference besides the size of the venue that they're playing, they always give it their all. If it's just them playing to me and Eggplant at some party or them playing to 10,000 people, they always give it their all."

But some things were different from the old days. "A lot of people want to talk to them, so they can't really hang out," says Yee. "They're always getting pulled in a lot of different directions. But we hung out some in their bus after the show, drinking. We drank beer and we talked about our friend Lucky Dog [a one-time roadie for Green Day who had killed himself]. That was the first time I got to talk to Billie Joe about that. He said the last time he saw him was perfect, and that's the way he wanted to remember him. Then everybody went to go see Neurosis because Neurosis was playing at the Great American Music Hall. Kevin and I didn't go in because we were pretty much, 'Just screw it.' Neurosis pretty much sucked at that point anyway."

On November 10, the band appeared on *The Tonight Show*, again performing 'Minority'. At the end of the month, the band returned overseas for more shows. *Warning* was certified Gold in December, and the year ended with the band doing four radio-sponsored shows in Fairfax, Virginia; Seattle, Washington; San Francisco at the Bill Graham Civic Auditorium; and the Universal Amphitheater at Universal Studios in LA. A Q&A the band filled out for the show's program was typically jokey: "Favourite album this year" was *Check Please* by The Influents; "Favourite stocking stuffer" was a "Jeff Striker Penis Pump"; "All I Want for Christmas is: Sox"; "Favorite food to eat while on tour: Whisky"; and "I would most like to tour with: Santa Claus."

In retrospect, *Warning* would come to be seen as a turning point in the band's career, a necessary developmental step that would lay the groundwork for their artistic breakthrough with *American Idiot*. But it's hard to recognise a turning point when you're going through one. And though *Warning* and the subsequent tours had achieved a measure of success, there would now come a growing sense of disatisfaction with the direction of the band's career. It was easy to overlook this as 2000 became 2001, for several months of touring in the US and overseas awaited Green Day after the Christmas break. After that, it would be time to write more songs and record the next album. Certainly no one would ever have guessed that the Green Day would not release another new studio album for four more years.

CHAPTER 9

Here A Superhit,
There A Shenanigan

"When I was doing Insomniac *I didn't want to do anything that sounded like* Dookie. *When I was doing* Nimrod *I didn't want to do anything that was like* Insomniac. *With* Warning *I didn't want to do anything like I did before, and now I don't know what the hell I want to do."*

— *Billie Joe to* RollingStone.com, *November 26, 2001*

In some ways, the next few years found Green Day in something of a holding pattern. Not that the band wasn't working; as the new millennium began, Green Day was where they could usually be found — on the road. A US concert tour opened January 11 in Dallas and ran through the end of the month. In March they played a short tour of Japan. Summer would also see a hectic round of touring. And there were plenty of new releases; appearances on compilations and soundtracks, non-album B-sides, unreleased material available on the group's website, and the release of both greatest hits and rarities sets, not to mention their innumerable side projects. But there would be no new full-length album released until the fall of

2004; not unusual for some big acts, but it would be a first for Green Day.

The year also began with a new single to promote, the title track from *Warning*, which peaked at number three Modern Rock, number 24 Mainstream Rock; in the UK, it reached number 27. Adeline released a vinyl single with the non-album B-sides 'Scumbag' and The Ramones cover, 'Outsider'; non-album B-sides on other versions of the single included 'Suffocate' and a cover of Hüsker Dü's 'I Don't Want To Know If You Are Lonely'. The video for 'Warning', directed by Francis Lawrence, was filmed in San Francisco and played off the track's lyrical suggestion of ignoring life's warnings. A young man is shown going about his daily routine, all of which involve a degree of risk — running with scissors, swimming immediately after eating, accepting candy from a stranger — and surviving all the potential dangers without consequence. The man's escapades are intercut with shots of the band performing the song in their house. The video had its premiere on MTV on January 22.

The group made a steady stream of TV appearances to promote the single, first appearing on *The Tonight Show* on February 2 performing the song. On February 23, they taped an appearance for *Mad TV*, again performing 'Warning' in addition to 'Blood, Sex, and Booze'. (Terry Linehan from The Frustrators played second guitar as Jason White was on tour with another of his bands, The Influents, at the time.) Billie Joe played an acoustic guitar during the former number, which, combined with the blue denim jacket he wore, made him come across as an earnest singer-songwriter type; he struck more traditional "rock star" poses with his electric guitar during the second song. The studio audience got an additional treat as the group also performed 'Brat' and 'The Ballad Of Wilhelm Fink' in between the two broadcast numbers.

The same month, Adeline Records held their first showcase at San Francisco's Fillmore on February 10. The Frustrators and The Influents were both on the bill, as were Fetish and One Time Angels. Pinhead Gunpowder also played occasional dates throughout the spring, at Oakland's Starry Plough on March 9 and at The Clock Tower in Benicia, California on April 16. Later in the year, Billie Joe would also sit in with The Influents for two shows in July. Meanwhile, Tré was occupied with the latest addition to his family; his wife, Claudia, gave birth to their son, Frankito, in February.

In between touring, the group shot the video for their next single, 'Waiting', over the weekend of April 14 to 15, at a house in the West Adams neighbourhood of Los Angeles. The video debuted on April 24, when Green Day appeared on Montreal's music channel Musique Plus, playing a 90-minute set for a studio audience. The clip, directed by Marc Webb, was a straight performance video, with the group seen playing in the living room of a comfortably lived-in house, while their friends dance and frolic around them. The song was the lowest charting from *Warning*, only reaching number 26 Modern Rock and number 34 in the UK.

On April 15, Joey Ramone, lead singer of The Ramones, succumbed to lymphatic cancer after a lengthy struggle. The band had been one of Green Day's biggest influences, and Mike quickly issued a public statement, noting that Ramone's death had occurred on Easter Sunday: "Ironically, religion gets its Icon back and American punk culture loses theirs. I think an end of an era has come and I've never felt as old as I do right now...Thanks always come a day late and a dollar short but my respect has and will always be there for the band that showed me that simple songs and a simple life could make you happy." He signed off, "Oh yeah!! and the kid in The Ramones T-shirt will always be cool... GABBA GABBA HEY." Billie Joe later told *Launch.com*, "If it wasn't for them, my band wouldn't exist. They're one of those bands that definitely had a direct influence or impact on the way we even look at songwriting." The band later provided a taped musical tribute that aired at a fiftieth birthday party celebration in honor of the late singer, held May 19 at New York's Hammerstein Ballroom. US Representative Gary Ackerman issued a congressional proclamation on the same date, declaring it "Joey Ramone Day."

The group's next visit to New York was more than a little hectic. They began April 26 by appearing on *The Howard Stern Show*. Then it was off to *The Late Show*. In reference to Tré's previous antics on the program, host David Letterman noted while introducing the group, "It's great that we have a pain management doctor in the audience, because every time on the show, the drummer — who's unstable — does something strange and he hurts himself. . . keep your eye on the drummer!" The band then launched into 'Waiting'. Tré didn't hurt himself, but toward the song's end, he did stand on his drum stool and dumped a box of potato flakes over his head to the audience's laughter and applause; even Billie Joe had a bit of difficulty keeping a straight face. At the song's end, Tré rolled over his kit, lay on the floor, then got up and ran into the audience, leaping on a lap or two before escaping out the back door. "A very troubled youngster!" Letterman observed.

And the band's day wasn't over yet. They next headed to the legendary venue CBGB's to see their friend Jesse Malin in his new band, Bellevue. (Malin, who'd also played with East Bay band D Generation, later signed to Adeline as a solo artist.) Green Day then took the stage for a surprise set of their own, playing to a delighted audience estimated to be around 100 people. Many of the songs were drawn from the group's first two albums, with only two songs from their new album. Though the size of the crowd meant it was less frenzied than their usual audiences, a young man did manage to briefly crowd-surf during '409 In Your Coffeemaker'. The band also chatted a lot more between songs, as they had in earlier years. "I like that song," Billie Joe said after playing 'Going To Pasalacqua'. "That's a good song. I like that one. If I do say so myself!" When someone shouted a request for 'Mahogany', Billie Joe responded with, "You don't think I can play that song, do you?" then proceeded to perform the song's first verse. "That is some creepy shit, ain't it?" Mike observed afterwards. "Reminds you of being molested by your fuckin' uncle or something!" Billie Joe regained control of the situation by putting in his own request. "I like this song, therefore, we're going to play it," he said by way of introducing 'She'. "This is not a democracy, fuck off!"

Later that week they attended the California Music Awards, held April 28 at Oakland's Henry J. Kaiser Auditorium. Green Day ended up walking away with "everything. . . but Carlos Santana's hat," wrote journalist Joel Selvin, winning an impressive eight awards: Artist of the Year, Outstanding Group, Billie Joe named Outstanding Male Vocalist and Outstanding Songwriter, Mike named Outstanding Bassist, Tré named Outstanding Drummer, and *Warning* named both Outstanding Album and Outstanding Punk Rock/Ska Album. The Outstanding

Songwriter award was especially notable for Billie Joe, given that the competition had included Neil Young, perhaps prompting him to note, "Punk rock is about writing songs!" on accepting the award. When Tré won his Outstanding Drummer award, he pulled off the same on-off stunt he'd done on *The Late Show*, dashing up, running across the stage, pausing briefly to snatch his award, and tearing right off again. What host Huey Lewis meant when he said, "That Green Day, they're all class — in a weird sort of way," wasn't exactly clear, but the group returned for a brief musical performance at the show's end.

Work on side projects also continued apace, with Billie Joe co-writing the track 'Unforgiven' for The Go-Go's reunion album, *God Bless The Go-Go's*, released May 15. The collaboration came about after Billie Joe joined the group onstage during a performance the previous August, singing along to 'Our Lips Are Sealed', then hung out with them after the show. He also appeared on a record released by his old OpIvy friend Jesse Michaels and his new band, Common Rider, whose EP — *Thief In A Sleeping Town* — was released on August 22 on Lookout. (Jason White also appeared on the EP.) In a "Top 5" list for *Rolling Stone*, Billie Joe had previously cited Common Rider's 1999 album *Last Wave Rockers* as one of his favourite records of the year. He also served as an engineer and mixer on Tilt's 2001 album *Been Where? Did What?*

The group's last US tour of the year started in June, with the band performing 'Waiting' on *The Tonight Show* on June 13 as a warm-up. The tour began June 17 in Minneapolis, ran until July 3, then picked up again on July 20 and ran until August 5. While in New York, they appeared on *Late Night with Conan O'Brien* on June 28, again performing 'Waiting'. On tour, Billie Joe was again announcing, "That's it for our set list. Do you have any requests?" after a few opening songs, encouraging audience suggestions. And once the band tired of honouring requests for Green Day songs, they urged the crowd to suggest covers. At a show at Milwaukee's Eagles Ballroom on June 18, for example, they ended up covering 'Blitzkrieg Bop', Ozzy Osbourne's 'Crazy Train', part of 'Eye Of The Tiger', and what the *Milwaukee Journal Sentinel* described as "a few quick jabs at Linkin Park and Limp Bizkit." When a fan was invited onstage to play guitar, the paper noted he had to "pass a rigorous test to prove his worthiness: jump from the balcony and crowd surf to the stage.

And although it took him a while to build up the nerve for the plummet, he eventually made it to the stage and proceeded to show up Armstrong with his guitar chops." The show ended with 'When I Come Around', the crowd singing along with gusto when it became apparent Billie Joe couldn't remember all the words. "Not surprisingly, fans found out what they already knew: the band is still the ultimate '90s punk-pop group," the *Sentinel* concluded. The *Washington Post* was somewhat less complimentary during the tour, saying of the group's June 24 date at Washington, D.C.'s Bender Arena, "Mostly it was just three guys telling noisy tales about boredom and horniness in the suburbs, with a very limited musical vocabulary," though the writer did concede, "It's an approach to rock that has survived the onslaught of hip-hop and electronica and outlived grunge and metal. As long as there are suburbs and guitars, it's going to inspire kids to pogo. And start their own bands." While in D.C., the group appeared on a local radio station and Tré performed an ode to fellatio that would've confirmed the *Post's* assessment of the band's "horniness."

After the completion of the US tour, the group returned to Studio 880 to record some more songs: re-recording of 'Maria' (a song they'd previously recorded in March and which appeared as a B-side on the vinyl version of 'Waiting', released by Adeline) along with a new song, 'Poprocks & Coke'. In an interview with *MTV.com*, Mike revealed the group was also working on other songs, ostensibly for their next album. "The songs are coming out quickly, but we don't want to force anything," he said. "Our thing is just get in there and pound the songs out and let them come out when they're ready." He added that the next record would not be as (relatively) low key as *Warning*: "I feel like the last record is so complete that to try to take over where that one left off would be kind of futile. . . I just think the fact that we've had a nice break from making hard and fast music has made us want to do it [again]."

The group had continued to drop by Studio 880, even when they weren't working. "Whenever they're home, they're here," says John Lucasey. "They always come by. If they're going to the airport, I'll get cars in my lots, and I'd be like, 'Who the hell's car is it? Oh, it's Tré's, he must be gone visiting New York or something.' Or they'll just stop by and get a burrito and just sit in and ask what's going on."

They even got involved in the studio's renovations, truly making it "the house that Green Day built" in more ways than one. "During *Warning* I started construction on a second room, which they love very much now," Lucasey says. "I've consulted Mike on a lot of things, like on the building of the spaces, and even the offices. Mike designed his house, and he's designed a couple of houses, and he's helped design a restaurant. It's just amazing, his artistic mind. So whenever I'd be stuck on something, he'd be the person I called, the only other person who I thought was wacked enough to understand what's going on. And he would say, 'No, what you're gonna do is. . .' He wouldn't suggest, he would tell you. A lot of the elements in this studio are Mike Dirnt-born. In fact, for a short time he had an office here. He even cut the ribbons for the front of the building here. I couldn't think of anybody better to do it!"

The group then headed to Europe. By late August, they hit the UK festival circuit, beginning with the Reading Festival on the twenty-fourth (where, after Tré's drum kit, a guitar, and a speaker stack were all set on fire, the group took up acoustic instruments to finish their set), Leeds on the twenty-fifth, and Glasgow on the twenty-sixth. The group recorded an interview for Steve Lamacq's *Evening Sessions* Radio 1 program and also attended the *Kerrang!* awards, having been nominated in three categories: Best International Live Act, Best Band in the World, and Classic Songwriter, winning in the latter category. The band then returned to the states.

As a result, they were at home when the September 11 attacks on America occurred. After hearing the news, they ended up going into Studio 880, though not to work. "They came in and just sat together for a couple days," John Lucasey recalls, "not wanting to record, or even watch the news anymore. They just needed each other, as well as their families."

In the immediate aftermath of the attacks, a list of "lyrically questionable" songs circulated among the 1,100-plus radio stations that were part of the Clear Channel Communications network, with a suggestion that they be temporarily pulled from playlists lest they prove too disturbing. Songs that referenced planes (Peter, Paul, and Mary's 'Leavin' on a Jet Plane', Steve Miller's 'Jet Airliner') were perhaps obvious contenders, but the inclusion of tracks like The Bangles'

'Walk Like An Egyptian' and Green Day's 'Brain Stew' were more puzzling. Even John Lennon's decidedly anti-war 'Imagine' and Frank Sinatra's 'New York, New York,' made the list, though these were songs that some might take comfort in hearing. Indeed, *E! Online* reported that one New York City radio station said both numbers were among their most-requested songs that week.

When news of the list was made public, Clear Channel hastily issued a press release denying that any of the songs were being censored, saying, "Clear Channel Radio has not banned any songs from any of its radio stations. It is up to every radio station program director and general manager to understand their market, listen to their listeners, and guide their station's music selections according to local sensitivities." They did admit that the list was compiled by one of their program directors, but added, "This was not a mandate, nor was the list generated out of the corporate radio offices. It was a grassroots effort that was apparently circulated among program directors." (The *New York Times* said that a "smaller list" of songs was generated by the corporate office, "but an overzealous regional executive began contributing suggestions and circulating the list via e-mail, where it continued to grow.")

It was indicative of a sea change in the cultural climate of the US; post-9/11, there was going to be no room for dissent. As President George Bush put it when he addressed a joint session of the US Congress on September 20, "Either you are with us or you are with the terrorists," and performers who later attacked the administration ran the risk of being penalised for their views. In one of the most reported examples, when Natalie Maines of The Dixie Chicks made the statement, "Just so you know, we're ashamed that the President of the United States is from Texas" (The Dixie Chicks' home state) at a London concert in March 2003, the group's songs were yanked from radio playlists across America.

But interestingly, the members of Green Day didn't face censure when they made similar remarks. The US began bombing Afghanistan on October 7 and Tré told *Launch.com* the same month: "I object to any killing at all. It's terrible what happened [on September 11] and I think retaliation definitely makes sense and it's definitely one option. But, personally, I prefer peace." Even more surprising was his blunt opposition to the Bush administration: "I knew the day that George Bush was elected President that we were in deep, deep shit." This was an exceptionally daring statement for a major artist to make at a time when Bush was enjoying record-high approval ratings of around 90%. Further, it was less than a month after then-US Press Secretary Ari Fleischer had ominously warned the American public that they "need to watch what they say, watch what they do" during a White House press conference. Tré was even brasher when talking to Joel McIver of *Record Collector*: "Take my personal freedoms, go ahead. I don't care. Tap my phone, Mr. Bush. Do whatever you want. Fuck my ass too, it's all right. God bless America!"

Adeline Records had previously scheduled a showcase at Gilman for September 16, with The Thumbs, Agent 51, One Time Angels, and The Influents on the bill. The show went ahead and Green Day also put in a surprise appearance, defying Gilman's "No bands on major labels" ban. "No one wants to think about what happened a few days ago," said Mike. "So let's try and have some fun." Yet the band's performance also showed that some grudges never die. "No one bitched on the night," Mike later told Q about their Gilman appearance, "but they sure debated it the day after." Still, not everyone felt that way; one attendee told *Spin*, "It was like they never left. Who they were and where they've been didn't even enter into it." Further Adeline showcases were held in October at the Showcase Theater in Corona on the twentieth (with The Frustrators, The Influents, One Time Angels, and Agent 51 on the bill) and the Troubadour in Hollywood on the twenty-first (with Fetish replacing Agent 51). The Frustrators also played a show with LA speed punks, The Dickies, on September 22 at the Minnow in Alameda, California.

In November, Green Day business was back to the forefront, with the release of the greatest-hits collections *International Superhits* (on CD) and the accompanying *International Supervideos* on DVD, on November 13 in the US (the day before in most of the rest of the world). The group hadn't initially been keen on releasing a greatest-hits set. "We were kind of indifferent about it," Billie Joe admitted to *Guitar World*. "We all felt it was perhaps too early in our career to release a best-of. But when we started to add up all of the successful singles we've had, we realised we had the makings of a pretty damn good record."

"We wrote them, you bought them, and now you're buying them again," Tré joked to another reporter. But along with the new songs 'Maria' and 'Poprocks & Coke', the CD included 'J.A.R.', which hadn't previously been featured on a Green Day album. 'Maria' was the first track on the album and opened with an excerpt from the interview a five-year-old Billie Joe had done for his 'Look For Love' single, which, by 2001, must have felt like it had been recorded a lifetime ago. The song was an invigorating slice of pop-punk, with surprisingly biting lyrics lurking underneath, the title character being an unabashed, free-wheeling insurrectionist. Conversely, 'Poprocks & Coke' was a straightforward love song that wouldn't have been out of place on *Warning*.

The cover of both the CD and the DVD featured the same image: the group's forms in silhouette, their name above them, and the release's title below. Both the band name and title emerged from a pop art-esque band of bright colours: pink, orange, and yellow. "Obviously, they were taking the piss out of the idea of doing a greatest-hits release in the first place with such an ostentatious title," says Chris Bilheimer of the design. ("We prefer to call [the album's songs] 'Superhits' in all ridiculousness," Tré confirmed to *Launch.com*.) "The first thing I thought of with *International Superhits* were those compilations you see advertised on TV. I thought, let's go over the top and do a really garish design that looks like those old compilations. I did one mock-up of that design, and the outline of the band is actually a photograph from the *Warning* photo sessions, because I didn't have a current photo session. So I just outlined that. Then I went to D.C. — they were playing a radio festival up there — with just this one idea. I showed up with one piece of paper, my first idea, and they were like, 'I love it, it's done.' For *Superhits*, they gave me the title and that was it." Bilheimer also put together another EPK for the record, hosted by comedian and writer Greg Behrendt. "I only spent a couple of days in the studio and just filmed them a little bit," he says. "For *Superhits* they only recorded two new songs, so there wasn't a whole lot going on."

The album only reached a surprising number 40 in the *Billboard* Top 200, but reached number 15 in the UK. In assessing the band's career, Billie Joe told *RollingStone.com*, "Everything that we've achieved has come naturally to us. And everything that has come to us, it wasn't about some huge marketing plan. I think people genuinely liked our songs. A lot of bands have to trade in their integrity to get what they want, and the gross thing about it is that they have no problems doing it at all. I think we've accomplished a true sense of independence."

The group made numerous TV appearances at the time of the *International* releases. The week of November 12 saw them in Vancouver, B.C., taping an appearance on *The Chris Isaak Show* (a connection undoubtedly fostered by Rob Cavallo's having produced Isaak's 1998 album, *Speak of the Devil*). The episode, entitled "The Wrong Number," had the band playing with Isaak on the songs 'Hitchin' A Ride' and Isaak's own 'One Day' in between trashing Isaak's home. It aired the following year, and the group also appeared on a subsequent episode, "Charity Begins at Home." Then it was back to Los Angeles, where the group performed a particularly intense 'Hitchin' A Ride' on *The Tonight Show* on November 19. Billie Joe let out a few sustained cries during the instrumental breaks, then motioned for the band to play softly during the break before the final chorus, meaning that when the group came back in at full volume, the effect was that of a punch straight to the gut. At the song's conclusion, Billie Joe stood on his left leg with his right cocked behind him as he played the final chord, then nonchalantly holding his right hand in the air. They also appeared on the radio program *Rockline*, playing live in the studio (including older songs like 'She', 'Scattered', 'Who Wrote Holden Caulfield?', and, the only track from *Superhits*, 'Minority') and taking questions from callers. The next day they appeared on *The Late Late Show*, performing 'Minority' and 'Maria', with Tré giving his drum set a "love tap" with a bat at the end of the latter song.

A video was shot at the end of October for the song 'Macy's Day Parade', which also appeared on the *International Superhits* CD, though it had not been released as a single. "That was just a simple one," says director Mark Kohr. "All it is, is a one-shot video of Billie walking through this defunct steel plant site that's been vacant for years. It was about, in a certain kind of way, leaving behind failures and having the hope to move on; and so it's just basically him walking through the ruins, and then saying, 'There's hope' and then leaving." The video was shot in black and white, underscoring the poignancy of the song, with Billie Joe looking unusually conservative with neat, closely cropped hair and wearing a suit and tie. The rest of the band plays in an uncharacteristically subdued fashion off to the side, and Billie Joe eventually joins them, but only strums the guitar for a minute before putting it down in favour of wandering through the industrial wasteland again. "It did get played some, but not that much," says Kohr. "It wasn't that popular." A video for 'Poprocks & Coke' was also prepared. As in 'Last Ride In', the band isn't seen performing the song; the video is a compilation of footage shot at rehearsals and studio sessions.

Green Day's fans were also pleased by the sudden appearance of some Billie Joe demos on the band's website, recorded in his basement studio. The quality was rough, but it was great fun to hear Billie Joe working out songs — none of which were later recorded by Green Day — at home. Soon after, three Christmas songs also appeared: 'The First Noel', 'Rocking Around the Christmas Tree', and 'Santa Claus Is Coming To Town'.

There was more touring coming up in 2002, but given that there was no new album to promote, the schedule was more relaxed. On January 19, the group appeared at the Winter X Games VI in Aspen, Colorado. Then came a gig they probably wouldn't have missed for anything in the world, when The Ramones were inducted into the Rock And Roll Hall Of Fame. The ceremony was held March 18, 2002, at New York's Waldorf-Astoria Hotel. Pearl Jam's Eddie Vedder, sporting a new mohawk, gave the induction speech, which rambled on for 17 minutes and prompted some booing from the audience (Vedder's response:"Fuck you"), but which also recognised the magic of what the group achieved, a quality Vedder saw as missing from the current music scene. "They were armed with two-minute songs that they rattled off like machine gun fire," he said, "and it was enough to change the Earth's revolution. Now it's Disney kids singing songs written by old men and being marketed to six- and seven-year-olds, so some kind of change might have to happen again soon."

And then it was Green Day's turn. With Billie Joe and Mike in "concert stance," pummeling their instruments fiercely as Tré pounded on his drum kit behind them, the group blasted through a powerhouse set of 'Rockaway Beach', 'Teenage Lobotomy', and 'Blitzkrieg Bop', which induced a number of the black-tie audience to jump to their feet, enthusiastically punching their fists in the air. "It was like Joey was in the room and we played our asses off for him," Billie Joe later told *Rolling Stone*. It was noted the group left the event immediately afterwards without heading backstage where reporters traditionally wait at the event to conduct interviews, but the band members claimed they weren't aware of this procedure. Instead, the group headed for a party upstairs, dragging Dee Dee Ramone into the elevator with them. Unfortunately, the elevator got stuck, forcing everyone to climb out, but as Billie Joe noted, "I would have been fine getting stuck in the elevator with Dee Dee Ramone any day of the week."

Later, on the group's website, Billie Joe addressed what he saw as a mistaken view about The Ramones; that they were ultimately "unsuccessful" because they were only critically acclaimed and had not sold many records. "I thought they were the most successful band in the world," Billie Joe's statement read in part. "The Ramones has this sort of good following everywhere. And everywhere, all these punk bands had started up — thousands and thousands of punk-rock bands. And I think that is way more important than having a hit single or a Platinum record. I would give that in a minute to have something like that. I think that is the most important kind of success that a band can ever have — the ability to influence." He also mentioned the thrill of finally meeting Dee Dee Ramone ("For some people, that might be like meeting Marlon Brando or something"), and was pleased that the green-haired "son of the rhythm section in The Talking Heads" (Chris Franz and Tina Weymouth) had so obviously enjoyed Green Day's set; in footage of the event, both the couple's sons, Egan and Robin Franz, can be seen bopping away in front of the stage.

At the end of the month, Green Day began a quick tour of Japan (a live seven-track album taken from the tour, *Tune In Tokyo*, was released that October in Japan only). It was then announced the band was joining forces with Blink-182 for what was billed as The Pop Disaster Tour (a name Mike had come up with), set to open April 17 at the Centennial Garden in Bakersfield, California and running through June 17. The initial suggestion for the tour had come from the Blink-182 camp. While batting around ideas for a summer tour, the band's bassist, Mark Hoppus, recalling the earlier Monsters Of Rock festivals (held in Castle Donington, England, featuring heavy-metal acts), had thought, why not a Monsters Of Punk Rock tour? Green Day proved to be receptive, while Reprise also thought the tour would be a good way of reminding audiences exactly who had influenced bands like Blink-182 in the first place. "There were a handful of new bands influenced by Green Day that a younger generation was paying more attention to than Green Day," Warner Bros. chairman and CEO Tom Whalley later told *Billboard*. "Before we lost that younger generation, we wanted to make them aware of Green Day."

Though officially co-headliners (and both would play 75-minute sets), Blink-182 closed the show, but bassist Mark Hoppus was gracious enough to tell *Rolling Stone* that Green Day was "a huge influence for us. Green Day breaking punk rock into the mainstream consciousness really helped us and opened up people's minds to our kind of music." For his part, Billie Joe joked about the "big production" the band was going to bring on the road: "We're going to be biting the heads off bats," he said. He added that he hoped Blink-182's presence would provide "a challenge... I'm looking for people to walk away saying, 'Whoa! That was a great show!'" Hoppus suggested the group consider swapping set lists on occasion, an idea unfortunately not taken up.

Darryl Eaton of Creative Artists Agency (CAA) — who booked both acts — was perhaps a little indelicate when, in reference to the tour's ticket price range of $30 to $35, he said to *Billboard*, "That's only $5 to $7 over what we charged on the last Blink tour, so in essence, they're getting Green Day for $5 to $7." In fact, reviews tended to favour Green Day over Blink-182. In reviewing the tour's April 24 date at the Forum in Inglewood, California, *Variety* said that Green Day "proved it is the better of the two veteran bands with a supertight showcase of its many hits," citing 'Waiting' as a particular highlight, "though Armstrong's poor harmonica playing should be removed from the tune." By comparison, the reviewer held his nose over Blink-182's "endless potty-mouth shtick [which] seemed even more gratuitous and juvenile than usual after Green Day's excellent set," and, even worse, noted that "the crowd appeared to grow restless long before the band's time was up."

On April 27, as the group was playing San Francisco's Shoreline

Auditorium, they were also being honoured across the bay at the California Music Awards, again held at the Oakland's Henry J. Kaiser Auditorium, winning Outstanding Group. Two days later, the band played even closer to home at the Oakland Arena, with profits from the show going to the city's Children's Hospital. Billie Joe told *Launch.com*, "We've been dicked over on some charities but this organisation is solid and everyone's money [from the] tickets is going directly to Children's Hospital... Plus, you know, Tré's been in and out of Children's Hospital his entire life, either breaking something or in the psych ward. And then my kids and his kids and Mike's kids will probably do the same thing."

In its review of the show, the *San Francisco Chronicle* unsurprisingly came down in favour of the home crew. "Green Day remains the hotter band," wrote Neva Chonin. With the group dressed in "fashionable black," "Billie Joe Armstrong was a consummate ham, leaping and bouncing across the stage, goading fans, climbing on stacks of speakers to shower the audience with a squirt gun, and leading the group through spastic punk jam sessions," while delivering "a string of greatest hits that kept the crowd singing along even as it danced itself breathless." Conversely, "Blink's 60-minute, paint-by-numbers set paled in the aftermath of the Oakland punk-pop pioneers' rousing performance." To Chonin's ears, the "fuzzy sound" only "highlighted the fact that many of Blink's songs sound depressingly alike" and she also took exception to Blink-182's vulgarity: "A few sex jokes are funny; nonstop scatology is a snooze."

The spring had also seen the release of The Frustrators' first album, *Achtung Jackass*, released March 5 on Adeline. "An awesome East Bay display of truly magnificent musical madness" read one ad for the record, though the subsequent questions the ad posed — "New wave? Punk? Country? Ball-busting rock? Stand-up comedy? All of the above?" — remained unanswered. In the summer came the release of another Green Day collection, *Shenanigans*, a compilation of B-sides and rarities that was released July 2. The album offered fans a chance to pick up stray songs they might have missed, given the number of non-album tracks the band had released over the years on import singles, compilations, and other types of releases. Songs like the '50s-flavored 'On the Wagon' and the cover of The Kinks' 'Tired Of Waiting For You' (which featured some wonderfully dreamy harmonies) dated back to the *Dookie* era. There were other fun covers, such as Fang's 'I Want To Be On TV' (B-side of 'Geek Stink Breath') and The Ramones' 'Outsider' (which had appeared on a Ramones tribute album and the soundtrack of *The New Guy*). 'Espionage' was another soundtrack number, an *homage* to the music of James Bond spy thrillers and perfectly suited for the spy film satire, *Austin Powers 2: The Spy Who Shagged Me*.

'Do Da Da' had been recorded during *Insomniac*, when it was then titled 'Stuck With You,' not to be confused with the song of that name that did end up on *Insomniac*. It first appeared as a 'Brain Stew' B-side. The raucous 'Desensitized' was recorded during the *Nimrod* sessions, and Billie Joe later admitted the band wished they'd put it on the album. Instead, it became a 'Good Riddance' B-side and as a bonus track on the import version of *Nimrod*, along with 'Suffocate', 'You Lied', and 'Do Da Da'. Mike had written lyrics for both 'Scumbag' (a 'Warning' B-side) and 'Ha Ha You're Dead' (which had also appeared on the Adeline compilation, *Every Dog Will Have Its Day*), a kiss-off to an enemy that brought the record to a satisfying close.

The cover of *Shenanigans* had a spray-painted portrait of the group on a wall next to a public telephone, created by Chris Bilheimer, an idea he got from a fashion spread in a magazine. "Instead of photographs of the clothing, the guy had spray painted pictures of models wearing the clothing," he explains. "It was such a great concept, that I took the band a copy of the magazine and said, 'What if we spray paint stencils of you guys?' and they said, 'Great.' I did it and that was it. That was another kind of easy one." Or, relatively easy. "Something that elaborate takes about an hour and a half," says Bilheimer. "I had fourteen stencils. Different big paper stencils. And I actually just spray painted it onto a sheet of plywood and then photographed a blank wall, and faked it on the computer. Which makes me feel like a big pussy, because if I was really punk rock I would have done it and gotten arrested. But it's not exactly something you can do very stealthily." If you look closely, you can see that the abandoned cans of spray paint that lie under the portrait are all labeled "Green Day." "That sort of expresses my obsessive compulsive side," says Bilheimer. "I still have some of those cans here in my office."

The inside cover features a collage of images, mostly drawn from the group's previous album covers, with individual portraits of the band spray painted on top. "With the inside of *Shenanigans* there's a sense of you're looking at a span of their career," says Bilheimer. "In a lot of cases, it's the cast-offs, the flotsam and jetsam of what they've been doing. That was the concept — it's posters from their career and you're just seeing parts of them, you're seeing the leftover scraps and pieces." The spray-painted portraits on top also give a sense of their work being defaced. "That's one of my favourite things about working with Green Day, there's a huge sense of humour in what they do," Bilheimer says. "Which there isn't so much in the stuff I do for R.E.M."

The album performed better than *International Superhits* had in the US, reaching number 27 on the *Billboard* Top 200 chart. But the record also got some mixed reviews; some described it as filler, simply released to squeeze more money from the fans, but others not only welcomed a collection that pulled together a number of rarities, they felt the songs were more than capable of standing on their own merits. "There are bands who write songs as and when the record company demands," said *Kerrang!*, "and then there are bands who just can't help but knock out gem after gem — on tour, off tour, and in their sleep. There's enough quality material here to suggest Green Day fall squarely in the latter category."

July also marked the start of another UK tour, which began July 11 in Manchester, and included shows in Ireland, Scotland, Wales, and England. The shows began with the spirited 'Maria', perhaps not as familiar, perhaps not a big hit, but with an invigorating guitar line and propulsive drumbeat that never failed to get the crowd stomping and cheering (the flash pot explosions after the first verse didn't hurt either). Audiences were always ready to sing-along with old favourites like 'Longview' and 'Basket Case', and newer live favourites like 'Hitchin' A Ride' and 'King For A Day' kept the pace lively. The setlist was split fairly evenly among Green Day's Reprise albums, though 'Brain Stew'-'Jaded' was usually the only number from *Insomniac*. In his review of the second of two shows at London's Wembley Arena for *DotMusic online*, Matt Thompson noted the band's usual antics (including flash pot explosions and Billie Joe spraying the crowd with an oversize water pistol), but added, "Between the madness it's easy to forget the sheer punk grandeur of Green Day's songs. . . there's no sign that the band have lost their love for this performing malarkey and after doing it for so long they sure have mastered their art, right down to the vacant stare in Billie Joe's eyes and the shake of drummer, Tré Cool's blue rinse hair. . . The show is both accomplished and ragged, but always top class, and by the time it's over there's not a single punter who isn't grinning like a dumb kid and wishing the band will carry on all night."

While overseas, the group also taped various radio appearances for the BBC. And then came another long break from live performance, at least in the guise of Green Day; another two years, in fact. Work on the next album continued, as did the band members' involvement in various side projects, such as Billie Joe's appearance on an episode of the TV show *Haunted*, playing a gambler. Mike took time out to have wrist surgery, as years of bass playing had finally resulted in his developing carpal tunnel syndrome.

He also entered the restaurant business, becoming co-owner of the Rudy's Can't Fail Café, which opened in Emeryville in September, at the corner of Park Avenue and Hollis Street. The site had previously been the location of Eugene's Ranch House, a diner that had opened in 1964 and had been patronised by the many factory workers in the area. But as the factories began closing, business had slacked off.

The owners decided to sell in 2002 and the building was purchased by Jeffrey Bischoff, the guitarist in Tilt. He also ran the merchandising company Cinderblock and had been a customer of Eugene's for many years. His partners in the venture were Zach Zeisler, his accountant; Steve Mills, a general contractor; and Mike, who was initially more of a silent partner ("Rumors of an anonymous, millionaire rock-star owner swirl around the place like meringue on a banana cream pie" said an early story on the restaurant), but his involvement eventually became publicly known.

The restaurant took its name from The Clash song, 'Rudie Can't Fail' (from *London Calling*), and its design was '50s-retro mixed with punk-rock touches, such as a display of Barbie dolls identically dressed as waitresses, vintage games, toys under the glass-topped tables, and a bulletin board with a Polaroid picture of the "Band Of The Month." The specials might have rock-themed names like "Mr. Roadie's Fish & Chips,"

"Give 'em Enough Meatloaf," and "God Save Southern Fried Chicken," but the generous portions and reasonable prices made the café an instant hit with the locals, such as businesses like Pixar Animation Studios, located across the street. (Coincidentally, Clash lead singer and guitarist Joe Strummer died that December of a heart attack; Billie Joe posted a version of The Clash's 'Bankrobber' he'd recorded on the band's website as a tribute.)

The state of the American union was also very much on the band's mind at the time. When the US began bombing Afghanistan in October 2001, fans who visited the group's website were solicited for their views. And as talk of a war with Iraq heated up in 2002, Green Day's opposition to the administration became even stronger. Billie Joe posted an audio message on the group's website that urged fans to sign a petition opposing the war (or, in his words, "strongly urging [President Bush] to re-think his plans for military invasion," adding, "This petition isn't only for people who live in America, but people all over the world. So, even if you know someone at work or at school who doesn't even know what Green Day is, tell them to log on to *greenday.net*, type in their name and where they're from. I want to get as many names as possible."

Billie Joe later wrote he was gratified by the response to his appeal: "All of the opinions were honest and polite and nasty, and for that I commend you," he said. The group's seemingly new interest in politics was but a taste of what was to come.

CHAPTER 10

At The Threshold

"Breaking up was an option. We were arguing a lot and we were miserable. We needed to shift directions."

— *Mike to* Rolling Stone, *February 24, 2005*

2003 did not begin on an auspicious note for Billie Joe, who was arrested on January 5 for driving while intoxicated. Taken into custody at the Berkeley County Jail, he paid his bail fee of $1,053 and was released.

More important was the looming crisis in the band's career. Since the release of *International Superhits*, the band had been asked repeatedly about the release of their next studio album and the answer was always some variation of, "We're working on it." *MTV.com* even reported that the band had "seven songs written and another three under construction." "The songs are coming out quickly, but we don't want to force anything," Mike was quoted as saying. "Our thing is just get in there and pound the songs out and let them come out when they're ready." But no release dates ever seemed to be forthcoming.

It was later said that the band had completed an album during this time, provisionally entitled *Cigarettes And Valentines*, but that the master tapes had been stolen, forcing the band to start all over again. There has always been some mystery surrounding this claim. Where exactly were the tapes stolen from? Several stories stated it was the band's recording studio, but owner John Lucasey insists this isn't so. "They were *not* taken out of Studio 880," he says. "We take so much pride about our security. Our front gates stay closed, you gotta check in once you're inside, we've got safes and everything. I had clients asking me about that, and I'm like, 'No, trust me. It's all good here.'" Were the police ever notified? Were only master tapes taken and not tapes of rehearsals, demos, jams? Were there no backup copies available? Nor did whoever took the tapes apparently know their value, for the tracks have never appeared on bootlegs or on the Internet. As *Q* noted, "Armstrong seems cagey on the subject and even says that perhaps [the tapes were] just 'mislaid.'" In addition, a December 2004 *Billboard* story said the tapes weren't stolen, but "accidentally erased from a computer drive" and quoted Mike as saying, "We still have some burned CDs but those are not good enough to release."

But for whatever reason, the group was now free to start over in a new direction. And not just musically; for the first time, the band members also decided to address the growing grievances between them. Mike told *Entertainment Weekly* that when he and Billie Joe were speaking on the phone after the Pop Disaster tour, Billie Joe had suddenly confronted him by asking, "Do you wanna fucking do this anymore?" "And I was like, 'Well, yeah, but we're fucking miserable a lot of the time, and we gotta get to the core of this shit.' A lot of it came from bundling shit up and not treating each other like grown men."

Green Day didn't go quite as far as Metallica did (hiring a therapist and filming the sessions, as seen in the 2004 documentary, *Metallica: Some Kind of Monster*), but found that more informal sessions of mandatory "talk time" were beneficial. "Admitting that we cared for each other was a big thing," Tré told *Rolling Stone*. "We didn't hold anything back." Billie Joe admitted feeling intimidated about bringing new ideas to the table, lest Mike and Tré make fun of them. Mike and Tré admitted their resentment at being shut out. As Mike explained to *Q*, he told Billie Joe, "We're not, like, staff. You're the President, but we're the cabinet and you've gotta consult us."

Airing their differences enabled the band to get back to work with a new confidence and determination. "At one point, they just kinda looked at each other and said, 'Fuck it, we've got to do the album we want, and we've got to do it on our time,'" says Lucasey. "'We're not in Hollywood and people aren't gonna prod us anymore.' So all of a sudden they just started having fun."

For a while, some of that "fun" involved Green Day's typical love of vandalism, as when Tré painted the walls of the studio's lounge with glow-in-the-dark paint. Lucasey finally noticed it when he was locking up the place one night. "Everything looked normal, then I turned out the lights, and I went, 'What?'" he says. "I turned back on the lights, nothing there. Turn them off. What the hell? It was all over all the walls. And the refrigerator! It was everywhere. It was horrible. So I took knives to the heads of his drums." It wasn't the first abuse inflicted on the fridge; it also bears numerous dents as a result of Tré driving golf balls into it.

Next to the lounge is a large room that was initially designated as a game room, where Green Day indulged in further horseplay. One of the doors is black, with the words "Painted Black" on it in red, a joking reference to The Rolling Stones' song, 'Paint It Black'. The walls are a deep red; one features a large mural by Bulgarian artist Vladimir Bibera that spells out the word "Oakland". A wide array of artifacts are hung throughout the room, such as a poster advertising a Charlie Chaplin Midnight Film Festival that has a picture of Green Day pasted on it, the photo altered to show Billie Joe sporting the Little Tramp's trademark moustache. Lucasey has painted gold stars in various places in honour of the star tattoos the members of Green Day have. And there's a collection of what can only be described as rock'n'roll action figures, with such names as "Goth Guy" and "The Geek," plus the requisite Beavis and Butthead figures. ("What's a rock studio without a Beavis and Butthead?" says Lucasey.)

As befits a game room, there's an air hockey table and a beautiful old billiards table, with black fringe dangling from the pockets and bear-claw legs, made by Golden West Billiard Manufacturing. And among the cast-off clothing, go-karts, and old guitar cases, there's also some workout equipment. At one time, the room also had an eight-lane slot car race track. "Seventeen feet wide by 32 feet long," brags Lucasey. "But it was taken out because Tré figured out a way to make a ramp for the slot cars — pretty ingenious, actually — and would run them on the strait and launch them across the room into my cinderblock wall. He destroyed roughly 25 cars in about an hour's time. Those cars cost me around 50 to 100 bucks per car, so I figured this could get quite expensive. So, with much regret, the track left." Crazy-looking cars were painted on the wall in compensation.

The room was also home to "a real insane game Tré and I used to play," says Lucasey. "We cleared this room out completely, and Tré and I used to play a little game of chicken. We'd open the doors on each side of the room. Then Tré would take his golf club, set up a golf ball, and hit it as hard as he could against the cinderblock wall on the far side. And the ball would come flying back at you, at maybe 150 miles an hour. And we'd each stand by a door, and whoever dodged out of their door would be the loser. I mean, it was almost risking our lives doing it. And everybody else thought we were just complete jackasses for doing it, but it was just something Tré and I liked to do."

But the game room eventually became a music room as well. "I gave the guys everything that any kid would ever want in a game room," says Lucasey. "And they said, 'But that's fun for a minute. Can we set it up so we can have jam sessions?' So I did, and they'd have blues sessions and jazz sessions. We'd walk in, and I'd be like, 'What the hell are you guys playing?' They'd be having jam sessions, they'd have a mariachi band come and jam with them or something. Just weird shit, because their fun, their release, was playing music. And then their work was going in the main studio and making music. So, the game room didn't get used that much as a game room."

But not all the release was musical, as the group's intense go-kart races on the premises revealed. "We were out there killing each other every night on go-karts, things like that," Lucasey recalls. "It was insane. Nobody was allowed to park in our parking lot, because we had a full Indy course set up. We had 10 go-karts, and people going to the hospital on a regular basis, because we weren't nice to each other. We were all wearing helmets and protective gear, and we're running each other off the road, and when I think about it, it was frickin' madness. There were a couple injuries, but nothing too debilitating. Some stitches — one of our guys got stitches because he got in a golf-kart crash. I think Mike aimed him into a wall; Mike hurt his arm pretty badly. Then there was a guest band from Japan who came over to visit, and one guy got total road rash. And Rob Cavallo, the first day he gets here, says, 'Okay, I'll try this freaking thing.' And somebody, Tré maybe, says to me, 'John, uh, you know, you better let Rob win.' And I pointed to Billie and I said, 'On stage you're a rock star. Rob, back in LA, you're a fucking big Hollywood producer. But when you're on my track, you're dead, you're nothing but meat.' And sure enough, the second lap, I flipped Rob, he just went tumbling in a go-kart, probably doing about 30 miles an hour."

But Lucasey feels the rough-housing had its therapeutic value. "Magical things happened because of all that," he says. "When they wrote and recorded songs, they were just so intense. There was a great energy, because they believed in their writing. I saw what you rarely see in the studio, which is a deep down satisfaction in their music. Some bands that come in here don't know how to have a good time in the studio. They're really uptight, they take it way too serious, and get angry at things because they're out of control. They don't know what they're doing, so they have to look like they know what they're doing by getting angry or acting too dominant, instead of just letting things happen. When you see a band who's totally with it and together, it looks like it's effortless, and it looks like they're just so happy, like they're having a great time. It's not like they're dancing or jumping for joy; they eat dinner when they're supposed to eat dinner, they sleep when they need to sleep. They go out and say, 'I'm gonna go hit golf balls.' They take it like it's a part of their lives, and that's what these guys did. It's a zone that very few achieve in the music business, and Green Day definitely hit that zone."

The group's creativity also spilled over into other ventures. They set up their own pirate radio station, broadcasting from their rehearsal space behind Adeline's offices. Iggy Pop recorded his 2003 album *Skull Ring* at Studio 880, and the group appeared on the two tracks Billie Joe co-wrote with Pop: 'Private Hell' and 'Supermarket'. Billie Joe also contributed backing vocals on 'Do Miss America' on Ryan Adams' album *Rock N Roll*, and had a hand in mixing *Kids Are Alright* by Link (both albums also released in 2003). And Green Day also seemingly created an alter-ego for themselves with the band The Network.

With little advance warning, The Network's debut album, *Money Money 2020* appeared on Adeline on September 30, 2003. (It was later released on Reprise.) The record was billed as "an anomalous synthesis of pop and sarcastic social commentary," created by five mysterious individuals "brought together by an ancient prophecy, which predicted their rise to world power and eventually their demise," and who were all disciples of the "Church of Lushotology." All wore bizarre costumes with some type of mask hiding their face and had equally bizarre names: Fink, Van Gough, Z, Captain Underpants, and The Snoo.

The 14 songs on the album were drenched in the new wave, synth-soaked sounds of the early '80s, complete with distorted, robotic vocals. A highlight is 'Spike', largely a spoken-word piece concerning the narrator's pathetic attempts to score drugs, and, after getting kicked out of his cool Oakland warehouse, borrow money from his mother — a sort of updated version of 'Welcome to Paradise'. The Reprise edition of the album featured a cover of The Misfits' kitschy 'Teenagers From Mars', which could easily be the theme song of some teen exploitation film put out by American International Pictures. The zany humour is in fact the key to The Network's appeal. Their rendition of new wave is clearly an affectionate parody, especially seen in their song titles ('Hungry Hungry Models' and 'X-Ray Hamburger') and in the "Manifesto" posted on their website, which read in part: "The Network has been sent here to rid us the mediocre music that has inhabited our planet for too long. Their quest is to dominate the airwaves, thus getting rid of the mindless shit that has been dominating the radio and television for the last 20 years." The Adeline edition of the CD also came with a DVD of music videos by Roy Miles which mixed together imagery of the band with soft-core shots of scantily dressed women, though the video for 'Transistors Gone Wild' more inventively recast the group as action figures.

With representatives at both Reprise and Adeline neither confirming or denying Green Day's involvement in the project, rumours began multiplying; Devo was said to be involved with the record, and another story had it that the album was indeed a Green Day record that Reprise had rejected, hence the decision to release it on Adeline. The two bands even engaged in a war of words on the Web. On The Network's site, a clip of a mock press conference was shown, which degenerated into chaos when a reporter unwisely mentioned the group's purported connection to Green Day. On Green Day's site, Billie Joe posted an audio message that said in part, "All I gotta say is fuck The Network. These guys are totally spreading rumours. I try to do those guys a favour by bringing them to this country and putting out their record and this is how I get repaid, by [their] talking shit about my band... the only thing I can say is, 'Fuck you Network — bring it on!'" the latter comment a not-so-subtle dig at the phrase President Bush had used to taunt the insurgency in Iraq, following the official "end" of the war in that country in 2003.

When it was announced that The Network would perform at the Key Club in Hollywood on November 22, Mike issued his own public statement: "I hope you enjoy your 15 minutes of borrowed fame, because where I come from, one good record doesn't mean dick. So keep runnin' your mouths 'cause it'll give me a good reason to come to the Key Club and kick all your circus monkey asses!!!!" If attendees at the show hoped to discover The Network's identity, they were disappointed, for the group kept their faces covered throughout. The show was filmed by John Roecker, an LA scenester and music fan who'd previously operated the "apocalyptic general store," You've Got Bad Taste with Exene Cervenka from the band X. Roecker himself appeared onstage during the show, tossing flyers into the audience as The Network played 'Spastic Society'.

2003 also saw the group picking up more honours at the California Music Awards, held May 25 at Oakland's City Hall Plaza, winning Outstanding Group, Band of the Year, and a special "Spirit of Rock" award. Billie Joe was also named Best Guitarist. But finally, the games, go-kart racing, and celebrations ended, and the group buckled down to work on their next album. Billie Joe later said that prior to the sessions he had a creative crisis and flew alone to New York, where by his own admission he indulged in copious drinking and a search for, as he put it, "something". The current state of the real world brought him no further reassurance. On March 20, 2003, America's war with Iraq began, and though it officially ended on May 1 of that year, American troops remained overseas, battling an increasingly hostile insurgency that eventually succeeded in killing more Americans after the "official" war ended than had been killed during it.

Though reporters were embedded with the troops in Iraq, their view of the war was severely restricted, a lesson learned from the days of the Vietnam conflict, when the gut-wrenching footage routinely broadcast on American TV during the dinner hour had helped change the public's mind about the war. Coverage of the Iraq war was more sanitized, but nonetheless available on a plethora of cable networks 24 hours a day. War coverage was also constantly interspersed with commercials, a juxtaposition that ultimately reduced everything, from the horrors of inhumanity to pleas to try a "new and improved" laundry detergent to the same level of banality. It was a dichotomy captured perfectly by a line in Margaret Cho's 2005 show *Assassin*, discussing media coverage of the death of Pope John Paul II: "He's not dead yet. . . but he might be when we come back from this commercial!"

Anyone with an awareness of the news outside America's borders could also not help but notice how America's stature had fallen around the globe in recent years. Immediately after 9/11, the United States had most of the world's sympathy. But this had steadily declined over the years. Foreign leaders were increasingly put off by, in the words of *Newsweek*, America's "imperial style of diplomacy." "Most [foreign] leaders who are consulted are simply informed of US policy," the magazine said. "'When we meet with American officials, they talk and we listen — we rarely disagree or speak frankly because they simply can't take it in,' explained one senior official." This directly translated into a lack of support for America's war with Iraq from countries usually friendly to America. And even countries that did support the war were often openly critical. After President Bush won re-election in 2004, Britain's *Daily Mirror* ran a picture of Bush on the front page with a headline that chided the voters who had returned him to office: "How can 59,054,087 people be so DUMB?" Brian Reade's accompanying editorial was equally damning: "They say that in life you get what you deserve. Well, today America has deservedly got a lawless cowboy to lead them further into carnage and isolation and the unreserved contempt of most of the rest of the world." It was a surprising statement to come from a nation that was traditionally one of America's staunchest allies.

Billie Joe was well aware of these attitudes. "I know how Americans are often viewed by the rest of the world," he told *Kerrang!* in July 2004. "We're seen as being dumb and arrogant, which is a pretty lousy combination. Americans talk about how their country is the best country in the world, which is something I don't notice people in a lot of other countries doing." All these different elements became themes of Green Day's new album, *American Idiot.* The thrust of the album was not simply an attack on a particular administration, but a denunciation of a entire cultural climate, spelled out in the title track via key words like "mania", "hysteria", "tension", "alienation", "propaganda", and "paranoia".

Though the final versions of the *American Idiot* songs were recorded in LA (at both Ocean Way Recording and Capitol Studios), the songs were written and first put together at Studio 880. References to Oakland appear throughout the album and its artwork. The title of 'East 12th St.' refers to the street location of the office where Billie Joe had gone to fill out paperwork following his DUI arrest. Lucasey felt the line in 'Jesus Of Suburbia' about "moms and Brads" being away referred to 880's studio manager named Brad, who would sometimes be "the enforcer" when the group's antics got out of hand (in the group's appearance on *VH1 Storytellers*, Billie Joe indicated the line referred to a stepparent). In the album's booklet, 'Jesus Of Suburbia' is datelined "Jingle Town USA," a locale also mentioned in 'We're Coming Home Again' (go-karts are also mentioned in the latter song).

Rob Cavallo was back on board as co-producer, and he also helped keep the group focused on their work. "He had his couple of days of fun when he got here, but he dedicated himself to this album," says Lucasey. "When he saw what it was, he spent four months here; he basically moved to Oakland. And he'd be like, 'Okay you guys, that's enough on the go-karts; you can do it maybe once a week.' So we just had go-kart night, when we'd barbeque and do go-karts. And it was kinda neat, because the guys could've said, 'No, F-off, we're gonna do what we want.' But instead they were more like, 'Okay, somebody really does care about us; somebody's gonna dedicate that much time and effort to us when they could be in Hollywood doing any project they want.' For him to really change his life and move away from his family for four months, that is sheer belief and dedication into what's going on here. So

I respect Rob like you wouldn't believe. Although I could kick his ass in a ping-pong match — he'll tell you different — everything that he does is focused and intense." Even so, Cavallo initially had his own doubts. "When they first came to me and said, 'Let's get the band back together and make the best rock record we can,' I wasn't totally sure they could do it," he admitted to *MTV.com*.

The spark for the album that ultimately became *American Idiot* came when Mike arrived at Studio 880 one day and found himself having to kill time while waiting for Billie Joe and Tré to arrive. "The engineer challenged me to write a 30-second song," he recalled to *Bass Player*. "So I laid down drums and wrote this quick little tune. My one goal was to make it as grandiose as possible. Just after I finished the song, everyone came back. Billie listened to it and went, 'Wow, that's fun! I want to do one!' Then, he threw the ball at Tré to do a quickie. After we had all done one, we started connecting them and screwing around with different ideas."

"It was funny at first," Billie Joe told *Entertainment Weekly*. "But then something more serious started happening." Serious indeed; from various scraps of songs, they pieced together the first of *American Idiot's* epic song suites: 'Jesus Of Suburbia'. The number was different from anything they had done before, and not just because of its length (nine minutes and eight seconds). While some of band's previous work had played with musical dynamics ('In The End' from *Dookie* comes to mind), 'Jesus Of Suburbia' goes through innumerable changes in mood and time signature (which the band would pull off flawlessly in concert). Billie Joe would later describe *American Idiot* as being the story of a character's emotional journey; the same could also be said of 'Jesus Of Suburbia', which distills that journey into a single song.

But there was also another inspiration for the name 'Jesus Of Suburbia' — the 13-minute short Lance Bangs had made when he was around 20, that shared the same title and had been one of the first pieces of his work he'd sent to Billie Joe. "It was just all this experimental Super-8 stuff of this kid that I was in high school with," he explains. "I sort of used him as this idea of this kid that was the reincarnation of Christ that no one was paying any attention to. And so he was kind of humiliated." In Bangs' film, "Jesus" is a high-school senior named Josh, with Bangs (who narrates) as his fellow student and devoted disciple. The two boys, stranded in the suburbs and attending a religious school, plot to galvanize the youth of the world. But their plans to commandeer a stage at Lollapalooza come to naught, and Josh's crowning as Prom King at the high-school dance proves to be equally anti-climactic. The boys' friendship is over, and they graduate from high school, each facing the world alone.

All in all, 'Jesus Of Suburbia' was a remarkable accomplishment. But it also presented a new challenge; to come up with material that was just as strong. The group realised this themselves. "We sort of looked at each other and said, 'Now we're onto something,'" Billie Joe told a reporter. "At the same time, there was no looking back. It was scary. You can't go, 'Now I want to make a regular record.' You have to keep going. As soon as you make the big leap, you're looking at a bigger mountain to climb. It was really exciting and scary at the same time."

The group were more than ready for the challenge, no matter how unlikely this new direction seemed: "We decided we were going to be the biggest, best band in the world or fall flat on our faces," Billie Joe told *Rolling Stone*. And though he later said the songs for *American Idiot* were largely written in chronological order, a March 2004 *RollingStone.com* story said the group had 35 songs from which to choose when they recorded the final version of the album in LA, suggesting the album's storyline was paired down from a surfeit of material (a handful of non-album tracks would appear as B-sides and on a compilation).

However it came together, the final line-up was judiciously chosen for maximum impact, making *American Idiot* an exceptionally well-crafted album. The opening, and title track, sets the stage much as an overture does in a traditional musical. The song grabs you immediately, with a few bars of opening guitar riff, the full band kicking in mere seconds later. As if to underscore the necessity of the lyrics being understood, the band uses an interesting technique during the verses, alternating between Billie Joe singing a line a capella (accompanied by a drumbeat) and the full band playing a line. This back-and-forth, ping-pong effect gives the verses an additional tension, making the resulting explosion of the choruses (which have the full band playing and singing together) that much more powerful.

And for all the debate about who the "American idiot" is supposed to be, the song's broad appeal is because it doesn't point to any one specific person. As the song would have it, an "idiot" is anyone who doesn't question the manipulative power of the media and the government. 'Warning' and 'Minority' were similarly themed songs, but 'American Idiot' is a more invigorating and urgent *cri de coeur*, decrying aspects of modern-day American life anyone might object to; the heightened sense of tension and fear, coupled with the feeling of being blindsided by information from all fronts. Only Billie Joe's allegiance to the "faggot America" and subsequent disavowal of a "redneck agenda" reveal his political stripes. Billie Joe said the title had a touch of self-deprecation as well, pointing out he'd worn T-shirts bearing the word "idiot" or "stoopid" in concert (indeed, he occasionally introduced 'American Idiot' in performance by saying, "It's about me").

Next comes 'Jesus Of Suburbia', which introduces *American Idiot's* main character. In the key opening phrase, our suburban Jesus proclaims himself the "son of rage and love," a push-pull dichotomy that runs throughout the album. Jesus is a true product of his culture, immersed in the kind of addictions that run in a straight line from childhood to adult life — soda pop, ritalin, alcohol, cigarettes, "Mary Jane", and cocaine (the last word was often censored when the group performed the song on TV; presumably the censors felt the youthful audience wouldn't recognise Mary Jane as being slang for marijuana).

After a brief musical interlude, the song segues into the next number in the suite, 'City Of The Damned'; if part one of the suite deals with Jesus himself, 'City Of The Damned' describes his dead-end environment. Jesus' hopelessness about his situation finally boils over into full on anger in 'I Don't Care', which rages against the world's hypocrisies. Another segue and we're into 'Dearly Beloved', the most light-hearted number in the suite (complete with sweet harmonies and a touch of glockenspiel) — until you listen to the lyrics, which are a heartfelt plea for help. The tempo surges forward again in 'Tales Of Another Broken Home', which has Jesus shaking off his old world and leaving it behind, striking out for a new life in the city.

Next is 'Holiday', easily the most bitter track on the album (and, along with 'American Idiot', the most obviously political). While a denunciation of the high cost of war (the luckless souls who "died without a name"), it also lashes out against those who would silence dissent, in a sequence that's also performed with minimal instrumentation to allow the words to be heard. Along with the potent imagery (*e.g.* the flag being used as a gag), the music is as harsh as the subject matter.

The album's best segue is arguably when the closing guitar chord of 'Holiday' takes on a shimmering effect and becomes the opening of 'Boulevard Of Broken Dreams' — not the Al Dubin/Harry Warren number written for the 1934 film *Moulin Rouge*, but a haunting portrayal of loneliness and desolation. Billie Joe said the title came from a picture of James Dean he'd seen captioned with that title, possibly referring to the cover of Paul Alexander's 1995 biography, *James Dean: Boulevard Of Broken Dreams*. (Interestingly, the song's opening line echoes the suicide note that inspired Elvis Presley's 'Heartbreak Hotel', which read, "I walk a lonely street.") 'Boulevard' makes a subtle use of the trademark alternative-rock formula of quiet verses/louder choruses, though one can easily imagine the number being played acoustically. It also features one of Billie Joe's most evocative vocals.

Cavallo was immediately impressed when he heard the song's demo. "I loved it from the first day I heard it," he told *MTV.com*. "Just the nature of it and the tempo and the way he sang the opening part. . . I knew it was going to be a smash." He also helped shape the song's ending, which the band had originally envisioned as along the lines of the cataclysmic ending of The Beatles' 'A Day In The Life' from their landmark *Sgt. Pepper's Lonely Hearts Club Band* album. Cavallo persuaded them to use guitars and just pound out the final chords as hard as possible. There's no segue into another song; 'Boulevard' simply crashes to a halt.

The next song, the anthemic 'Are We The Waiting', finds Jesus still stranded alone, until the track segues into the song that introduces the next character in the album, 'St. Jimmy'. Or, more intriguingly, as some theories would have it, this is the moment when Jesus of Suburbia *becomes* another character — St. Jimmy — in a case of split personality à la *Fight Club*. Either way, St. Jimmy's song is a rollicking, out-and-out stomper, painting a vibrant picture of a personality that's brimming with brio — you can practically see him strutting down the street.

But the next track, 'Give Me Novacaine', slows down the pace, as

Jesus/Jimmy seeks solace in numbing oblivion. The song dies down to a single drum beat, which leads — *bam!* — straight to Whatsername, the star of 'She's A Rebel', a character whose love is the counterpoint to St. Jimmy's rage. Billie Joe described Whatsername as representing "Every girl I've been involved with," and in 'She's A Rebel' she's as daring and as bold as St. Jimmy is. It's love at first sight and Whatsername sets up a new challenge Jesus/Jimmy can't wait to try and live up to.

But the flipside of this new relationship comes all too soon in 'Extraordinary Girl'. The bittersweet number pictures the couple at a turning point, where she's tired of being disappointed and he feels like simply giving up. The final note hangs in the air, unresolved, and then, coming from a distance, is the mocking sound of Whatsername's voice, taunting from the sidelines. The four-line sequence was sung by Kathleen Hanna of Bikini Kill, a singer (and band) Billie Joe was a big fan of. "She's one of my favourite singers in the world," he told *The Advocate*. "If they made a car called Kathleen Hanna, I would drive one."

But this relationship isn't one that peters out quietly. 'Letterbomb' is Whatsername's kiss-off letter, which starts out at a brisk clip, then appears to get faster and faster, as if the one who's moving on can't wait to leave this burning wreckage of a romance behind. The final break is even felt in the last chord, which slowly fades into nothing.

Billie Joe has said the next number, 'Wake Me Up When September Ends', departs from the album's narrative, for this song of loss was inspired by the death of his father, marking the first time he'd written about the event. But its placement on the album also means it serves just as effectively as a post-breakup song, crystallizing that moment when it seems things will never get better. It provides a more downbeat counterpoint to the Green Day song it's most often been compared with, 'Good Riddance'; where 'Riddance' looks back with nostalgia, 'September' looks ahead without hope.

'Homecoming' is the second of the album's nine-minute-plus song suites, opening with 'The Death Of St. Jimmy', as Jimmy's bright spark is laid to rest for good. The music surges neatly into 'East 12th St.', which has Jesus, personality whole once again, stuck in an anonymous office building, already missing his previous existence, squalid as it was living among those in the "underbelly". And 'Nobody Likes You' (written by

Mike) suggests Jesus is as lonely and alienated as ever. There's a momentary upswing with 'Rock And Roll Girlfriend', written by Tré, a succinct slice of autobiography that tells his story in less than a minute. But the concluding 'We're Coming Home Again', which has the sound of triumph in its ringing bells and bold tympani, also carries with it a sense of defeat; Jesus, back in Jingle Town, may be older and wiser, but not necessarily happier or better off. Especially as the song's last words repeat Whatsername's parting taunt: We're having fun — and you're not.

The final song, 'Whatsername', provides a resigned postscript to the story. The song begins with a restrained, melancholy musical backing, breaking out halfway through in a rush of emotion, a desperate desire to hang on to a memory that's already fading. Jesus looks back at the love of his life, but can't even remember her name anymore. And if the passing of time has meant the pain is no longer as sharp, the regrets still remain. It's on this despondent note that *American Idiot* comes to an end.

The story is almost an hour in length, making *American Idiot* nearly twice as long as Green Day's debut album, *39/Smooth*. And not only is the record the band's most thematically cohesive album, it's also a work that — aside from some moments of anger and elation — is surely the saddest release in the group's canon to date.

All of which made *American Idiot* quite unlike anything the band had previously released. "It's weird; when they first started playing me the songs, I was blown away, but I didn't know what to think," Lucasey confesses. "I thought they were fantastic, but I was really nervous for them. Because it was so different from what I was expecting. When you think about what Billie Joe wrote and how it all comes together, it's crazy. These rock operas or concept albums — we're in a time where a song's got to be three minutes and it's got to be set so you can make a short, cute little video to it; it's a turn 'em and burn 'em kind of time. But yet, they did the most punk thing you can ever imagine. They did the opposite of what everybody's doing, and they just said, 'We don't care if it flies or if it doesn't. This is something that's in our hearts.' That's what I saw out of it."

It was also ironic that the most outspoken album of the band's career initially came together at a studio where American flags are so conspicuous; an enormous one covers an entire wall of Studio 880's large Studio

A (a shot of which can be seen in the *Warning* EPK). "I'm very patriotic," Lucasey says "Maybe I'm the American Idiot!" He also readily admits to not sharing the group's political sensibilities. "I don't like the political part," he says. "When they were here there were a lot of anti-George Bush stickers everywhere. They were definitely anti-Bush, and I wasn't playing into that at all — I wasn't going go to there, as they say. But I saw history in the making, which is just fantastic for me. That's why I'm in this business. It's not for the money, because I could make a hell of a lot more money doing something else. But to be a part of musical history, that's fantastic."

Billie Joe acknowledged the album's political angle, but emphasised that it was only one element of the overall story. "The atmosphere can be anti-Bush, and I definitely had that in mind, but when you get down to it, it's a human story," he told *Rolling Stone*. "This album is about feelings. I didn't want to make a rage against the machine record. I wanted to make an album of heartfelt songs." Because the record's influences were so far ranging — everything from *Tommy* and *Ziggy Stardust And The Spiders From Mars* to more traditional musicals like *Grease*, to name a few ("I think this whole record has more in common with *The Rocky Horror Picture Show* than it does with The Clash's *London Calling*," Billie Joe told *Kerrang!*) — any number of interpretations could be given to its story. There were autobiographical elements as well. But at its core, *American Idiot*'s political commentary just provides a backdrop, a context, for the larger tale, one that's been told before and will be again — the story of the protagonist's coming-of-age. It's a story that can be endlessly retold, for while the emotions felt while growing up are similar for every generation, the times in which those emotions are experienced are different. Thus, each generation feels compelled to tell the story in its own voice. And this is the key to why *American Idiot* became a classic album; it tells a story that's both of its time, and is timeless.

By the time Green Day left Studio 880 to record the final versions of the *American Idiot* songs in Los Angeles, they were as tight a unit as they'd ever been, even getting the same tattoo — the letters E.B.P.M. (for "East Bay Punk Mafia") — to illustrate their renewed bond. They also left some new graffiti on 880's walls: the words "Green Day" written in gold.

The group's excitement continued to mount as they worked on the

Billie Joe at the Reading Festival, August 24, 2001. *(Jon Super/Redferns)*

Billie Joe with his side project band, Pinhead Gunpowder,
at the Starry Plough, Oakland, March 8, 2001. *(Anthony Pidgeon/Retna)*

Green Day in disguise? The mysterious band The Network, following the group's performance
at the Key Club, Los Angeles, November 22, 2003. *(Jay Blakesberg/Retna)*

In between recording introductions for their appearance on *Sessions @ AOL*, New York, September 20, 2004. *(Clay Enos/Retna)*

American Idiot photo session, 2004. The baggy shorts and t-shirts were gone, in favor of designer wear. *(Pamela Littky/Retna)*

The band's political outspokenness on *American Idiot* was controversial,
but gave the group their biggest hit in a decade. *(Ross Halfin/Idols)*

Jason White backstage at the *Billboard* Music Awards, Las Vegas, December 8, 2004. Jason played his first show with Green Day in 1999, and has been the group's second guitarist on tour ever since. *(Mark Sullivan/WireImage)*

"But you can call me… *asshole!*" Billie Joe bashes his favourite American idiot at Irving Plaza, New York, September 21, 2004. *(Kevin Mazur/WireImage)*

Mike at an outdoor concert in front of New York's J&R Music World store, 22nd September 2004. *(Eddie Malluk/WireImage)*

Mike and Tré enjoying a rare moment of relaxation, backstage at the Voodoo Music Experience festival, New Orleans, October 16, 2004. *(Jason Squires/WireImage)*

The infamous pink bunny gets the crowd going before Green Day's show at the Hammersmith Apollo, London, February 6, 2005. *(Debbie Smyth/Retna)*

Billie Joe and his wife Adrienne, at the Grammy Awards, Staples Center, Los Angeles, February 13, 2005. The band picked up their first Grammy when *American Idiot* won the Best Rock Album award. *(Christina Radish/Redferns)*

Picking up yet another honor at the MTV Video Music Awards, American Airlines Arena, August 28, 2005. 'Boulevard of Broken Dreams' would win six awards, including Video of the Year; the 'American Idiot' video also won the Viewers' Choice award. *(John Shearer/WireImage)*

We Are The Champions: Billie Joe at Milton Keynes Bowl, June 18, 2005. The two shows held at the venue were proclaimed "Gig of the Year" by the readers of the *New Musical Express*. *(Rowen Lawrence/WireImage)*

We're A Happy Family: clockwise, Billie Joe, Adrienne, Joey, and Jakob at the Nickelodeon Kids' Choice Awards, April 1, 2006. The band was named Favorite Music Group and 'Wake Me Up When September Ends' Favorite Song. *(LFI)*

Displaying their Record of the Year Grammys for 'Boulevard of Broken Dreams' at the Grammy Awards, Staples Center, Los Angeles, February 8, 2006. *(Steve Granitz/WireImage)*

Back On Top: after 10 years of declining sales, Green Day's *American Idiot* eventually topped the 10 million-plus sales of 1994's *Dookie*. *(Spiros Politis/Retna)*

album in LA, especially at the prospect of playing the new songs live. Already sensing the album's importance, the band arranged to have the sessions filmed by John Roecker for a later documentary. Some of the footage was aired as part of a "making of" program on the fuse network; one sequence shows the group parodying Bob Dylan's classic 'Subterranean Homesick Blues' proto-video, the different band members seen standing next to a building holding up signs with lyrics from 'American Idiot', as a go-go dancer, clad in an American flag-patterned bikini, dances in the background.

As the sessions were coming to a close, the group had yet to decide on cover art. Chris Bilheimer had previously been contacted to do artwork for the band's earlier, aborted album. "Billie called me and said, 'Hey, we're just finishing up this record, why don't you start working on some covers?'" he recalls. "'And I think maybe a band photo on the cover again.' So I came up with a couple of ideas and sent them to him and he liked them. That's when the record got stolen. Then he's like, 'Oh well, we're not putting this record out. I'll let you know what's happening.' Then I didn't hear from him for a year. I was kind of like, 'Oh, that's weird.' Then I heard they actually hired a couple of other people to come up with ideas for *American Idiot*. And when I heard that I was like, 'That kind of sucks.' I was pretty bummed out for awhile. But I'm not on any kind of retainer, or any kind of employee of theirs; I work project to project."

But after assuming he wouldn't be working on the album, "The same thing that happened with *Nimrod* happened," he says. "They said, 'Hey, we've gone through a couple of people and everything they've done has been terrible and we don't like it. Can you help us out?' So I was going into a pretty difficult situation because they'd already seen a bunch of stuff and they hated it — it was kind of daunting."

Bilheimer flew to Los Angeles, where the group was now working, to listen to the record. It didn't take him long to realise that *American Idiot* was not just another album. "I was really blown away," he says. "I was like, 'Holy crap, there's not a bad song on the record, there's not any filler. This is a really tight concept, from start to finish.' Not to sound like a know-it-all, but when I heard that record I thought, 'There's no *way* this can't be huge! If this doesn't do incredibly well, all hope is lost for our culture. If people don't recognise that this is a phenomenal album, then we're in trouble.' I had my doubts that in the Britney Spears world we're living in that, God, maybe this record won't do well. But then when I heard it, I was like, there's no way that it can't do well. They were so focused in the studio; they were so focused, they really seemed like they were on a mission. They were getting along better than I've ever seen them get along. They just all seemed to be on the same page. I'm not surprised that it created what it did."

Now it was Bilheimer's turn to try and come up with a workable concept for the cover, continuing his work for R.E.M. during the week and flying out to meet with Green Day on the weekends. "It wasn't easy," he admits. "Billie told me, 'There's a story, there's kind of a narrative, with the characters going through the journey of the album. We want something big, we want something epic. Almost like a movie poster.' So I did a bunch of covers, threw out a bunch of different concepts. Some of them were of fat Americans sitting and watching TV, that sort of thing — the literal American idiot! Some were more focusing on the St. Jimmy character, focusing on this person being lost in the world. In one of them I think we had one of those 'Kick Me' signs taped to his back that said 'Idiot'. Things like that. But nothing seemed quite as epic as they wanted. I started to get the feeling I was going to get fired; I would be another in a line of people who couldn't figure out what this record was going to look like."

Billie Joe called Bilheimer's attention to an image he liked; a hand grenade shaped like a heart that he'd seen on friend Jim Theibaud's Real Skateboards website. "He'd given me this heart/hand-grenade idea, and I'd done some stuff that looked vaguely like Banksy, a phenomenal British artist, one of my favourite graffiti artists of all time," says Bilheimer. "*Thinktank* had just come out, by Blur; that's a Banksy image on their cover. I was thinking, 'Well, we can't put out a record that looks a lot like the Blur record that just came out two months before.' It just wasn't working. That's when I thought, 'God, I'm going to get fired!'

"Then Billie Joe called me up one night and said, 'You know, I just saw this movie poster by a graphic designer,'" he continues. "'Have you ever heard of an artist named Saul Bass?' Saul Bass is my favourite graphic designer. I have tons of books of his work. He could not have said anything to make me happier than Saul Bass. I drove to my office, did one comp and e-mailed it to him and within 45 minutes of that phone call we had the cover." The end result went on to be the most widely reproduced graphic image associated with the band; against a black background, a white hand holds up the red heart/hand grenade, which is oozing blood onto the palm. The image was so strong that it immediately resulted in a lyric change in the song 'She's A Rebel' that directly referenced the image.

"When we got the cover done, Billie Joe was just so excited," says Bilheimer. "He was like, 'This is it, this is absolutely it!' The colours [red, white, black] were a somewhat obvious choice, since they are the colours you think of when you think about communist propaganda posters. It seemed to fit the theme of *American Idiot* perfectly, a big theme of the title song being governmental propaganda." Saul Bass' movie poster for *The Man With The Golden Arm* was another influence, its central image being a crooked arm and hand. "That's one of my favourite movie posters," Bilheimer says. "A little of the style is refer-encing that. And I had actually designed an entire typeface font that was based off of the lettering Saul did for the movie *Vertigo*. Apparently the Warner Brothers legal people thought it was too close, so I had to scrap it." The lettering of the words "Green Day," which are worn through in places, was "vaguely inspired by the letters of the *West Side Story* poster," says Bilheimer. "I liked the idea of this record being a rock opera, and *West Side Story* also being a musical." Even the way the album's name is presented echoes the movie poster idea; the cover reads, "Green Day Presents *American Idiot*," like the opening credits of a film. "It was about making this its own entity," Bilheimer explains. "This album exists as its own piece. They definitely wanted you to think of the record as a whole. It isn't an album, it's a produc-tion. It's not about the band; it's its own entity."

The lyrics in the booklet are dated to create the impression that the booklet is the journal of the main character. "They basically span a year of his life," says Bilheimer. "They're kind of chronological; you're looking at this person as he's going through this journey. That's why the pens change, the style of writing changes; sometimes you write 'harder' when you're really angry, like for 'I Don't Care'. I really wanted it to look like you found someone else's journal." Tellingly, the date for the last song, 'Whatsername', is January 1, indicating a new beginning in the lead character's life. The lyrics were also all handwritten by Bilheimer, "Which sucked," he says. "Every time there was a title change, or a lyric change, or a spelling change you had to start over. I would start writing it and all of a sudden it would take up 18 pages and we only had 16 pages for the booklet so I'd have to start over again and try and cram in more and more. I probably wrote it out six times."

The journal idea was expanded on the limited-edition version of the album, packaged as a hardcover book. The book's style was inspired by Jim Goldberg's book, *Raised By Wolves*. "He'd spent years living with the kids who live on Hollywood Boulevard, the gutter punks, and documented their life," Bilheimer says. "He'd have all these Polaroids of the kids, and then there'll be a studio portrait of their jeans jacket with all this shit written all over it, and blood on it. It's sort of a mix between a diary of time passing and living with these kids, and then these objects, representing certain parts of the journey. You read some of the stories in the book and you go, 'Oh, he got knifed out in front of Pink's,' and then 20 pages further in the book you actually see the guy hanging out in front of Pink's Hot Dogs two weeks after and you're like, 'Holy crap.' There's this weird connection to the story when you actually get to see a little element from it. That's sort of what we did with the special package. Billie Joe wrote a bunch more journal entries from the point of view of the characters that are interspersed with the song lyrics. And there's just a lot of photos, and things like pieces of bus tickets that makes you feel like you've been part of the journey. It's the best thing I've ever done. It's really what I'm most proud of in my whole career."

Bilheimer admits it's "a little weird" to realise how widely produced the cover image has been. "I'm pretty isolated down here [in Athens, Georgia]," he says. "It's like, I'll draw something and I'll e-mail it. Then maybe I'll see a poster in the corner record store and I'll go, 'Oh hey, there it is.' I'm pretty isolated from the fact that, 'Wow, they made a million of these billboards, it's in all these magazines.' I don't really see it that often, so it's pretty much a shock when I do. I'll go to New York and I'll see it on the side of a 20-story building, and I'll just kind of go, 'Holy crap.' Like those large foam heart/hand grenade oversize gloves that people wear; I didn't know that they were doing those, that's one of the few merch items I didn't design. I saw those and I was like, 'Oh my God, amazing!' It is very weird. It's not something I've gotten used to, I try not to think about it very much."

While working on the cover, Bilheimer had told Bangs the new album had a song called 'Jesus Of Suburbia' and Bangs was somewhat concerned. "In my mind, I thought that meant Billie Joe had written a song about the character or the movie," he explains. "I thought it was a little weird. I haven't really circulated that film that much. I showed it a lot as a teenager, then gave copies to people and bands back at that time, but since then I've been kind of protective of it. I've never been super self-promoting with it; I've never tried to show it at film festivals or gone out of my way to call attention to it. And I just had a weird feeling, like it was going to get turned into a title or phrase that other people were going to have access to, that it wasn't my little precious thing anymore. I thought it was going to be a rock opera about this character that I identified with and that was now being co-opted or turned into this huge thing, without anyone bothering to ask me about it or mention it to me."

Bangs was in Portugal working on a film at the time and he and Billie Joe played a frustrating game of phone tag for a few days. "I was just getting weird voice-mail messages that I wasn't able to return," he says. "It would be like a day later in the middle of the night when I would get the message, and I wasn't able to talk to them directly or use a pay phone there on a phone card. I left messages back and forth, saying, 'Do I understand you right, is this the whole record?' Eventually, I got this message where Billie Joe said yes, he'd written the song and called it 'Jesus Of Suburbia', and he'd been wondering where the title came from. Then he came home and was going through all his old video tapes, and he found my tape, and he was like, 'Oh, that's where that name came from!' So he explained that he had definitely come across the title because of that, and that it had been more subconscious than deliberate. In the end, of course, it turned out that the record wasn't called 'Jesus Of Suburbia' and there were lots of other characters and stuff. It's a great record and when I finally heard it was like okay, this isn't as weird of a deal as I thought it was originally."

With the music and cover art in place, the last step was making an equally exciting video to give the album an appropriate launch. The group found exactly the right man in Sam Bayer, who would ultimately go on to direct all the *American Idiot* videos. Bayer's first major piece of work, the video for Nirvana's 'Smells Like Teen Spirit', had been key to that group's massive success. But Bayer had eventually stopped making videos. "I felt I'd outgrown it," he told *Adweek*. "It wasn't the medium I grew up with. And I think MTV had outgrown me. I didn't like the music I was being sent; I didn't like the images I was seeing on MTV. I felt like it was a bad marriage and time for a separation."

Green Day had been soliciting treatments from directors for over a year. Bayer, who cited Sam Peckinpah, Stanley Kubrick, Martin Scorsese, and Fritz Lang as influences, impressed the band by coming in with ideas not only for the first video, but the album's subsequent videos. "It showed us he was emotionally invested in the record," Mike explained to *MTV.com*. "We didn't know if we wanted to switch directors from song to song, it just worked so well with Sam, it just seemed like he was really progressive with his ideas," Billie Joe said in the same article. "There is a thread with all the videos, as with the album. They don't look alike, but there's something that ties them all together."

'American Idiot' was the obvious choice for the first single. And the accompanying video is, essentially, a straightforward performance video. But in its execution, it's nothing less than stunning, and, as its director hoped, as timeless as the album. As Bayer put it to MTV, "If a band can't perform, you don't have a video."

The video was shot over two days at Pechiney Cast Plate, a former aluminum factory located in Vernon, California, just south of LA. The building provided an industrial setting, its huge windows letting in plenty of natural light. The "set" was minimal; mics for Billie Joe and Mike, a riser for Tré's drum set, a few camera monitors, and two large banks of speakers, flanking an enormous American flag. The flag hung vertically, not horizontally, and instead of bearing the colours of red, white, and blue, this flag's colours were green, white, and black. The band members themselves also had a homogenous, unified look; for the first time in a video, they were all wearing the same colour of clothing, black, marked by individual touches — Billie Joe's red tie, Tré's black-and-

232

white striped tie, Mike wearing a tight sleeveless shirt. The band's clothes were also well tailored and later articles would name-check designer brands like Dior Homme and Duncan Quinn in discussing the group's new look; gone were the days of T-shirts and baggy shorts.

As the band mimed to the song, Bayer shot from numerous angles in his efforts to give the video a true live feel. And one of the most effective visual techniques was the use of motion control, which allowed the band members to be filmed at different speeds, yet having them all remain synchronised in time to the music. As motion-control operator Mike Leben explained to *Studio Daily online*, "Since the motion control was triggered by the corresponding time-coded music track for each frame rate, we were able to keep the camera moves and the band's performances in sync, no matter what speed we chose to shoot at. Each of the band members performed at various speeds, and editorial was able to choose which sections of the song would have which members of the band performing at which frame rates, all mixed together seamlessly."

After the second chorus of the song, the stripes on the main flag the band performed in front of began to run, eventually disintegrating completely (the flag had been painted with acrylic paint mixed with Joy dishwashing liquid, which kept the paint from washing away too quickly once water was poured over it). Green paint also gushed from the speakers, eventually drenching the band. Bayer later noted the flag had been inspired by the opening scene from the film *Patton*, where George C. Scott as the legendary WWII general addresses the audience in front of a large flag, while the green paint pouring from the speakers was a nod to the waves of blood cascading down the hall in Stanley Kubrick's horror classic, *The Shining*. The band members were also shot individually in front of another large green, white, and black flag that extended onto the floor.

At the end of the shoot, Bayer had 60,000 feet of footage to work with. Along with the different performance shots, there were also shots of the band seen in grainy black and white on monitors. Working with editor Tim Royes, the footage was edited down to a fast and furious three minutes. There were a few visual jokes; the word "faggot" in the line about "faggot America" was usually censored when the video played, but directly after the line is sung, there's a quick cut to Mike shooting Billie Joe a quizzical look, as if to say, "I don't know about this guy..." (Billie Joe told *The Advocate* that in addition to worrying people might think he was using the word "faggot" as a demeaning term — "I thought of it as empowering," he insisted — he also thought censors would be more likely to bleep the phrase "redneck agenda"). The end of the song had Billie Joe throwing down his guitar in the puddles of green paint now covering the floor, then cutting to a wider shot of the band members walking away. In the last shot, someone walks right in front of the camera, conveying the feel of watching a documentary; the camera then jerkily pans to focus on the water-streaked flag.

With release of the album still three months away, all elements were now in place for what would amount to a full-scale resurrection of Green Day's career. Tom Whalley, Warner Bros. chairman and CEO, admitted to *Billboard* he had some concern about the album's political content, especially considering "the way other artists were condemned for speaking out." But, he added, "the music was so great and it wasn't overly political to the point that it was obviously picking a side. It speaks more to where the band saw the state of the country." It was the first of many attempts to reconcile the difficulty in dealing with a popular — and money-making — band taking a potentially unpopular stance in their music. Phil Costello, Reprise's senior vice president of promotion, was quoted in the same article about his wondering how a "punk-rock opera" could be marketed. "When I first spoke to Billie Joe about it at the beginning of the project, I was left with the impression that there was going to be little if anything for radio," he said. "Then, lo and behold, when I was invited to the studio, I was speechless, because I heard so many singles."

And the fun was just beginning.

CHAPTER 11

Return Of The Conquering Idiot

"To me, it doesn't feel like it's just another rock record that somebody put out. It feels like we tapped into the culture a little bit."
— *Billie Joe to* Billboard, *October 9, 2004*

Green Day wasn't present when the California Music Awards were held June 6 at Frank Ogawa Plaza in Oakland, where they earned another four awards: Outstanding Male Vocalist, Outstanding Bassist, Outstanding Drummer, and Most Downloaded Song for 'I Fought the Law' (the song had first appeared in an iTunes/Pepsi commercial that had aired during the 2004 Super Bowl). Billie Joe had also been nominated for Outstanding Guitarist but lost to Kirk Hammett of Metallica. The Network's *Money Money 2020* was also nominated for Best Debut Album. (The CD would be reissued by Reprise on November 9, along with a DVD of the November 2003 show, entitled *Disease Is Punishment*. The DVD also featured the six videos packaged with the original Adeline CD release, and The Network's raucous press conference.)

But the band wouldn't be under wraps for much longer, for *American*

Idiot was now ready to be unveiled to its eagerly awaiting public. As was their custom, the band played a few warm-up shows, beginning on July 29 at the Olympic Auditorium in LA, followed by August dates in Japan and the UK, including appearances at the Leeds Festival on the twenty-seventh, and the Reading Festival on the twenty-ninth. The shows were intended to get the band back into performing mode, and so featured little of *American Idiot*'s material.

Their old friend and "boss" from Lookout Records, Lawrence Livermore, caught up with the band during their appearance at the Reading Festival. "It was very cold and windy up on the stage," he recalls, "and although the crowd was going crazy, they seemed so far away that I marveled at how the guys could put such incredible energy into their performance. Because it seemed almost like playing in a big, empty warehouse while watching the audience on television, if that makes any sense."

Stories had been circulating for months about the new album. The album's title track was the obvious first choice for a single and went to radio on August 4, quickly topping *Billboard*'s Modern Rock Tracks chart. It also reached number five Mainstream Rock, number 14 on Hot Digital Songs, and number 16 on the new "Hot Ringtones" chart. The song also appeared on the *Maddon NFL 2005* video game, later winning an award for Best Song in a Video Game at Spike TV's Video Game Awards.

The US CD single was released August 31, and eventually reached number 61 on the Hot 100, an inauspicious sign of the chart action soon to come. The cover art was also as striking as the artwork for the album's cover had been, with white silhouettes of a couple holding a small child over a trap against a black blackground, which Chris Bilheimer explains, was meant to reflect "the concept of being raised by 'rage and love,'" he explains. "In your childhood, it seems that at any second you can be scarred for life by chance, especially from something like a divorce. You trust your parents to protect you from harm, and so often it is your parents that do the scarring. So that image is really about how you think you and your family are safe, but you never know what is around the corner."

The US single also featured the non-album bonus track, 'Too Much

Too Soon', a mid-tempo number which detailed some of the further frustrations in Whatshername's life. Two versions of CD single were released in the UK, one of which also featured 'Too Much Too Soon' and the other having two more non-album tracks. 'Shoplifter' was a poppy lament about an activity one could easily imagine St. Jimmy indulging in, while 'Governator' was a bitter critique of California's movie-star-turned-politician, Governor Arnold Schwarzenegger, which threw in lines from the Terminator's hit films — 'California Über Alles', indeed.

The video had its world premiere August 16 on mtvU (a station only available on college campuses; the station would award the group honourary degrees the following year), then hit MTV2 on August 18, following a "Making The Video" special, which further heightened anticipation for the rest of the album. And just under a month later, the band would perform the record live in its entirety for the very first time at the Henry Fonda Theatre in Los Angeles on September 16 (the only songs from the album they'd previously played live were 'Holiday' and 'American Idiot').

On the night of the show, Billie Joe admitted to some pre-show nerves, saying he felt like "a deer in the headlights." Meanwhile, in the auditorium, songs from *The Rocky Horror Picture Show* soundtrack filled the sold-out room as the audience took their seats. The show started much like the stage version of *Rocky Horror* had begun as well, with two black-and-red-clad hostesses emerging from the wings to sing the lines Kathleen Hanna performed on the record. (*The Rocky Horror Show* had opened with an usher coming on stage to sing the first number, 'Science Fiction-Double Feature'.) The hostesses also reappeared during the show to hold up signs reading "Act 2" and "Finale" at the appropriate times (before 'Novocaine' and 'Homecoming', respectively), as if the concert was an old-time vaudeville performance.

The curtains dropped and a mosh pit formed the moment Green Day launched into the title song. The band members were equally animated throughout the night. Billie Joe, one reviewer described, "jumped around like the stage were a trampoline, his red tie flying from side to side," while Tré was seen lustily singing along with each song in spite of not having his own microphone. Billie Joe was also taking more advantage of the band's having a second guitarist in Jason White. Now, if he was caught up in running around the stage, he didn't have to worry about missing a guitar line, and in some songs he played little guitar at all. The band was also wearing the *American Idiot* colours of red, white, and black, as they would for every subsequent date on the tours supporting the album, which would continue through the end of 2005. The stage sets, designed by Justin Collie of the Artfag Design Co., used the same colours and at the larger stadium shows, huge banners would depict the heart/hand grenade logo from *American Idiot* and the zapped man logo from *Warning*.

"Welcome to *Green Day Presents American Idiot*, our record-release party — slightly glorified," Billie Joe said after the first song, then, aware that the audience was mostly unfamiliar with the material, helpfully provided brief explanatory comments about each number. "Which brings us to our next character, he's a son of a bitch," he said, introducing 'Jesus Of Suburbia'. Afterwards he explained, "That song's about telling your home, your family, whatever, to fuck off. And here's something else that can fuck off. The next song's about the war going on in Iraq," leading into 'Holiday'. 'Wake Me Up When September Ends' was dedicated to Johnny Ramone, who had died of prostate cancer the day before.

For the encore, the band served up some back catalogue classics, performing 'Longview', 'Brain Stew' (which Billie Joe ended up singing on his knees when his mic fell over), 'Minority', and Queen's 'We Are The Champions'. Said *RollingStone.com*, "It proved to be a fitting finale, as on this night Green Day earned the right to declare itself champion. . . of a whole new genre."

When the album was finally released in the US on September 21 (September 20 in the rest of the world), it hit with the force of a full-scale explosion, debuting in the *Billboard* charts at number one, having sold 267,000 copies in its first week. ("It's pretty sweet," Billie Joe said of the achievement.) It also debuted at number one in the UK, Ireland, Canada, Australia, and Japan, racking up sales of 1.5 million worldwide in the first week. The reviews were overwhelmingly glowing, from music magazines (*Guitar World*: "This is a multi-layered, literate narrative that effectively wields anger, wit, and bombast to expose the ugliness that seeps below the surface of this country's patriotism, commercialism, and nationalism") to mainstream periodicals (*Newsweek*: "This is one of the best rock albums and the biggest surprise of the year — a punk-rock opera and one of the only mainstream offerings to really address the emotional, moral, and political confusion of our times").

"Tell the truth: did anybody think Green Day would still be around in 2004?" marvelled Rob Sheffield in *Rolling Stone*. "But here they are with *American Idiot*: a 57-minute politically charged epic… all this from the boys who brought you *Dookie*." Sheffield didn't think the album was perfect, but felt that added to its strengths ("*American Idiot* could have been a mess; in fact, it is a mess… But the individual tunes are tough and punchy enough to work on their own"). He also picked up on the wealth of musical influences — naming Hüsker Dü, The Clash, Cheap Trick, The Beach Boys, and Bruce Springsteen among them — and described 'Wake Me Up When September Ends' as "a sadder, more adult sequel to 'Good Riddance (Time of Your Life)'." And if he didn't like every song (calling 'Homecoming' "monstrously awful… like The Who's 'A Quick One While He's Away' without any of the funny parts"), he nonetheless concluded, "Green Day have found a way to hit their thirties without either betraying their original spirit or falling on their faces. Good Charlotte, you better be taking notes."

Many of their peers and colleagues also felt the album ranked among Green Day's best work. "*American Idiot* was the best record of the year and should be recognised as the best record of this decade, certainly dependent on what else comes out," says Jennifer Finch. "As far as craftsmanship, that record is great." Frank Portman remembers first hearing the title song while on a solo tour of Europe. "I went to a radio station when they were playing it and I was like, 'This sounds totally great,'" he says. "You could tell that it was going places. I think it has some great songs. Personally, I like it in spite of the hype, rather than because of it. I'm not that big of a fan of political concept albums, and I think it works if you forget that; it works better for me personally." "As far as I'm concerned, *American Idiot* is their best record by far, an absolute classic in the history of rock'n'roll," says Lawrence Livermore. "I found it really inspiring that a band could do its greatest work after so many years together. Most bands might as well break up after their first two or three albums; by the time *American Idiot* came out, Billie and Mike had been in Green Day half their lives and still managed to make their greatest record yet."

Accolades soon went beyond the album, encompassing a reevaluation of Green Day's entire career. *Entertainment Weekly* called Green Day "the most influential band of their generation." Q magazine had published three special editions chronicling "50 Years of Rock 'n' Roll" in 2004 that didn't have a single mention of the band; by early 2005 they were calling Green Day "the biggest band in the world." At the same time, some were seeking to downplay *American Idiot's* political sensibility. "Don't let the album's political agenda put you off — *Idiot's* appeal is actually mostly non-partisan," *Entertainment Weekly* reassured its readers. Not everyone agreed with that assessment. *Billboard* quoted Mike O'Connor, program director for Denver radio station KTCL as saying, "Denver-Boulder is a split market politically, so when a record like Green Day comes out, we always get accused of Bush bashing."

Nor did the "political agenda" necessarily put everyone off. "It's *got* a political edge," musician/journalist John Robb says of the record. "'American Idiot' is one of the finest punk records ever made. The single is absolutely fantastic — if The Clash had made that single in '78, it'd be looked on as one of the greatest Clash songs ever written. But because it's Green Day, all the rock snobs wouldn't take it seriously. It's not a direct political song, but it taps into what America's like in the Iraq war times, the way the media's being really controlled, etc. America's a very rich country, but it's a country you can very easily be left out of, and I think the song, and the record, picks up on that as well. There's a lot of broken homes, kids not having proper upbringings, it's a selfish society maybe. And Green Day pick up on the things that in your mid-teens you feel like; you feel disenfranchised by American society. But also it's been picked up among loads of kids who have completely happy back-grounds, and just want to go to gigs and jump up and down and sing along to the songs. They just write really great anthems. The best political rock'n'roll is always small 'p' politics. You don't say, 'Bush out! Bush out!' You sing a song that sums up those feelings of people in a more subtle way."

But politics were very much on the American agenda in 2004, another presidential election year. The results of the 2000 election had been (and remain) much disputed, and there was a new divisiveness among the population that spanned generations, as opposed to the anti-war movements of the 1960s that were dominated by younger people — many of whom were not even eligible to vote at the time (prior to the American voting age being lowered to 18 in 1971). In fact, those aged 18 to 24 were now the least likely to vote. In a presidential election year, generally between 50% to 60% of those eligible do cast a ballot, while among 18-to-24-year-olds, the percentage is 20% to 30% less.

In an effort to raise awareness about not only the importance of voting, but also the need to defeat Bush, Green Day contributed the song 'Favorite Son' to the compilation *Rock Against Bush Vol. 2*, released August 10 on Fat Wreck Chords. The label, run by "Fat Mike" Burkett of NOFX, had released *Vol. 1* of the series in April. Proceeds from both CDs were earmarked for Punkvoter, an organisation Burkett had founded, that, in the words of *Vol. 2*'s booklet, was formed to create "a united front in opposition to the dangerous, deadly, and destructive policies of George Bush Jr. [sic]." "I hope that Punkvoter makes [the democratic process] seem a little bit cooler to some of these kids," Billie Joe volunteered by way of endorsement.

Vol. 2 featured a total of 28 bands, including Foo Fighters, Sleater-Kinney, and Bad Religion, among others; "28 more Bush-hating bands give you a slew of unreleased and rare songs that will make you wanna march on D.C. with pitchforks and torches," boasted the label's website, adding the humourous cautionary note: "We don't suggest you do that however, 'cuz they'll come get you and torture the shit out of you." 'Favorite Son' opened the album with an invigorating blast of pop-punk, even as the song disparaged the title character's life of privilege. 'Unity', from Operation Ivy's *Energy* album also appeared on the compilation, with Jesse Michaels writing in the CD's booklet, "George Bush and his administration are responsible for the most destructive pattern of arrogance, corporate servitude, and belligerent warmongering in recent history." The set also came with a DVD featuring a number of short documentary films, including *Unprecedented*, about the 2000 election in Florida; *Independent Media In The Time Of War*; and *Honor Betrayed*, a documentary about US troops fighting in Iraq.

The band played a handful of other preview shows showcasing

American Idiot in its entirety, before the first US leg of the official *American Idiot* tour began, including shows September 18 at The Vic in Chicago and September 24 at Toronto's Phoenix Theatre. A two-day stretch in New York saw them making a number of appearances. On September 20 they taped an appearance for *Sessions @AOL*, which aired Oct 1, followed by an appearance on *The Late Show*. They were photographed with Democratic presidential candidate Senator John Kerry, who was also a guest on the program, and performed 'American Idiot', of which *Salon* noted, "Green Day played as if their music had the power to pick up Bush and Cheney by the throat and shake them lifeless."

On September 21, they appeared at Irving Plaza, a show that was also filmed and recorded, the songs used for single B-sides and film clips appearing on TV music stations. The performance, said *Rolling Stone*, "felt like it was shot out of a circus cannon." While admiring the high-energy songs on the album, reviewer Pat Blashill also noted, "The real beauty, however, could be found in the pathos the group wrung between the power chords, especially in wistful tunes such as 'Wake Me Up When September Ends'... Armstrong, who usually mugs like a silent-film villain, played it straight as he sang the beautiful lyric...At moments like this, the band achieved the sort of punk-rock greatness some critics have accused it of merely imitating. Green Day, surprisingly, have become sublime." It was as clear a sign as any that their days as "snotty-nosed punks" were over. From hereon in, it would be taken for granted that the band had finally achieved unqualified artistic credibility.

The first leg of the American Idiot tour began October 19 in Fort Worth, Texas. Before heading out on the road, the band made their next two videos, 'Boulevard Of Broken Dreams' and 'Holiday'. Both videos were shot at the same time, as 'Boulevard' was meant to be a sequel to 'Holiday', though 'Boulevard' would be released first. "If you think about our country and the specter of war and the problems we're having, then 'Boulevard Of Broken Dreams' is the state of the union," Sam Bayer told *MTV.com*. "And 'Holiday' is the wild trip that got us here."

Both videos show the group passing through two different landscapes, but where 'Holiday's' is the garish neon-lit world of the Las Vegas Strip, 'Boulevard's' is desolate and barren. Both were shot in the same fashion, at an airplane hanger in LA, with the group walking on a treadmill, with moving footage projected on a screen behind the band, conveying the impression they're driving or walking. This technique, called rear-screen projection, has been used in countless older movies and Bayer liked what he called "the surreal and dreamlike" effect it could create. The footage used in the rear-projection shots was filmed by Bayer, shooting out the window of a van driving through the nearby desert, and the streets of downtown Los Angeles.

As 'Boulevard' begins, the open-topped convertible the group was roaring down the road with in 'Holiday' comes to a rolling halt on a deserted road. The band gets out of the car and walks down a "lonely road" of empty houses and urban blight, populated by defeated, broken-down souls; underscoring the overall bleakness is a shot of a vulture (actually a King vulture named Ethel) perched on a post between battered mailboxes. Given that the song's lyric is one of despair, the video becomes a sad travelogue of that other America its citizens don't like to think about — not the land of opportunity, but a wasteland of shattered hopes. In a final touch, Bayer mutilated the film, scratching it with a razor blade, burning it with cigarettes, even throwing it in his shower: "I dare any other directors to try and rip me off on this!" he declared in a documentary on the making of the video. Bayer's handiwork emphasised the video's raw feel, capturing a world on the verge of disintegration.

The video debuted on AOL on November 13, then premiered on MTV2 November 15, as part of a "Making The Video" program. The single proved to be an across-the-board smash, going all the way to number two on the *Billboard* Hot 100, and topping the Modern Rock, Mainstream Rock, Pop 100, Pop 100 Airplay, Adult Top 40, Top 40 Mainstream, and Hot Digital Songs charts, reaching number 30 on the Adult Contemporary chart, and number five on the Hot Ringtones chart. The single's cover, a spray-painted image of a downcast young man with wings on a fading blue wall, readily matched the desolation of the song. The man was actually Chris Bilheimer, and the image was inspired by a painting he'd seen of a homeless man with wings done by Banksy, the UK artist whose work Bilheimer (and Green Day) admired. "Since the song says the line, 'I walk alone' 5000 times, it seemed the obvious element from which to base the content of the cover," he says. "I had very little time to pull this package together, so I photographed myself, cut a stencil, ran down the street and painted it, photographed it and laid it out in a matter of two hours." Royalties from the song's sales on iTunes later went to the Red Cross International Response Fund, benefiting victims of the tsunami disaster in Thailand at the end of December 2004.

By the time the video was released, President Bush had been re-elected, to the band members' dismay. Billie Joe had taken to wearing a Bush mask onstage at concerts, and was particularly disappointed that so few young people had turned out to vote. The turnout ended up being 17% in some places, he told *ContactMusic.com*, but optimistically added, "But of those people, 54% ended up voting for Kerry, which is pretty overwhelming." The same interview also quoted him as saying, "I think George Bush is more of a threat to the freedom of America than Saddam Hussein ever was," a sentiment he continues to voice.

By November 2004, *American Idiot* was certified Platinum and the fall tour was in full swing. During the tour, the group also made two rare in-store appearances, signing memorabilia at Circuit City electronic stores in Rochester, New York and Lynnwood, Washington (a suburb of Seattle), on November 5 and November 16, respectively. At the latter event, teacher John Goar finally managed to meet up with his one-time student. "When I found out he was doing the in-store signing, I jumped at that," says Goar. "I wanted to see if he would recognise me and remember me." Goar brought a Frank Kozik-designed poster of the October 17, 1995 show he'd seen in Seattle, as it featured three bunnies and Goar liked the tie-in with the person cavorting onstage in a bunny suit at the start of Green Day's recent shows.

"I put it down in front of Billie Joe, and he goes, 'Oh, nice poster,'" says Goar. "He hadn't looked up and looked at my face. I said, 'Hey, Billie Joe, do you remember me from John Swett?' and then he looked up and said, 'Mr. Goar!' That was really cool! I kind of half expected that he wouldn't remember me or recognise me, but he did. He reminded me that he got a D in my class. That was something I didn't remember. He indicated that he considered it a gift, that maybe he really didn't even deserve the D — he was thankful I showed him some mercy!

"One of the band members made a joke like, 'Hey Billie Joe, why didn't you try to sell him drugs?' something like that," Goar continues.

"He asked if I was going to the show, and I go, 'Oh, yeah!' Each guy signed one of the bunnies on the poster."

The show that night was at the Everett Event Center in Everett, Washington, "a very large indoor venue," says Goar. "Like all the Green Day shows I've seen, it was awesome. This was the first live rendering I experienced of *American Idiot*, and was nearly the same set as the show I would see a year later at Tacoma Dome [on September 26, 2005]. The Tacoma show was the first Green Day show for my daughters. They both love Green Day, especially my youngest, 13-year-old Julia. Green Day is her favourite band."

On November 22, the group appeared on *Jimmy Kimmel Live*, performing 'Boulevard' and 'American Idiot'. Following a November 24 show at San Francisco's Bill Graham Civic Auditorium, there was a break for the Thanksgiving holiday, then the band went right back to work with a hectic two weeks of performances and appearances. On December 1, they taped an appearance for *VH1's Big In '04* show at the Shrine Auditorium in LA, which would air December 5. On December 3 and 5 there were two shows in Mexico. They then returned to the states where they played a show at The Joint in Las Vegas on December 7, where journalist Jonathan Cohen found Mike in enthusiastic spirits, telling him, "Our shows are bigger than they've ever been. We just played to 18,000 kids in Mexico City. I feel honored by our fans, especially those who have stuck around since the beginning. The fact that this album has done so well really verifies their belief in us." That night they would again play *American Idiot* in its entirety. "This is something we want to revisit the rest of our career," Mike told Cohen. "It's like a new bullet in our arsenal, and it's great to step outside of our regular tour set." The same day, it was announced that Green Day had been nominated for six Grammy Awards, the most nominations they'd ever secured. *American Idiot* was nominated for Album of the Year and Best Rock Album, while the title track was nominated for Record of the Year, Best Rock Performance By A Duo Or Group With Vocal, Best Rock Song, and Best Short Form Music Video. Rob Cavallo was also nominated for Producer of the Year.

They remained in Las Vegas another day to appear at the *Billboard* Awards, then returned to Los Angeles on December 9 (Tré's thirty-second birthday) for an appearance on *The Tonight Show*, followed by an appearance at KROQ's Almost Acoustic Xmas show on December 12. New Year's Eve found them in New York, where they appeared on MTV's *Iced Out New Year's Eve*. The group's mood was giddy, with Tré excited by the blinking ice cubes specially designed for people's drinks at the event ("These things are Satan!"), while Billie Joe blithely smoked backstage in violation of the "No Smoking" rules. The group performed 'American Idiot' and 'Longview' (with Snoop Dogg joining in on the latter number), then got up to more hijinks during the commercial breaks, performing quick cover versions of such unexpected choices as Salt-N-Pepa's 'Push It' and Sir Mix-A-Lot's ode to women's posteriors, 'Baby Got Back'. As the ball fell in Times Square at midnight, marking the start to another new year, *American Idiot* had sold 1.8 copies in the US — an average of 17,476 copies a day.

On January 3, they returned to *The Late Show*, performing 'Boulevard' and two days later were in the studios of MTV, taping a short live set for the music channel. Billie Joe was also a participant in The Fourth Annual *New York Times* Arts & Leisure Weekend, held January 7 at CUNY (City College of New York), interviewed before a live audience by Jon Pareles, the *Times* music critic. Other participants included Susan Sarandon, Bill Murray, and Keifer Sutherland.

The week of January 9, *American Idiot* returned to the top of the *Billboard* charts; sales of the album had reached two million domestically and five million worldwide. Then, on January 11, the first tour of the year began (and the group would play shows every month throughout 2005) with a month-long European/UK tour starting in Berlin. Along the way, there were further TV appearances, including Germany's *TV Total* on January 13, performing 'Boulevard' and Britain's *Top Of The Pops* on February 6, performing 'American Idiot'. On February 9, they appeared at The Brit Awards ceremony, held at Earl's Court in London; nominated for Best International Group, they lost to Scissor Sisters. The tour concluded with a February 10 date in Glasgow, Scotland, by which time *American Idiot* had hit number one on the European Top 100 albums chart for the first time.

Then it was back to the US for the Grammy Awards, held at the Staples Center in LA Green Day turned in an especially tight performance of 'American Idiot'; Billie Joe had told *Inside Bay Area* they planned to "kick some major ass, even if we lost." But this night they wouldn't go away empty handed, taking home the Best Rock Album award. "Rock'n'roll can be dangerous and fun at the same time," Billie Joe assured the audience as the group collected the honor. He later admitted to *Inside Bay Area* he'd been "stunned" at winning, adding, "The reason why I appreciate it so much is just because I feel like all the hard work that went into it was real. There wasn't anything fake about it, so I felt like they were appreciating something for the right reasons." He also participated in the All Star Tsunami Relief Tribute during the ceremony, which had artists including Bono, Alicia Keys, Stevie Wonder, and Norah Jones performing The Beatles' 'Across The Universe'. The song was later offered as a download on iTunes, with the proceeds going to the Red Cross for Tsunami Relief.

On February 15, the group appeared on *Last Call With Carson Daly*, performing 'Jesus Of Suburbia'; again, the studio audience was treated to a few other songs that were not broadcast. On the same day, the group taped a set for *VH1 Storytellers*, a program that features a musical act performing before a live audience, taking breaks in between to talk about the creation of the songs. The band performed the entire *American Idiot* album, and a number of the questions were not just about specific songs, but also about the band's own viewpoints. One attendee asked if the band felt "that anyone who voted for Bush is an 'American idiot.'" Billie Joe smiled and replied, "No, no. . . Just a misinformed idiot." The album's politics were downplayed in places, as when Mike asserted that the record was "speaking from an individual standpoint. It's not pointing fingers necessarily." And during the intro of 'Holiday', Billie Joe announced that the number "is not anti-American, it's anti-war," though the force with which he screamed out "*waaaaarrr!*" left no doubt about his anger regarding the issue. But the group also addressed the record's potential for controversy. "What you going to do?" said Tré. "Are you going to lay down and roll over and be safe and put something out that no one's going to have any questions about being safe? Or are you going to stick your neck out, and let them bleep out what they want to bleep out, and say what's supposed to be said?" Mike also expressed his belief in the power of music; "People say rock'n'roll can change things. If it changes your mindset for one second, or makes you question anything then, yes, I think so." *Storytellers* later aired April 2.

'Holiday' was the group's next single, which continued the group's winning streak, performing well on the various US charts; peaking at number 19 in the *Billboard* Hot 100; it also topped the Modern Rock and Mainstream Rock charts, reached number five on the Adult Top 40 chart, number 18 on the Pop 100 chart, number six on the Hot Digital Songs chart, and number 35 on Hot Ringtones. In the UK, it reached number 11. The cover was a photograph of Billie Joe with dynamite strapped to his chest, meant to symbolize, Bilheimer explains, "How everyone has felt, at some time in their life, as if they were going to explode."

The video debuted on MTV2 on February 5. The video's ominous opening shot is that of a bomb labelled "Green Day" being dropped from a plane (also bringing to mind the cover of *Dookie*). Then the band is seen seemingly cruising down the Las Vegas Strip at lightning speed (in reality, it's another rear-screen projection trick). The band's cavorting in the car is intercut with scenes from one of the best sequences in any Green Day video — a bar full of colourful characters, each one played by a different member of the band: Mike plays a long-suffering bar-tender and a cop who hauls a drunken Tré out of the bar. Billie Joe plays a variety of bar patrons, two of whom get in a fight with each other. Tré gets into drag once again, becoming a floozy blonde in a tight, blue-spangled dress. But the group's fun comes to a grinding halt when their car rolls to a stop — the point at which the 'Boulevard' video began.

A more off-the-wall-venture also had its premiere in February, when John Roecker's film *Live Freaky Die Freaky*, which featured voice-overs from each of Green Day's members, debuted at The Roxy in San Francisco on February 17. The film utilised stop-motion animation and grotesque puppets in relating its story of the power of myths — in this case, the mythology surrounding Charles Manson. Manson, a convicted criminal, and his mixed-gender gang who dubbed themselves "The Family," gained international notoriety for their crime spree on the nights of August 9 and 10, 1969, when The Family (minus Manson) murdered a total of seven people in their Los Angeles-area homes (including actress Sharon Tate, the wife of film director Roman

Polanski). There has long been an inextricable link between Manson and the rock world. Manson was an aspiring musician (an urban legend persists that he auditioned for *The Monkees* TV series) and he finally released an album, *LIE*, after his arrest. He and his "Family" had lived with Dennis Wilson of The Beach Boys for a time; Manson's song 'Cease To Exist' was re-written by Wilson, and, retitled 'Never Learn Not to Love', was recorded and released on The Beach Boys' *20/20* album. Manson has since been referenced in numerous rock songs and controversy still erupts when artists cover his own songs, as when Guns N' Roses recorded Manson's 'Look At Your Game Girl' for their 1993 album *The Spaghetti Incident?*

Prosecuting attorney Vincent Bugliosi wrote the best-selling book *Helter Skelter* about the trial, which further popularised Manson's story and eventually provided the kernel of the idea for Roecker's film. Roecker had noticed how prevalent copies of the book were in used book stores and later speculated that "when the apocalypse comes, all they are going to find is a copy of *Helter Skelter* and the new inhabitants on the earth going to make this their bible." *Live Freaky* opens with just such an post-apocalypse survivor discovering a copy of the book buried in the desert; the film then flashes back to the Family's murder crimes, though the characters are renamed Charlie "Hanson" and Sharon "Hate". The film ends with the apocalypse survivor convinced of the wisdom of Charlie's "message" and he returns to his tribe of fellow survivors, determined to spread the word.

The film's message, Roecker explained to *Filmjerk.com*, was "how you can read anything and make it your own. Good or bad. Take for example, the Bible. A book that was supposed to make people come closer together but more blood was shed from that book than anything else". Indeed, Manson's Family had done just that, interpreting The Beatles' songs 'Helter Skelter' and 'Revolution 9' as foretelling "an impending race and nuclear war, based on Biblical prophecy in the Book of Revelation." Roecker insisted that *Live Freaky*'s message was "think for yourself," but it was a message that was arguably buried underneath the unabashedly profane and scatological antics of the film, which were replete with crude stereotyping, foul language, gory violence, and "explicit puppet sex."

Unsurprisingly, Roecker had difficulty raising money for his film; even Troma Entertainment, known for producing such low-budget cult film fare at *The Toxic Avenger*, turned him down. Eventually, Hellcat Films, the film division of Hellcat Records — run by Rancid's Tim Armstrong — put up the funding. Armstrong also provided the voice-over narration for the film and soon other musicians signed on to participate as well, including one of Armstrong's Rancid band mates, Lars Fredrickson, Jane Weidlin of The Go-Go's, Benji and Joel Madden from Good Charlotte, John Doe from X, and Kelly Osbourne (credited as "Nelly Posbourne") as Sharon Hate, among others.

Actor Viggo Mortensen was originally planned to voice Charlie, but his work on the *Lord Of The Rings* films precluded his participation, so Roecker approached Billie Joe, who readily agreed. Billie Joe recorded his lines in one day, turning in a very convincing performance; "I don't know where that voice came from" he told *Rolling Stone*. "It was like I was possessed by the character." He also recorded a song for the film, 'Mechanical Man' (itself the title of a Manson song, though the song in the movie is a completely different number written by Faith No More's Roddy Bottom). Mike and Tré also had small parts in the film.

When it was completed, Roecker then had more trouble in getting his film seen. It was rejected by every film festival he submitted it to; "I was told I was morally irresponsible," Roecker told the *LA Weekly*. After the film's premiere, it played at a number of independently owned theatres and was finally released on DVD on January 31, 2006. US chains like Wal-Mart refused to carry it, but at least the film had received stateside distribution (as well as release in Canada and Japan); as of this writing, no UK distributor had been found.

In March came a story that was nearly as bizarre as the antics in Roecker's film — the news that Green Day's music had actually awakened a boy in a coma. Nine-year-old Corey George of Aberaman in Aberdare, South Wales, had been hit by a car on his birthday and spent two weeks in a coma on life support. Knowing that Green Day was George's favourite band, his parents played *American Idiot* at his bedside. "He loves Green Day and is always playing their records," said George's father Martyn. "The title track we played is his favourite — he listens to it all the time." In less than an hour, it was said, George emerged from the coma. The band sent George a get-well package of Green Day items and one of the band's representatives stated, "The boys are incredibly pleased that one of their tracks has brought Corey out of his coma. They hope he continues with his recovery and makes a full return to health."

The group played Japan and Australia in March, picking up two more prizes at the MTV Australia Awards on March 3, for Best Group and Best Rock Video for 'American Idiot'. The following month, they picked up two more, winning Favorite Music Group at the Nickelodeon Kids' Choice awards, and International Album of the Year at Canada's Juno Awards. On April 9, they appeared on *Saturday Night Live*, performing 'Boulevard' and 'Holiday'. The entire band was in black, for a change (aside from Tré's striped tie), which struck a somber note during the first number, though Billie Joe broke the mood by shouting "New York City!" during the instrumental break. That same week, the Marriott Marquis in New York's Times Square refused to allow a promotional banner advertising *American Idiot* to be hung on the side of the hotel. In the words of a Marriott representative, "We have the right to review all advertising that goes on our buildings, and if we feel it has any political, pornographic, or inappropriate content, we have the right to reject that ad." The nearby W Hotel had no such reservations and displayed the banner instead.

Then it was back to touring. On April 15, the band began another leg of the US tour in Miami, which ran until May. Another European tour began in June, which ran until July. The highlights included two sold-out shows before a total of 130,000 people at the Milton Keynes National Bowl in England, Saturday June 18 and 19. "A lot of bands have a problem with playing in front of that many people and trying to create intimacy," Billie Joe told *NME*. "But you just try to create an effect. You try to create a spectacle or a splash. It's about just having something that's massive." Still, Mike admitted the band had momentarily wondered if they'd be able to attract a sufficient audience — until both shows sold out. Both concerts were also filmed for the documentary DVD/CD, *Bullet In A Bible*, released that November.

Though Green Day's set — and concluding fireworks display — could be scaled down to accommodate an arena with a capacity of "only" 20,000, the Milton Keynes performances gave the shows the space to live up to their full potential and the group showed they had little difficulty in commanding such a huge stage. Certainly *American Idiot*'s dramatic songs were tailor-made for just such an enormous setting, and live favourites like 'Hitchin' A Ride' and 'Brain Stew' translated to the big stage just as easily. Flashpots, explosions, and fireworks routinely drew screams of approval from every audience; at Milton Keynes, as the sun set and darkness fell over the enormous field, the effects were even more impressive. And certainly a call to "sing so loud that every fuckin' redneck in America hears ya tonight!" was going to be warmly received in a country where even respectable daily newspapers referred to Bush as a "war criminal" in their pages.

As usual, the first part of the show consisted of the *American Idiot* songs, then reached back into Green Day's extensive catalogue. Longtime fans might have noticed, as 'Longview' began, that Billie Joe was playing the guitar he'd named Blue when he first received it, all those many years ago. In a nice nod to the British audience, Billie Joe began singing the chorus of 'Always Look On The Bright Side Of Life' from *Monty Python's Life Of Brian* during the 'little bit softer now' part of 'Shout' as he lay face down on the stage, his head hanging over the steps leading down to the catwalk; the crowd quickly joined in. 'Minority' closed the main set, with Billie Joe proclaiming, "I just want to say that England is now the official home of Green Day from now on!" during the song's instrumental break. He also interjected his standard message of self-empowerment: "Regardless of who the powers that be are — the people that you elect, the people that I elect into office — remember you have the fuckin' power, we're the fuckin' leaders! Don't let these bastards dictate your life or try to tell you what to do!" It was a message audiences were hungry for; as one young man who was interviewed at the show said, the release of *American Idiot* "proved that rock bands can be honest again. And people want to hear it. People want the voice."

The encore of 'Maria', 'Boulevard Of Broken Dreams', and Queen's 'We Are The Champions' followed, with red and white confetti flying after the latter number. It was almost anti-climactic to see Billie Joe return alone, accompanying himself on guitar on 'Good Riddance', but the song had long since become Green Day's equivalent of 'Yesterday' — it was impossible for them to do a show and not perform it. On the last chord, a spectacular fireworks show filled the sky, and Mike and Tré joined Billie Joe on the catwalk to take their final bows, and the show that *NME's* readers would later vote Best Gig Of The Year came to a close.

Green Day then faced a worldwide audience on July 2, when they played a short set at the Live 8 concert staged at Berlin's Siegesse Victory Column. (There were a total of ten Live 8 concerts held in nine countries.) The Live 8 event was organised by Bob Geldof, who had also organised the landmark Live Aid concerts of 1985. The Live 8 concerts were intended to draw attention to global poverty and the AIDS crisis, especially in Africa, and were held the same week world leaders were meeting at the G8 summit in Scotland (July 6 through 8). The London concert generated the most excitement, opening with Paul McCartney joining U2 for 'Sgt. Pepper's Lonely Hearts Club Band' (whose opening line about "20 years ago today" provided an appropriate nod to Live Aid), and also featuring a reunited Pink Floyd, together for the first time in 24 years. Only one song from Green Day's set, 'American Idiot', would be featured on the four-disc DVD set of the event released in November, so fans would miss out on what *Entertainment Weekly* called the "most winning musical statement" of the day. It was Green Day's closing song of the set, 'We Are The Champions', with *Entertainment Weekly* saying of the performance, "From what we saw of Live 8, they really were." It had been a bright, sunny day and the audience needed little encouragement to raise their arms and wave them back and forth as Green Day performed the anthemic song that had also closed Queen's Live Aid set 20 years before. Just before hitting the final chord, Billie Joe looked up at the audience and went, "I say heeeey-oh!" "Heeeey-oh!" the crowd shouted right back. The band finished the song, and Billie Joe held his guitar up over this head, like the champion he was.

CHAPTER 12

And Into The Future

"My goal is to be one of the biggest bands in the world, and I have never been bashful about saying that."

— *Billie Joe to* Alternative Press, *June 2002*

In early August, it was announced that Green Day had reclaimed the rights to the recordings they'd released on Lookout Records, citing lack of royalty payments. Other artists on the label had similar complaints, and the previous few years had seen a number of Lookout acts (including Pansy Davison, Screeching Weasel, and Blatz) leaving for other labels. Green Day had apparently let the matter go in the hopes that it would one day be sorted out, but eventually grew tired of waiting. "There comes a time where you're like, 'Okay, how long do you want to support your record label?'" Mike said to the *East Bay Express*.

Losing Green Day was indeed a blow for Lookout. At the time Green Day reclaimed their recordings, *1,039/Smoothed Out Slappy Hours* had sold over 550,000 copies (and was averaging sales of 900 copies a week), and *Kerplunk!* had sold over 650,000 copies (averaging sales of 800 copies a week). The year after *Dookie's* release, sales of the two albums had resulted in Lookout being awash in cash, with a reported $10 million in sales in 1995. At one point there were as many as 18 staffers —who enjoyed full health benefits and a 401(k) plan — working for the label, and the company even owned its own record shop on University Avenue in Berkeley. As noted in the *East Bay Express*, the label "seemed financially set for life."

But ironically, the influx of cash played a role in the label's later troubles. The label began sinking money into various promotional efforts that never paid off financially. And Lawrence Livermore became increasingly unhappy at having to deal with the pressure of trying to run an unexpectedly successful label. "I was sick of it, partly because I was feeling like Lookout was turning into something very different from what I had intended," Livermore told journalist Rob Harvilla. "I didn't enjoy… sitting in an office fielding requests and demands to spend ever-increasing amounts of money on what I thought was a foolish attempt to mimic the bloated excesses of the major labels." In 1997, he turned ownership over to another employee, Chris Appelgren, Appelgren's now ex-wife [and Bratmobile drummer] Molly Neuman, and Cathy Bauer.

In an open letter posted on Lookout's website on August 2, Appelgren admitted to "bad decisions and poor judgment" leading to Lookout's current problems, "most strikingly in hoping that things would all somehow magically work out, that the shortcomings in operating income, and the fact that our new bands were not selling as many records as we hoped would all somehow just turn out okay on their own if we just kept working hard and doing the best job we could." He added there was no undue animosity between the parties, and indeed, Green Day has not, as of this writing, filed any legal complaint regarding their unpaid royalties. In the meantime, most of Lookout's staff was laid off, as part of a major reorganisation to keep the label afloat. By the end of 2005, the company had moved out of its office on Adeline Street.

On a more positive note, the video for Green Day's latest single, 'Wake Me Up When September Ends', had its US debut on *AOLMusic.com* on August 8 (it was released earlier in Europe). The seven-minute version of the video, which had been shot by Sam Bayer the previous March, had an extended prologue before the music even began, making it something of a mini-movie; indeed, Bayer later said he approached making the video "exactly like a major motion picture," taking a month to cast it (a five-minute edit was also put together). The prologue featured two young actors, Jamie Bell and Evan Rachel Wood (the latter of whom had appeared in the indie film, *Thirteen*), exchanging their vows of love in what was meant to seem an archetypical field somewhere in the American Midwest (in reality, Ojai, California). Bell enlists in the army to his girlfriend's distress; the final shots have him battling in (presumably) Iraq while Wood pines for him at home, sitting on the high-school bleachers. Shots of the band are intercut throughout, each member (including Jason White) on his own raised white circle, as if in some darker version of a 1960s TV variety show.

The end result conveyed a decidedly mixed message; though *RollingStone.com* had Green Day "making their most powerful anti-war statement yet" with the video, the *New York Times'* Kelefa Sanneh noted that "it also works pretty well as a support-our-troops statement for the emo age." Certainly, the "protest" seemed to be aimed more at the unfairness of the young lovers having to be separated; there was no explicit dissent expressed regarding any particular war. One could even argue whether the video had an anti-war message at all. Bayer felt that it did. "I'm not taking a political stance about whether the war in Iraq is right or wrong," he told writer Steve Knopper. "But I'm definitely saying war is a terrible thing." The band members agreed. "The video is like a commercial for free thought — or peace — using the same tactics that the government uses to get people in the Army," Tré told *Rolling Stone*. "We turned the machine on itself."

The song itself did nearly as well on the US Hot 100 as 'Boulevard' had, peaking at number six. It also landed at number two Modern Rock, number four Pop 100, number 12 Mainstream Rock, number 13 Adult Contemporary, number four Hot Digital Songs, and number 14 Hot Ringtones, along with appearances on the Hot 100 Airplay, Pop 100 Airplay, and Top 40 Mainstream charts. In the UK, it also hit the Top 10, peaking at number eight.

On August 10, Green Day kicked off an arena tour in Chicago, and they'd remain on the road for much of the rest of 2005. But the tour schedule was interrupted by plenty of other appearances, particularly at an increasing number of awards shows, with a new award of some kind being given to the band nearly every month for the rest of the year. The US tour precluded their appearance at the *Kerrang!* Awards in London in August, where they won Best Live Act and Best Band On The Planet. But they had arranged to attend that year's MTV Video Music Awards ceremony, held at the American Airlines Arena in Miami on August 29. They arrived in style, driving up in the same green convertible that had appeared in the 'Holiday'/'Boulevard Of Broken Dreams' videos, and, on entering the Arena, each received a specially designed Gap Weekender bag given out to attendees, containing such souvenirs as an iPod (bearing a VMA logo), a solid gold Shu Uemura eyelash curler, a Frederick's Of Hollywood bustier, a Paul Frank orange vinyl Moonman watch, and a paid vacation to South Carolina's Inn at Palmetto Bluff, among other luxury items.

The band also had the honour of opening the show, which they did with a flourish, performing 'Boulevard' utilising a dazzling array of flash-pots and fire and water effects. The song's video then went on to receive an impressive number of honours: Video of the Year, Best Group Video, Best Rock Video, Bayer winning both Best Direction in a Video and Best Cinematography, and Tim Royes winning Best Editing in a Video. The 'American Idiot' video also won the Viewers' Choice award. The only category in which they lost was for Best Art Direction in a Video, which was won by Gwen Stefani's 'What You Waiting For?' "It's nice to know rock music still has a place at MTV," Billie Joe said while accepting the Best Rock Video award. He later dedicated the last award the group accepted to the US troops, saying, "Here's to our soldiers, let's bring them home safe."

Earlier that day, Bayer had received another honour, a Kodak Lifetime Achievement Award for his work in music video, given out at a special luncheon held for those nominated for the VMA Best Cinematography award; though recognising all his work in video, Bayer's projects with Green Day had certainly given him a higher profile. And though again saying the 'September' video was anti-war, not anti-Iraq war, he nonetheless made a more outspoken anti-Iraq war statement himself. "I'm pissed off about the war," he told *Shoot*. "Maybe I'm pissed off that a media channel like MTV isn't doing more to energize kids... I'd like [the 'September' video] to start discussions. I'd like to have kids on TRL not talk about what Gwen Stefani is wearing, but maybe about the Iraq war."

On September 8, the group performed 'Boulevard' at the NFL Opening Kickoff game at Gillette Stadium in Foxboro, Massachusetts. The group had played the same venue in a show of their own on September 3; the performance was filmed and a clip of 'September' from the show was shown as part of *ReAct Now: Music & Relief*, a telethon benefitting victims of Hurricane Katrina. A download of the song, with proceeds also going to the cause, reached number 32 on *Billboard*'s Hot Digital Tracks chart.

Meanwhile, the US tour was proving to be wildly successful, the group routinely being greeted by rapturous sell-out crowds. Billie Joe's constant jabbing at President Bush received an equally enthusiastic reception; in addition to 'Holiday' being regularly introduced as a "big fuck you" to the President, Billie Joe would usually conclude his introductions of the band by saying, "... and I'm George W. Bush. But you can call me... *asshole!*" One wonders about the reaction to such statements of the more conservative parents escorting their children to the show, who may not have previously paid much attention to the music their kids were listening too, much less read any interviews with the band. Indeed, Mike told *Rolling Stone* Billie Joe's anti-Bush comments sometimes prompted a negative response. "We see a guy throw us the finger — but then they'll change it into a fist and start pumping the air," he said. "Maybe they suddenly figure, 'Fuck, yeah — he *is* an asshole."

There was also a subtle backlash of another kind, as a variation of the old "sell out" argument resurfaced and mainstream critics questioned how far the group had strayed from their punk roots now that they were headlining arenas. A *New York Times* review of the band's September 1 show at Giants Stadium in East Rutherford, New Jersey, was titled, "Now A Band That It Once Would Parody." The reviewer, Jon Pareles, went on to point out the irony that practitioners of punk, a genre he called "a corrective to bloated 1970's stadium rock" would go on to become stadium rockers themselves, "reveling in big-event shtick." "What may have been a fond parody of rock excess started to turn into, well, a stadium concert," Pareles wrote and while conceding, "Standard punk was made for clubs, not stadiums, and a full set of three-minute punk blasts wouldn't suit the band or the place," he couldn't help adding, "But Green Day's own catalogue of songs include such diverse material... that the band could have played a stadium concert with far less filler." Still, he also admitted that the material on *American Idiot* was "music that has no use for punk-rock orthodoxy."

And even in the wake of their latest round of massive success, Green Day remained a band more than willing to laugh at themselves, seen most readily when they allowed The Network to open for them for three shows, October 6 in Las Vegas, October 11 Los Angeles, and October 13 in San Francisco. Adeline Records remained as tight-lipped about The Network as always, a statement on their website confirming the opening dates but adding "Green Day's management declined to comment on the ongoing feud between the bands." In an additional twist, the statement was said to have been written by writer/actor George Plimpton, who had died in September 2003.

Insomniac cover designer Winston Smith attended the Green Day/Network show at the Warfield in San Francisco, "an old-fashioned theatre, the kind of place where Sinatra and other people would play when they were nobodies," he says. "It's not gigantically big, it's just a regular theatre. I think the band liked the idea of playing a small club. It wasn't like Gilman or anything, but it was a small club compared to the giant venues and stadiums that they've been accustomed to." He was surprised that the age of the crowd was older than the teenagers he'd been used to seeing at other Green Day shows, which he attributed to the fact that tickets for these special shows were only available on line. "The people who got the tickets were computer geeks or computer wizards," he says. "Usually 14-year-olds are the slickest at that stuff, but maybe they didn't have their gold card out! I don't mean that in any derogatory way. I'm just saying that the tickets evaporated within seconds of being offered."

Smith had not seen The Network before, nor was he aware that the group was, as he puts it, "Green Day in mummy drag." "At one point I was sitting backstage sketching, working on an album cover for Ben Harper," he says. "I was in this quiet, well-lit area; you could put your beer down and not have to worry about anyone knocking into it. I was sketching, and this guy walks up, he was wrapped head to toe in plaster, and he goes, 'Hey Winston, how are you?' I said, 'Is that Mike in there?' He said, 'Could be!' And the same thing happened with Tré coming down the hallway, he gives me a big hug, and I was thinking, 'Who is this, oh, it's you, Tré, you're wrapped up like the invisible man!' I was thinking, 'Man, that has to be really hot to perform under lights and also be wrapped up.' It would be like putting on a rubber Halloween mask, and after an hour you're thinking you've lost nine pounds because of the claustrophobic wrap job. I was amazed that they managed to make it through. It'd be like being in a miniature sauna, a Turkish bath. Maybe that's how they keep their weight down! What a clever thing, too, they open up for themselves."

As far as the band being too tired to headline after also being the opening act, Smith says, "When people who aren't musicians think about that kind of exertion, they think it's just more work. But in their case, they are just thrilled with the opportunity to perform. We artists would probably do it for free if we had to. We *do* do it for free for years before anyone recognises whether we have talent or skills. And that was their thing, that was why they couldn't go off the stage when they were supposed to at the end of the night, they just kept on grooving. Then afterward they were just completely high on the adrenaline charge. You'd think backstage after the show they'd want to have it all quiet and all the people gone but no, that's when they came out and wanted to socialize. From my point of view, I'm an artist, so when I create something, it can take me 10, 12, 14 hours, two weeks, whatever. And at the completion of it, instead of feeling totally drained and tired like you've been running for four miles, you feel this exhilaration for having dived in and completed this thing. Whether it's a work in progress or not, you have this, it's probably a dopamine high people get. That's why musicians can play until their fingers bleed, or artists can stay awake 22 hours at a time to finish a picture. It's because you are driven. Unlike the rest of us who have a 9-to-5 gig, who just can't wait until it's over with and we can unwind. I think they are unwinding while they are on stage. Everyone else is a beneficiary of that."

Smith also experienced the full force of the band's power that night. "Generally when I'm backstage, I stay backstage and hang out there, and I only hear the music from the backstage," he explains. "But this time, I went out front and I couldn't really turn myself away from the front view of the band because it was so compelling. They really know how to perform, and not in a pop or 'show business' way either, it's done completely sincere. They didn't want to stop when they were supposed to stop. Usually shows at the Warfield stop around midnight, maybe one o'clock if someone does a long encore. But these guys went on till they had to be dragged off. And the crowd completely enjoyed it. It was a mutual admiration society.

"When they came backstage, I gave Bill a big hug and I said, 'That was one of the best, if not the best show I've ever seen,'" he continues. "I used to be a roadie for any band you could ever think of, all kinds of wanna-be bands, and I've seen some great shows. Sometimes I think, that's the top, nothing is ever going to get any better than that. Then something else will come along and top it. This show surpassed some of the best stuff I've ever seen. I felt, he must hear this all the time, but it was completely sincere. I never said it to anybody else. I usually just say, great performance, good show, well done. But not so effusively as I felt that time. It was definitely heartfelt. And he definitely took it that way. I think he was kind of glad to hear it from an old-timer like me. A geezer like me, that I actually thought the show was not bad."

In November, the group was back overseas. On November 3, they picked up two more awards, winning Best Rock Act and *American Idiot* winning Best Album at the MTV Europe Awards, held at Lisbon's Pavilhão Atlântico, though losing Best Group to Gorillaz. The band also performed 'September' during the show. Then it was off to the UK, where on November 6 the group performed 'Jesus Of Suburbia' in its entirety on *Top Of The Pops*, making it the longest song performed on the show to date. Fans in attendance at the BBC TV studios were then treated to a short set by the group.

The next day a special advance screening of *Bullet In A Bible*, the concert film of their Milton Keynes concerts, was held at London's Vue Cinema (advance screenings of the film had been held November 1 in the US). The band members attended the screening, with Billie Joe making a few comments before the film was shown, thanking their tour crew, and adding, "It's been the best year we've ever had and most of all thank you, thanks a lot, we really appreciate it, and we will be back."

The *Bullet In A Bible* DVD/CD set was released November 14 in the UK and Europe (the same day the 'Jesus Of Suburbia' single was released in the UK), and November 15 in the US, where it debuted at number eight in the *Billboard* Top 200 chart. The cover was designed by Chris Bilheimer, who reversed the colour scheme used on *American Idiot*; instead of a black background, the package had a red background. The clear plastic "O" card that encased the package featured the title and the band's name in white lettering, with a shot of Billie Joe facing the massive audience, fist raised in the air, in black. "I tried to keep the same theme as the *American Idiot* album," says Bilheimer. "It's the same type-face, and I wanted it to still have the revolutionary propaganda poster effect with the raised fist sort of thing. And it was the best photo they had. Nothing else was that iconic, had that much of an impact, and didn't just look like every other live record — a dude with the guitar. This has an epic feeling to it."

The back cover has a bullet entry hole, and when you open the sleeve up, there's a shot of the bullet coming through the other side. "My father collects guns," Bilheimer says. "So I called him and said, 'Can you shoot some books for me and mail them to me?' So that is an actual bullet on the inside."

Both the DVD and CD had the same songs, but the show itself was incomplete (missing were 'Knowledge', 'She', 'Maria', and 'We Are The Champions'). On the DVD, the concert was intercut with interview seg-ments, backstage footage, and interviews with concert attendees. Billie Joe was seen confidently proclaiming Green Day the "hardest-working band in rock. Ever!" while Mike revealed, "I gotta break a sweat before I hit the stage. Because it's like jumping on to a moving train." Some of the segments struck a surreal note, as when Tré was seen, wearing a Canadian Mounties's hat, sitting behind a table of doughnuts, in a scene that could have come from David Lynch's *Twin Peaks* TV series (equally Lynchian was the moment he inexplicably blurts out, "No man can eat 50 eggs!"). There was also a sequence of the band walking around London's Imperial War Museum, which Billie Joe described as "a big gallery of someone else's nightmare." One shot had Billie Joe standing in front of a tank, his head blocking out the letter "D" on the machine, so that instead of reading "DEVIL" you see the word "EVIL". In another,

Billie Joe bangs his fist against a replica of one of the bombs dropped on Hiroshima, creating a mournful sound like the tolling of a funeral bell. The group also looks at a display featuring the item that gave the release its title; a Bible a soldier had been carrying in his coat pocket, which saved his life when it stopped a bullet. Though interesting and insightful, the interview segments do break up the flow of the concert, making it a shame that the first official live DVD by the group, capturing what will surely be considered a landmark engagement, didn't come with a "performance only" option.

Back in the states, the band performed 'September' on *Late Night with Conan O'Brien* on November 11. They also attended the US release party for *Bullet In A Bible*, held on the day of its release at LA's ArcLight Cinemas; among other celebrities, Danny Bonaduce, of TV's *The Partridge Family*, turned up with his kids, citing *Dookie* as his favourite Green Day album. November also saw the premiere of the last video from *American Idiot*, 'Jesus Of Suburbia', initially in a nine-minute edit. But like the video for 'September', additional footage was also shot and edited into a 14-minute version. Billie Joe referred to the video as "the new 'Thriller'." The video has the title character (played by Lou Taylor Pucci), disaffectedly going through his day, passing the time in his room, at the local 7-11, and at parties, an environment permeated by dilapidation. Even before working on the clip, Bayer had cited Larry Clark's bleak film *Kids* as having the look he wanted to achieve. What comes through is a strong sense of isolation; though he's frequently with other people, this "Jesus" is unable to make any kind of real connection with anyone, even his girlfriend (played by Kelli Garner; both she and Pucci had appeared in the indie film *Thumbsucker*). Cleverly, Green Day is only seen in passing, on the various TVs that sit in the background. The nine-minute version of the video had its US broadcast premiere November 28 on fuse, another music cable network; the longer version was available on Music Choice, a video-on-demand service.

Bayer felt the video set a new standard for him. He'd previously told *MTV.com* that he considered the 'September' video "hands down the greatest thing I've ever done." Now he amended that view, calling 'Jesus Of Suburbia' "the greatest Green Day video that's ever been done." Bayer also announced 'Jesus Of Suburbia' would be his last music video.

"I can't think of a better way to end my video career," he told *MTV.com*. The single itself reached number 27 on *Billboard*'s Modern Rock chart (making them their third act to hit the chart with five singles pulled from the same album) and number 17 in the UK. The single's cover art, the white silhouette of a dog, head hanging down, against a black background amply reflected the isolation of the song's title character. The idea was inspired by imagery Bilheimer had seen in Lance Bangs' films. "His film work has explored the concept of a stray dog symbolizing childhood alienation from one's family," he explained. "This seemed to mesh perfectly for the story of the Jesus Of Suburbia."

Green Day wasn't on hand to pick up their next awards at the American Music Awards ceremony, held November 22 at the Shrine Auditorium in Los Angeles. They won in two categories: Favorite Artist - Alternative Music and Favourite Album - Pop/Rock for *American Idiot* (losing Favourite Band, Duo or Group - Pop Rock to Black Eyed Peas). But they were in attendance for VH1's *Big In '05* show, taped on December 3 at LA's Sony Studios, winning the Big Music Artist award (the show aired the following day). And they performed at the *Billboard* Music Awards, held at the MGM Grand Hotel in Las Vegas on December 6, turning in a fierce rendition of 'Holiday'; not broadcast was a bonus performance of 'St. Jimmy'. Billie Joe also gave the magazine's Century Award to Tom Petty, saying, "I love music. I love rock'n'roll, therefore I love Tom Petty And The Heartbreakers," by way of introduction. And Green Day picked up six awards for themselves: Album Group Of The Year, Pop Group Of The Year, Rock Artist Of The Year, Hot 100 Group of the Year, and Modern Rock Artist of the Year, with 'Boulevard Of Broken Dreams' winning Rock Song Of The Year.

The *American Idiot* songs soon crossed over into another realm— mash-ups, when parts of two or more songs are combined to create a new recording, a technique that gained infamy when DJ Danger Mouse created the *Grey Album*, a mash-up of *The Beatles* (commonly known as the "White Album," due to its all-white cover) and Jay-Z's *The Black Album*. As mash-ups are generally done without permission and then distributed freely over the Internet, they violate copyright law.

In November 2005, two DJs, "Party Ben" from San Francisco and Australian "Team9," working under the joint name Dean Gray did a mash-up of *American Idiot* they entitled *American Edit*. The mash-ups showed the usual inventiveness: 'Holiday' drew on Gary Glitter's 'Rock and Roll', the theme from the UK TV series *Dr. Who*, and soundbites from President Bush's speeches; 'Novocaine' added 'Bohemian Rhapsody' to the mix (appropriately, given that the song had long been a favourite of the band's, "A rad song no matter how much they play it," Mike had told *Flipside*); and, in the most unlikely pairing, 'Boulevard' with The Eagles' 'Lyin' Eyes'.

Dean Gray posted the songs on line, soliciting no payment, but asking that fans make a donation to charities Green Day had supported. "Originally, the goal was to point out just how similar some of the songs on *American Idiot* are to other rock songs," Ben told *MTV.com*. "But there are also some tracks we did that created entirely new songs and they're amazing. So we decided to put the entire mashed-up album on line and on November 18 we did." Within 10 days they received a cease-and-desist order from Warner Music, though the band members themselves may not have minded the infringement as much. Billie Joe was said to have called the mash-ups "really cool," and, in reference to downloading songs for free via services like Napster, he'd said in 2001, "It was never really about getting paid. It was just getting people to hear my music and say, 'Hey, I like your song.' So if Napster wants to put my song out so people can download it or whatever, let 'em do it."

Nonetheless, after receiving the letter from Warner's, Dean Gray took the mash-ups down on November 28. In response, a DJ named Noisemaker, based in Portland, Oregon, organised what was called the "American Edit Gray Tuesday Protest" on December 13, which had websites around the world offering the songs as free downloads for a single day. On his website, Noisemaker contended that the protest "was not intended to be a mass organization of music piracy but, rather, one single display of the consumptive power of the mash-up and home remix community in the hopes of encouraging the labels, publishers, and artists who are curious about the mash-up community to consider giving the high-quality productions of 'illegitimate' music a legitimate consideration as a promotional avenue for all music." He added, "What can I say? It's the best promotion Warner and Green Day never wanted."

On the more legal front, US fans could content themselves with the screening of a new hour-long live performance taped for fuse on November 12 at their New York City studios. The concert, which aired December 4, was the culmination of an entire week of Green Day programming on the network. Afterwards, the band headed Down Under for another successful series of shows, with Billie Joe still delighting audiences by shouting phrases like, "My name is Billie Joe Armstrong and I was sent to make George fucking Bush's life a fucking nightmare!" A review of their December 17 performance at the Telstra Dome in Melbourne, where they played before 37,000 people noted, "This was the Green Day at their best." At the same show, Billie Joe Armstrong mentioned how Australian band The Living End had sent him a demo tape during Green Day's first Australian tour, then brought out the band's singer/guitarist, Chris Cheney, who played guitar on a cover of The Bobby Fuller Four's 'I Fought The Law'.

The show was also the very last date of the *American Idiot* tour. "It's going to be kind of sad for [the tour] to end, but, you know, we don't have any regrets." Billie Joe told *Billboard*, looking back on what he called "the best year of our career." The magazine also noted that the band had grossed $36.5 million from touring in 2005 alone. (*Forbes* put the touring income figure at $34.8 million, out of $99 million total the group had earned during the year.) And in a year that had seen album sales in the US continue to drop, *American Idiot* had remained a top seller, selling another 3.4 million copies. And there were still more awards to be received before the year was over. On December 19, the group won a clutch of honours at the Radio Music Awards, with 'Boulevard' chosen as Song of the Year in the Adult Hit Radio, Rock Radio, Alternative and Active Rock Radio categories, and Artist of the Year in the Alternative, and Active Rock Radio.

As they remained in the public eye, Billie Joe continued his anti-Bush statements; *NME* quoted him as saying, "This is the worst US administration in our history." And now, instead of being regarded as controversial, it was a sentiment being echoed openly by US elected officials, as when Senator Hillary Clinton, addressing a rally in Harlem on Martin Luther King, Jr.'s birthday on January 16, 2006, said, "I predict to you that this administration will go down in history as one of the worst that has ever governed our country." A tide was turning in America, and Green Day had been in the vanguard of change.

As 2006 began, there were no concert dates on Green Day's schedule for the first time a year and a half. But there were more awards waiting to be accepted. In the *Kerrang!* Reader's Poll they were named Best Band, the Milton Keynes concerts Best Live Show, 'Jesus Of Suburbia' winning Best Single and Best Video, and Billie Joe Best Dressed Star, as well as Hero Of The Year. On January 10, Green Day won the Favorite Group at the People's Choice Award. On February 8, they were back at LA's Staples Center for the Grammy Awards, with 'Boulevard Of Broken Dreams' winning Record Of the Year. When Billie Joe, Mike, and Tré came up to the stage, they hugged each other, then Billie Joe stepped forward to speak for the group, his first words being, "Oh my God!" Standing onstage with them were Rob Cavallo, Doug McKean (who'd engineered the album), and Chris Lord-Alge (who mixed the record). Billie Joe thanked them all, as well as Mike and Tré, whom he called his "brothers for life." He ended by saying, "I just want to acknowledge that pop radio playing rock music is a very big deal to me, so thank you very much." Lord-Alge had time to shout, "Green Day rules!" into the mic before the station cut to a commercial.

Six days later, on February 14, they finally won two Brit Awards, *American Idiot* winning Best International Album and the group itself winning Best International Band. ("When Paris Hilton presented the best international album prize to Green Day at the 2006 Brit Awards, many must have loved the irony of hearing the heiress scream out 'American Idiot!'" *ChartAttack.com* jokingly noted.)

And there were still more awards to be picked up. On March 9, the band received an Icon Award from the non-profit organization Music for America, at a San Francisco fundraiser honouring politically progressive musicians and politicians (other honourees included San Francisco Mayor Gavin Newsom, Death Cab For Cutie, and Oakland-based Youth Movement Records). Nirvana's bassist Krist Novoselic handed the group their award, and Billie Joe, pleased to be at an awards show "that actually has a fucking purpose," added that he anticipated getting the "racist, war-hungry, corporate fascists out of the White House" in 2008, the year of the next US presidential election. March 19 found them at a dinner held by the Recording Academy's San Francisco Chapter at the Westin St. Francis Hotel, "Honoring Bay Area Music Professionals." "It's an honour to be here because it's an honour," Billie Joe quipped as the group posed for pictures in the press room. My Chemical Romance played a medley of Green Day's songs by way of tribute at the show, which included 'When I Come Around', 'American Idiot', and 'Wake Me Up When September Ends'.

On March 23, it was announced that *Esquire* magazine named the group Best Band in their annual ESKY Awards for Musical Achievement. On April 1 they were named Favourite Music Group and 'September' Favourite Song at the 19th annual Nickelodeon's Kids Choice Awards. The same day it was announced the group would now be promoting a way for their fans to register to vote with their cell phones via text messaging at future shows.

But the band members were winding down from the excitement of the previous years and were quietly preparing to go back into the studio to start work on the follow-up to the most impressive album of their career. It was a prospect anyone would find intimidating. "It's just getting to this point where we're finished with this cycle, and sort of looking down and saying, 'OK, what's next?'" Billie Joe told *Rolling Stone*. "That's always the scariest moment in a band's career, and it's happening to us in a big way."

He could've said "happening to us again," as this was precisely the situation Green Day had faced after *Dookie's* explosive success. But it was a decade on, and the band, and their coping skills, had both matured, meaning they'd be able to face the next chapter in their career with a renewed sense of confidence. And they'd also be working, at least initially, in a very familiar setting, Studio 880, where playing hard and working hard went hand in hand, with some pretty spectacular results.

The group had over a dozen new songs to work on when they went in the studio, though Billie Joe stressed they'd be taking it slow; no potential release dates were even hinted at. "We're gotta take our time," Billie Joe told the *NME*. "[2005] was such a big year for us. I think it's a good time to regroup and have good substance to write about instead of hopping into something really fast." To *Billboard.com* he said, "Right now, it's that no-pressure/fun stage of just getting on a 4-track and coming up with some goofy stuff. Eventually, something sort of unfolds. It's exciting. The juices are always flowing."

In addition to the album, the band has expressed an interest in touring places where US rock bands don't usually go: Russia, perhaps, or many Cuba. A film version of *American Idiot* is also in the works, though at the time of this writing, the project was still in its initial planning stages, though the band members have said they have no plans of starring in the film. But there will be another film project released during 2006; as of this writing, John Roecker's documentary about the making of *American Idiot*, entitled *Heart Like A Hand Grenade*, is scheduled for release late in the year.

So many people have tried to explain what it all means, how a band whose members came from two small California towns most people had never heard of managed to turn the rock world upside down not just once, but twice. It's a remarkable and impressive story, all the more exciting for not being over yet. And in the end, it's a story best summed up by the band members themselves. Mike made the following comment to the Dutch magazine *Oor* in 1995, but it's just as true today, over 10 years later: "The name Green Day is living a life of its own now. Green Day is now an item to describe something, to support an idea or whatever. But I know what Green Day really is: three guys in a room and Billie Joe writing the songs."

Acknowlegements

Thanks to Chris Charlesworth, for commissioning this book, and to Andrea Rotondo for her editing. Many thanks to all of my interviewees: Murray Bowles, Dean Carlson, Jennifer Finch, Jon Ginoli, Steve Hart, Kevin Kerslake, Neill King, Mark Kohr, Ken Leslie, Jesse Michaels, Robin Paterson, Frank "Dr. Frank" Portman, John Robb, Michael Rosen, Winston Smith, Toxsima, and Eric Yee; extra special thanks to Lance Bangs, Chris Bilheimer, Jason Funbug, John Goar, Lawrence Livermore, and John Lucasey for their help in providing materials and answering repeated inquiries. My transcriptionists/researchers also merit major kudos for their efforts: Katie Hansen, Nick Tamburro, Julia Voss, and especially the nimble and relentless fingers of Carrie Stamper. Thanks also to Marc Melfi and Nick Hoffstedde for their help in many areas, Jeff Apter, Rick Buttle and Tam Johnson for their additional assistance, and Dr. Christopher Belcher and Carol Nicholson for keeping my hands and arms working. And, of course, my greatest supporter — mom.

Bibliography

Articles

Ali, Lorraine. "Wow, What An 'Idiot'!," *Newsweek*, September 20, 2004.

Appleford, Steve. "Tour Report: Green Day/Blink-182," *Rolling Stone*, April 25, 2002.

Aledort, Andy. "Basket Case," *Guitar World*, February 2002.

Armstrong, Billie Joe. "Sex Pistols: *Never Mind The Bollocks*," *Rolling Stone*, April 21, 2005.

Armstrong, Mark. "'Imagine' All The Inappropriate Songs," *eonline.com*, September 18, 2001.

Augusto, Troy J. "Blink-182; Green Day," *Daily Variety*, April 26, 2002.

Baird, Kirk. "'Warning' — Don't Call Green Day A sellout," *Las Vegas Sun*, July 20, 2001.

Baltin, Steve. "Green Day Cranking Out Songs," *RollingStone.com*, March 19, 2004.

Baltin, Steve. "Green Day Craft Punk Opera," *RollingStone.com*, May 26, 2004.

Baltin, Steve. "Green Day Unveil 'Idiot'," *RollingStone.com*, September 17, 2004.

Barbieri, Kelly. "Addition Of Green Day Pays Off For Vans Warped As Dates Added," *Amusement Business*, May 8, 2000.

Basham, David. "Frustrators Clarify 'Midget Toss' After NBA Flap," *MTV.com*, June 22, 2000.

Bauder, David. "The Best Thing Green Day Has Ever done," Associated Press, February 2, 2005.

Bird, Ashley. "Flicking the 'B's," *Kerrang!*, June 29 2003.

Blashill, Pat, Curtis, Anthony De Curtis, Ben Edmonds, Gavin Edwards, et al, eds. "Billie Joe Armstrong: My Top 10," *Rolling Stone*, December 11, 2003.

Blashill, Pat. "Green Day," *Rolling Stone*, October 28, 2004.

Boehlert, Eric. "New Acts Rewrite Book On Touring," *Billboard*, March 11, 1995.

Boehm, Mike. "Weekend Reviews; Green Day Sizzles During Bland Weenie Roast," *The Los Angeles Times*, June 22, 1998.

Borzillo, Carrie. "As Reprise Set Rises, It's Easy Being Green Day," *Billboard*, April 9, 1994.

Borzillo, Carrie. "Rocketing Off The Chart; Tracking The Development Of Heatseeker Impacts," *Billboard*, July 16, 1994.

Bradman, E. E. and Terry Buddingh. "Ready Set Go!," *Bass Guitar*, March 2006.

Brown, Mark. "Warped Tour Heralds Dawning Of New Day For Oakland Punkers," *Rocky Mountain News*, July 7, 2000.

Browne, David. "Insomniac (review)," *Entertainment Weekly*, October 20, 1995.

Browne, David. "Rock & Roll Story Hour: Green Day And Elvis Costello Concept CDs? How Punk! (review)," *Entertainment Weekly*, September 24, 2004.

Brunner, Rob. "NBC Sees Green," *Entertainment Weekly*, June 5, 1998.

Campbell, Jason. "Warning! Green Day Busy With Albums, Side Projects," *MTV.com*, August 7, 2001.

Cantu, Bob. "Green Day," *Flipside*, May/June 1992.

Carman, John. "D-Day Has Finally Arrived," *The San Francisco Chronicle*. May 6, 1996.

Chonin, Neva. "The Spirit of Punk Burns On At Saturday's Warped Tour," *The San Francisco Chronicle*, July 3, 2000.

Chonin, Neva. "A New Dawn For Green Day," *The San Francisco Chronicle*, October 22, 2000.

Chonin, Neva. "Green Day Eclipses Blink-182 (review)," *The San Francisco Chronicle*, April 29, 2002.

Clark, Michael. "Pop Pain: It's Not Easy Being Green," *The Houston Chronicle*, May 9, 2002.

Cohen, Jonathan. "Green Day's 'Idiot' Fueling Banner Year," *Billboard*, December 7, 2004.

Cohen, Jonathan. "Green Day Not Ready To Rest 'Idiot'," *Billboard*, July 26 2005.

Colapinto, John. "Working Class Heroes," *Rolling Stone*, November 17, 2005.

Colapinto, John. "Billie Joe Armstrong: Rock's Rude Boy," *Rolling Stone*, December 29, 2005-January 12, 2006.

Davis, Darren. "Green Day's Billie Joe On Joey Ramone's Legacy," *Launch.com*, April 19, 2001.

Davis, Darren. "Joey Ramone's 50th Birthday Celebrated," *Launch.com*, May 22, 2001.

Di Perna, Alan. "Far From The Maddening Crowd," *Guitar World*, December 2000.

Di Perna, Alan. "Combat Rock," *Guitar World*, Holiday 2004.

Doerschuk, Andy. "King Of Punk Rools," *Drum!*, July 1996.

Dougherty, Steve. "Pop Go The Punks," *People*, March 20, 1995.

Dowdy, Zachary R. and Jim Sullivan. "Abrupt End To Green Day Concert," *The Boston Globe*, September 10, 1994.

Duffy, Thom and Wolfgang Spahr. "Warner's Biohazard, Green Day Promoted, Welcomed In Europe," *Billboard*, June 25, 1994.

Editors; *Time*. "The Best & Worst Of 1994: The Best Music Of 1994," *Time*, December 26, 1994.

Elwood, Philip and Craig Marine, "Green Day's Big Night," *The San Francisco Examiner*, March 12, 1995.

Elwood, Philip. "Chris Isaak, Inka Inka Big Winners At Bammies," *The San Francisco Examiner*, March 10, 1996.

Elwood, Philip. Bay Area Scores Over 30 Grammy Nominations," *The San Francisco Chronicle*, January 8, 1997.

Enriquez, Kelly and Jen Gore. "Interview With Mike From Green Day," *Alter/Native*, April 4, 1994.

Epstein, Dan. "When They Were Green," *Guitar Legends*, Spring 2005.

Farber, Jim. "Green Day's Pin-Up Punk, Billie Joe Armstrong, Talks Just Like He Plays — Fast And Furious," *Seventeen*, April 1996.

Farley, Christopher John. "Not Your Parents' Punk," *Time*, October 16, 1995.

Fiore, Raymond. "Is 8 Enough?," *Entertainment Weekly*, July 15, 2005.

Fischer, Blair R. "HFS Fest," *MTV.com*, May 18, 1998.

Foeger, Alec. "Green Day," *Rolling Stone*, December 28, 1995- January 11, 1996.

Foerster, Jonathan. "Green Day Lets Fans Dictate Show," *The Milwaukee Journal Sentinel*, June 20, 2001.

Ganahl, Jane. "Green Day's Manic Energy Intoxicating," *The San Francisco Examiner*, December 15, 1995.

Ganahl, Jane. "Has Billie Joe Grown Up?," *The San Francisco Examiner*, December 14, 1997.

Ganahl, Jane. "'Twas A Bloody Bash!," *The San Francisco Examiner*, April 18, 1998.

Ganahl, Jane. Keeping It Real At the Bridge benefit, *The San Francisco Examiner*, October 31, 1999.

Giardina, Carolyn. "Samuel Bayer Earns Kodak Lifetime Achievement Award for music videos," *Shoot*, September 9, 2005.

Gordinier, Jeff. "It's Not Easy Being Green Day," *Entertainment Weekly*, June 10, 1994.

Grunwald, Michael. "For Fans Young And Old, A Scary Night On Esplanade," *The Boston Globe*, September 11, 1994.

Hajela, Deepti. "Clinton Blasts House Leadership, Bush," Associated Press, January 17, 2006.

Harris, Chris. "Green Day Pull Catalog From Lookout! Records, Label Lays Off Staff," *MTV.com*, August 4, 2005.

Harvilla, Rob. "Kerplunk: The Rise And Fall Of The Lookout Records Empire," *East Bay Express*, September 14, 2005.

Helbig, Bob. "Prosecutors Delay Action On Mooning Incident," *The Milwaukee Journal Sentinel*, November 23, 1995.

Helbig, Bob. "City Won't Pursue Case Against Singer," *The Milwaukee Journal Sentinel*, December 6, 1995.

Heller, Greg. "Green Day In, Jello Biafra Out For San Francisco Rally," *RollingStone.com*, November 1, 2000.

Heller, Greg and Denise Sheppard. "Green Day, Shelby Do Isaak Show," *RollingStone.com*, December 10, 2001.

Hendrickson, Matt. "Green Day And The Palace Of Wisdom," *Rolling Stone*, February 24, 2005.

Herrera, Jonathan. "Mike Dirnt: Punk Patriot," *Bass Player*, September 1, 2004.

Hiatt, Brian. "Shades Of Green Day?," *Entertainment Weekly*, November 7, 2003.

Hiatt, Brian. "Under Their Influence," *Entertainment Weekly*, September 17, 2004.

Hiatt, Brian and Evan Serpick. "Music Tanks in '05," *Rolling Stone*, January 1, 2006.

Hicks, Tony. "Big As Can Be, Green Day Sticks By Its Roots," *Contra Costa Times*, September 26, 2005.

Jackson, Derrick Z. "A Double Standard On 'Fun'," *The Boston Globe*, September 16, 1994.

Jamieson, Amie and Hyon B. Shin, Jennifer Day. "Voting And Registration In The Election Of November 2000," U.S. Census Bureau, February 2002.

Kaufman, Gil. "Green Day And 50 Cent Dominate Billboard Music Awards," *MTV.com*, December 7, 2005.

Kava, Brad. "Green Day Delivers At Sold-Out Concert," *The Mercury News*, September 25, 2005.

Kemp, Mark. "Shenanigans (review)," *Rolling Stone*, August 22, 2002.

Kennedy, Sharon and Iain Blair. "Green Day's 'American Idiot'," *Studiodaily.com*, May 1, 2005.

Knopper, Steve. "Green Day, Beyonce Hit Web," *RollingStone.com*, April 7, 2004.

Knopper, Steve. "Green Day Go to War," *RollingStone.com*, August 23, 2005.

Kot, Greg. "Billie Joe's New Day," *Rolling Stone*, October 10, 2000.

Krissy, "Green Day at Music for America's Icon Awards," sfist.com, March 14, 2006.

Lanham, Tom. "The Band You Love To Hate," *Rip*, April 1996.

Lanham, Tom. "Green Day's Billie Joe Armstrong Sounds Off," *Inside Bay Area*, September 23, 2005.

Lecaro, Lina. "Billie Joe Channels Manson," *RollingStone.com*, February 25, 2004.

Lecaro, Lina. "Starring Members of Green Day, Rancid, X And More, *Live Freaky! Die Freaky!* Is Guaranteed To Offend," *LA Weekly*, March 1, 2006.

Livermore, Lawrence. "Life With Larry," *MaximumRockNRoll*, June 1994.

Livermore, Lawrence. "Interview With Billie Joe," *Hit List*, July 18, 2001.

Livermore, Lawrence. "The Early Days," *Metal Hammer Presents Green Day*, Fall 2005.

Mancini, Robert. "Green Day To Issue 'Warning' In October," *MTV.com*, May 30, 2000.

Marinucci, Carla. "Technology, Star Power Energize Youth Vote," *The San Francisco Chronicle*, April 1, 2006.

Marks, Craig. "An American Family," *Spin*, December, 1995.

McGrory, Brian. "MDC Ponders Rock Ban At Hatch Shell," *The Boston Globe*, September 11, 1994.

McIver, Joel. "Go Ahead, Punks…Make My 'Day!," *Record Collector*, February 2002.

McPhee, Michele R. and Renee Graham. "Violence Halts Green Day Concert," *The Boston Globe*, September 10, 1994.

Melia, Daniel. "Green Day Go Bush Bashing…They love it!," *gigwise.com*, November 10, 2005.

Mikkelson, Barbara and David P., eds. "Radio, Radio," http://www.snopes.com/rumors/radio.htm, September 18, 2001.

Missio, Erik. "No Songs Banned After All?," *ChartAttack.com*, September 19, 2001.

Montgomery, James. "Ashlee Attacks Green Day, Lindsay Nearly Loses Her Dress: Backstage At MTV's New Year's," *MTV.com*, January 3, 2005.

Montgomery, James. "It's A Dark Day For Green Day In Somber 'September' Video," *MTV.com*, April 19, 2005.

Montgomery, James. "Green Day Shoot American Documentary In British Suburbia," *MTV.com*, June 17, 2005.

Montgomery, James. "'Teen Spirit' Director Calls Green Day Clip His Career Highlight," *RollingStone.com*, August 9, 2005.

Montgomery, James. "Green Day's 'Dreams' Slashed And Dumped In A Shower," *MTV.com*, August 13, 1995.

Montgomery, James. "Are Green Day Their Own Worst Enemy? Only Time — Or Concerts — Will Tell," *MTV.com*, October 5, 2005.

Montgomery, James. "Green Day Mash-Up Leads To Cease-And-Desist Order, Grey Tuesday-Style Protest," *MTV.com*, December 20, 2005.

Montgomery, James. "Road To The Grammys: The Making Of Green Day's 'Boulevard Of Broken Dreams'," *MTV.com*, February 1, 2006.

Moss, Corey. "Vans Warped Tour Turns 10 — So What's Its Secret?," *MTV.com*, June 24, 2004.

Moss, Corey. "Total Idiot : Green Day Perform Their Punk Opera In Hollywood," *MTV.com*, September 17, 2004.

Moss, Corey, and John Norris. "Green Day Shoot 14-Minute Short Film For 'Jesus Of Suburbia'," *MTV.com*, October 12, 2005.

Moss, Corey. "New Found Glory, Taking Back Sunday Turn Out For Green Day DVD Premiere," *MTV.com*, November 16, 2005.

Mundy, Chris. "Green Daze," *Rolling Stone*, January 26, 1995

Odell, Michael. "Three Kings," Q, May 2005.

Nelson, Andrew. "Rock 'n' Ribs Beginnings," *San Francisco*, October 2004.

Newman, Melinda. "Green Day," *Billboard*, April 29, 1995.

Newman, Melinda. "Pat's Own Imprint: Green Day Manager Teams With Universal For Label," *Billboard*, July 17, 2004.

Newman, Melinda. "A Smart Start For Green Day," *Billboard*, October 9, 2004.

Newman, Melinda. "Green Day Seeks Some Quiet After High-Energy Year," *Billboard*, Dec 30, 2005.

Pareles, Jon. "O.K., Not Quite as Bratty, But They're Still Rowdy," *The New York Times*, October 9, 2000.

Paterson, Robin. "JS Alum Rocks At SBC Concert," *John Swett Signal*, October 2005.

Porosky, Pamela. "Fear & Loathing In A Post-9/11 America," *Guitar Player*, February 2005.

Reade, Brian. "God Help America," *Daily Mirror*, November 5, 2004.

Reighley, Kurt B. "Green Day Dawns Anew," *The Advocate*, November 23, 2004.

Ritchey, Joy. For The Love Of Green Day," *Arkansas Times*, November 24, 2005.

Robbins, Ira. "Green Day, The Merry Pranksters Of Punk," *Newsday*, December 5, 1994.

Robbins, Ira. "Jingle Bell Rock At the Garden," *Newsday*, December 7, 1994.

Rosen, Craig. "New Acts Help Modern Rock Avoid Teenage Identity Crisis," *Billboard*, July 16, 1994.

Rosen, Craig. "MCA Links With Green Day Mgrs. For (510) Label," *Billboard*, March 11, 1995.

Rosen, Craig. "Green Day grows beyond punk on 'Nimrod'," *Billboard*, September 20, 1997.

Russell, Deborah. "R.E.M., Aerosmith Videos Win Big," *Billboard*, September 17, 1994.

Russell, Deborah. "Warner/Reprise's Green Day shows 'Maximum Vision'," *Billboard*, November 19, 1994.

Sanneh, Kelefa. "A Protest Song Does Double Duty As A Love Note To Soldiers In Iraq," *The New York Times*, August 21, 2005.

Saraceno, Christina. International Superstars, *RollingStone.com*, November 26, 2001.

Schaffer, Athena. "Green Day Taking Extra Steps To Secure Mosh Pits, Fan Safety," *Amusement Business*, January 8, 1996.

Scoppa, Bud. "*Taxi* A&R Interview: Rob Cavallo," http://taxi.com/faq/ar/cagallo.html.

Segal, David. "3 Guys, 4 Great Chords; Green Day's Participatory Punk," *The Washington Post*, June 26, 2001.

Selvin, Joel. "Five In '95: Banding Together, Green Day Managers Jeffrey Saltzman And Elliot Cahn," *The San Francisco Chronicle*, January 1, 1995.

Selvin, Joel. "For Green Day, It's A Solid Gold Night," *The San Francisco Chronicle*, April 30, 2001.

Selvin, Joel. "Green Day Plays Its Home Turf, Smacking Punk Out Of SBC Park," *The San Francisco Chronicle*, September 26, 2005

Sheffield, Rob. "Berkeley Calling," *Rolling Stone*, September 30, 2004.

Sinclair, Tom. "Green Day: Sitting On Top Of The World," *Entertainment Weekly*, February 11, 2005.

Snyder, Michael. "Lively Arts — Lots Brewing At Fantasy Studios," *The San Francisco Chronicle*, May 21, 1995.

Snyder, Michael. Lively Arts — Green Day's 'J.A.R.' Unsealed," *The San Francisco Chronicle*, July 30, 1995.

Solman, Gregory. "Sam Bayer: On The Spot," *Adweek*, September 5, 2005.

Sprague, David and Jana Eisenberg. "Green Day And Other Shades Of Punk," *Newsday*, December 12, 1994.

Strauss, Neil. "After the Horror, Radio Stations Pull Some Songs," *The New York Times*, September 19, 2001.

Sullivan, James. "Lively Arts/Nightlife — A Place for Punks to Hang," *The San Francisco Chronicle*, October 13, 1996.

Sullivan, James. "Fresh Fury From Green Day," *The San Francisco Chronicle*, December 16, 1997.

Sullivan, James. "Artists, Musicians Protest Rents," *The San Francisco Chronicle*, November 6, 2000.

Sullivan, James. "Green Day, Hammett, Eitzel Rock For San Francisco," *RollingStone.com*, November 7, 2000.

Sullivan, Jim. "For Police And Promoters, A Mosh Misunderstanding," *The Boston Globe*, September 11, 1994.

Sullivan, Jim. "Rich, Famous...And Punk," *The Boston Globe*, October 25, 1995.

Taylor, Rebecca. "Success Won't Stymie This Band's Adolescent Charm," *Birmingham Post-Herald Reporter*, 1995.

Temchine, Benjamin. "Rudy's Can't Fail Cafe Takes Over For Eugene's," *The San Francisco Chronicle*, November 15, 2002.

Terrell, Kristopher. "An Epic Interview With John Roecker," *Filmjerk.com*, August 8, 2003.

Thompson, Matt. "Green Day (live review)," http://uk.launch.yahoo.com, July 22, 2002.

Tucker, Ken. "Ever Green," *Entertainment Weekly*, October 6, 2000.

Turner, Lauren. "Green Day Awakens Boy From Coma," *South Wales Echo*, March 8, 2005.

Uhelszki, Jaan. "Lively Arts/Nightlife — It's Not Easy Being Green Day," *The San Francisco Chronicle*, October 1, 1995

Uhelszki, Jaan. "Pop Quiz — Q & A With Billie Joe Armstrong Of Green Day," *The San Francisco Chronicle*, November 19, 1995.

Uhelszki, Jaan. "Green Day Gets Bigwig Manager," *The San Francisco Chronicle*, July 28, 1996.

Uhelszki, Jaan. "Pop Music — Green Day — Still a Bunch of Punks," *The San Francisco Chronicle*, October 12, 1997.

Uhelszki, Jaan. "Secure This!," *RollingStone.com*, January 13, 1999.

Uhelszki, Jaan. "Green Day to Work With R.E.M. Producer," *RollingStone.com*, January 12, 2000.

Uhelszki, Jaan. "Warped Tour to Hit Thirty-Eight Cities," *RollingStone.com*, March 28, 2000.

Uhelszki, Jaan. "Warning: Green Day Have Grown Up . . . a Bit," *RollingStone.com*, October 4, 2000 .

Uhelszki, Jaan. "Day Tripper: An Interview With Billie Joe of Green Day," drdrew.com, 2001.

Van Luijn, John and Tom Engelshoven (translation by Nick Hoffstedde), "Green Day Interview," *OOR*, August 1995.

Vaziri, Aidin. "Green Day Pulls The Plug On Iconic Berkeley Indie Label Lookout Over Unpaid Royalties," *The San Francisco Chronicle*, August 6, 2005.

Vaziri, Aidin. "From Jazz To Punk, 'S.F. Grammys' Is A Meeting Of Great Musical Minds, Talents," *The San Francisco Chronicle*, March 21, 2006.

Villeneuve, Phil. "Kaiser Chiefs Take Over Brit Awards," *ChartAttack.com*, February 17, 2006.

Vineyard, Jennifer. "Green Day Plays 'Request Hour' In New York," *RollingStone.com*, October 6, 2000.

Waddell, Ray. "Green Day, Blink-182, Others Team In The Name Of Modern-Day Punk For Pop Disaster tour," *Billboard*, March 2, 2002.

Walters, Barry. "Young Fans Flock To Benefits By Green Day," *The San Francisco Examiner*, May 29, 1995.

Weiss, Neal. "Tré Cool Blasts Thanksgiving," *Launch.com*, November 22, 2001.

Weiss, Neal. "Green Day's Tré Cool On Afghan Bombing, Bush Presidency," *Launch.com*, October 16, 2001.

Weiss, Neal. "Green Day Releases Its 'Superhits'," *Launch.com*, November 13, 2001.

Weiss, Neal. "Green Day Bassist Dirnt Has Wrist Surgery," *Launch.com*, September 19, 2002.

Weiss, Neal. "Green Day's Armstrong Honors Strummer; Thanks Fans For Anti-War Petition," *Launch.com*, January 3, 2003.

Werth, Edward Richard. "Rodeo: A Brief History," www.rodeoca.org/about/, 2001.

Wieder, Judy. "Coming Clean," *The Advocate*, January 24, 1995.

Wiederhorn, Jon. "Green Day Offer Preview Of Demos Online," *MTV.com*, November 13, 2001.

Williams, Joe. "Green Day Singer Arrested At Show," *The Milwaukee Journal Sentinel*, November 22, 1995.

Winwood, Ian and Dan Martin. "Blood, Sex And Booze: 25 Smashing Facts About Green Day," *New Musical Express*, June 18, 2005.

Zakaria, Fareed. "An Imperial Presidency," *Newsweek*, December 19, 2005.

Zulaica, Don. "Tré Cool of Green Day," *liveDaily.com*, November 13, 2001.

Other magazines

The Advocate, Alternative Press, Bass Player, Billboard, e.p., Entertainment Weekly, Guitar Legends, Guitar Player, Guitar World, Magnet, New Musical Express, Rolling Stone, Oor, The San Francisco Chronicle, The San Francisco Examiner, Spin and *Metal Hammer Presents Green Day*, Future Publishing Ltd., 2005.

Books

Arnold, Gina. *Kiss This: Punk in the Present Tense*. New York: St. Martin's Griffin, 1997.

Brown, Tony and Jon Kutner, Neil Warwick. *The Complete Book Of The British Charts*. London: Omnibus Press, 2002.

Cometbus, Aaron. *Despite Everything: A Cometbus Omnibus*. San Francisco: Last Gasp, 2002.

Dafydd, Rees and Luke Crampton. *Q: Rock Stars Encyclopedia*. London: Dorling Kindersley Ltd., 1999.

Edge, Brian, ed. *924 Gilman: The Story So Far*. San Francisco: MaximumRockNRoll, 2004.

Ewing, Jon. *Green Day*. Miami: Music Book Services/Carlton Books Ltd., 1995.

Myers, Ben. *Green Day: American Idiots & The New Punk Explosion*. Shropshire, UK: Independent Music Press, 2005.

Novoselic, Krist. *Of Grunge and Government: Let's Fix This Broken Democracy!*. New York: RDV Books/Akashic Books, 2004.

Perry, Tim and Ed Glinert. *Rock & Roll Traveler USA*. New York: Fodor's Travel Publications, 1996.

Small, Doug. *Green Day*. London: Omnibus Press, 2005.

Whitburn, Joel. *Top Pop Albums 1955-2001*. Menomonee Falls, Wisconsin: Record Research, Inc., 2001.

Whitburn, Joel. *Top Pop Singles 1955-2002*. Menomonee Falls, Wisconsin: Record Research, Inc., 2003.

Web Sites

adelinerecords.net; allmusic.com; americanedit.org; billboard.com; contactmusic.com; drdrew.com; fantasystudios.com; greenday.com; greenday.net; greendayauthority.com; greendaydiscography.com; theinfluents.net; launch.com; lookoutrecords.com; mtv.com; mvwire.com; thenetworkband.com; 924gilman.org; nme.com; operationivy.com; pinheadgunpowder.com; rollingstone.com; studio880.com; thenetworkband.com; vh1.com; wikipedia.com.

Discography

All recordings released on CD unless stated otherwise.

GREEN DAY — EPs

1,000 Hours
Lookout! Records (1989)
1,000 Hours / Dry Ice / Only Of You / The One I Want
Note: Released as 7-inch vinyl only.

Sweet Children
Skene Records (1990)
Sweet Children / Best Thing In Town / Strangeland / My Generation
(Who cover)
Note: Released as 7-inch vinyl only.

Slappy
Lookout! Records (1990)
Paper Lanterns / Why Do You Want Him? / 409 In Your Coffeemaker /
Knowledge
Note: Released as 7-inch vinyl only.

Live Tracks
Reprise Records (1994)
Welcome To Paradise / One Of My Lies / Chump / Longview / Burnout / 2,000 Light Years Away
Note: Made for Japanese release.

Bowling Bowling Bowling Parking Parking
Reprise Records (1996)
Armatage Shanks / Brain Stew / Jaded / Knowledge / Basket Case / She / Walking Contradiction / Dominated Love Slave★
★bonus track on Japanese version only

Foot In Mouth
Reprise Records (1997)
Going To Pasalacqua / Welcome To Paradise / Geek Stink Breath / One Of My Lies / Stuck With Me / Chump / Longview / 2,000 Light Years Away / When I Come Around / Burnout / F.O.D.

Tune In Tokyo
Reprise Records (2001)
Church On Sunday / Castaway / Blood, Sex & Booze / King For A Day / Waiting / Minority / Macy's Day Parade

GREEN DAY - Albums

39/Smooth
Lookout! Records (1990)
At The Library / Don't Leave Me / I Was There / Dissappearing Boy / Green Day/ Going To Pasalacqua / 16 / Road To Acceptance / Rest / The Judge's Daughter
Note: Released on vinyl and cassette.

1,039/Smoothed Out Slappy Hours
Lookout! Records (April 19, 1991)
At The Library / Don't Leave Me / I Was There / Disappearing Boy / Green Day / Going To Pasalacqua / 16 / Road To Acceptance / Rest / The Judge's Daughter / Paper Lanterns / Why Do You Want Him? / 409 In Your Coffeemaker / Knowledge / 1,000 Hours / Dry Ice / Only Of You / The One That I Want / I Want to Be Alone
Note: Released on CD and cassette.

Kerplunk!
Lookout! Records (January 17, 1992)
2,000 Light Years Away / One For The Razorbacks / Welcome To Paradise / Christie Road / Private Ale / Dominated Love Slave / One Of My Lies / 80 / Android / No One Knows / Who Wrote Holden Caulfield? / Words I Might Have Ate / Sweet Children / Best Thing In Town / Strangeland / My Generation

Dookie
Reprise Records (February 1, 1994)
Burnout / Having A Blast / Chump / Longview / Welcome To Paradise / Pulling Teeth / Basket Case / She / Sassafras Roots / When I Come Around / Coming Clean / Emenius Sleepus / In The End / F.O.D. / All By Myself

Insomniac
Reprise Records (October 10, 1995)
Armatage Shanks / Brat / Stuck With Me / Geek Stink Breath / No Pride / Bab's Uvula Who? / 86 / Panic Song / Stuart And The Ave / Brain Stew / Jaded / Westbound Sign / Tight Wad Hill / Walking Contradiction

nimrod.

Reprise Records (October 14, 1997)

Nice Guys Finish Last / Hitchin' A Ride / The Grouch / Redundant / Scattered / All The Time / Worry Rock / Platypus (I Hate You) / Uptight / Last Ride In (instrumental) / Jinx / Haushinka / Walking Alone / Reject / Take Back / King For A Day / Good Riddance (Time Of Your Life) / Prosthetic Head / Suffocate / Do Da Da / Desensitized / You Lied

Warning

Reprise Records (October 3, 2000)

Warning / Blood, Sex, and Booze / Church On Sunday / Fashion Victim / Castaway / Misery / Deadbeat Holiday / Hold On / Jackass / Waiting / Minority / Macy's Day Parade

Note: There is also a limited special edition version, which contains a 52-page color book and a green *Warning* slipcover.

International Superhits!

Reprise Records (November 13, 2001)

Maria / Poprocks & Coke / Longview / Welcome To Paradise / Basketcase / When I Come Around / She / J.A.R. / Geek Stink Breath / Brain Stew / Jaded / Walking Contradiction / Stuck With Me / Hitchin' A Ride / Time Of Your Life / Redundant / Nice Guys Finish Last / Minority / Warning / Waiting / Macy's Day Parade

Note: A compilation of their videos, *International Supervideos!,* was also released. The DVD/VHS includes videos from 'Longview' to 'Waiting'.

Shenanigans

Reprise Records (July 2, 2002)

Suffocate / Desensitized / You Lied / Outsider / Don't Wanna Fall In Love / Espionage (instrumental) / I Wanna Be On TV / Scumbag / Tired Of Waiting / Sick Of Me / Rotting / Do Da Da / On The Wagon / Ha Ha You're Dead

American Idiot

Reprise Records (September 21, 2004)

American Idiot / Jesus Of Suburbia / Holiday / Boulevard Of Broken Dreams / Are We The Waiting / St. Jimmy / Give Me Novacaine / She's A Rebel / Extraordinary Girl / Letterbomb / Wake Me Up When September Ends / Homecoming / Whatsername

Note: There is also a limited special edition version, which contains a 52-page color book.

Bullet In A Bible

Reprise Records (November 2005)

American Idiot / Jesus Of Suburbia / Holiday / Are We The Waiting / St. Jimmy / Longview / Hitchin' A Ride / Brain Stew / Basket Case / King For A Day / Shout / Wake Me Up When September Ends / Minority / Boulevard Of Broken Dreams / Good Riddance (Time Of Your Life)

Note: This is a live CD and DVD release of Green Day's concerts at Milton Keynes, England on June 18 and 19, 2005. The DVD includes interview footage in between songs.

About The Author

Seattle-based author **Gillian G. Gaar** has written the book *She's A Rebel: The History of Women in Rock & Roll*, served as a consultant on the Nirvana box set *With The Lights Out*, has appeared in *The Nirvana Companion, Trouble Girls*, and the *Goldmine Beatles Digest* (both volumes) among other anthologies, and has written for music/entertainment magazines/online sites around the world.